POLICE, PROBATION AND PROTECTING THE PUBLIC

Mike Nash

BLACKSTONE
PRESS LIMITED

First published in Great Britain 1999 by Blackstone Press Limited,
Aldine Place, London W12 8AA. Telephone 0181-740 2277

20168772

ISBN: 1 85431 735 0

British Library Cataloguing in Publication Data
A CIP catalogue record for this book is available from the British
Library

Typeset by Montage Studios Limited, Horsmonden, Kent
Printed by Livesey Ltd, Shrewsbury, Shropshire

Contents

POLICE, PROBATION AND PROTECTING THE PUBLIC

Preface

This book concerns the protection of the public from dangerous offenders, particularly those who have committed serious sexual and violent crimes. As such it therefore deals with a relatively small percentage of those convicted. However, despite their comparative rarity, these offenders, it is argued, have been used to drive the criminal justice agenda in an increasingly punitive direction. They have also had a considerable impact upon the working practices of the two agencies primarily charged with offering the public protection in the community, the police and probation services. The public protection agenda discussed in this book is therefore quite specific and should not be confused with the broader community safety agenda now being pursued by the Labour Government. In many respects this agenda differs from that of the public protection one discussed here, by its use of research and evidence, in contrast to the often knee-jerk policy making characteristic of recent years.

The book is divided into two parts. Part one revisits the dangerous debate, originally held in the late 1970s and early 1980s, and also examines the way in which politics have influenced the public protection agenda both in Britain and many other countries of the world. Part two examines public protection in action and considers the way in which agencies such as the police and probation services have had to change their working practices to take on the onerous task of public protection. Readers are invited to consider the types of situations faced by practitioners on a daily basis using the information provided in the book.

In many respects the public protection agenda discussed here may
have been a child of its time, although its impact upon the criminal
justice process will be long lasting and undoubtedly will offer benefits
in terms of effective multi-agency collaboration. The move to the
community safety agenda promises to be more evidence based and
potentially innovative. Nonetheless, potentially dangerous offenders
will not disappear and the challenge for any government will be to
manage this problem in a rational and considered manner.

Acknowledgements

My thanks go to many police, probation and prison officers who have, over several years, contributed to my knowledge and understanding of dangerousness. Their willingness to give of their time and experience is greatly appreciated. Also giving of their time, although not perhaps in such a voluntary way, were numerous dangerous and potentially dangerous offenders, who crystallised my thoughts about society's response to dangerous people.

My thanks to Dr. John Coker for inviting me to speak on dangerousness in prisons many years ago and thereby kindling my interest in the subject (and developing my interest in an academic career). I am also grateful to Professor Stephen Savage for his thoughtful and helpful comments on earlier drafts. Blackstone Press have been extremely professional and supportive and my thanks to all concerned.

Finally to Karen, Will and Lindsay, my gratitude for allowing me to spend the summer of 1998 in the attic and giving the encouragement that I needed.

Mike Nash
January 1999

Introduction

The 1990s has been the decade of the predatory sex offender, at least in terms of constructing a demon. Across the world a range of legislation has been set in place which seeks to single out this group of offenders for greater punishment, fewer rights and potential exclusion from society. In so doing, many jurisdictions have closed the door on the possibility of rehabilitation with its associated impact upon the working of probation and other therapeutic services. Although the political debate has discussed dangerous offenders in more general terms, and along with this the need of the public to be protected from them, it is predatory sex offenders, especially paedophiles, who have driven key parts of the public protection agenda, although, as indicated in the preface, not so much the emerging community safety agenda. This demonised group of offenders has been used to develop and implement a wide range of punitive and restrictive legislative and policy measures aimed at reducing the risk such offenders pose to the public. These measures have not only impacted upon practitioners operating within the criminal justice system, but have also had a wider impact upon citizens' rights. Many of these measures have been or will be implemented before the United Kingdom passes its own Bill of Rights and it is pertinent to ask if all would have passed the type of criteria to be included in that Bill. Yet outside of the House of Lords and an occasional querying voice from civil liberties groups, there has been an almost deafening silence in terms of offering a reasoned argument to the government of the day. The public protection argument has swept all before it and hardly any person in the public eye has dared to voice any dissent. The result has been one of the most rapid creations of formalised multi-agency working ever witnessed in this country. A wide range of agencies has been drawn into the public protection network and the proposals contained in the Crime and Disorder Act 1998 extend the range. However, two agencies in particular have been charged with the onerous task of 'protecting the public', namely the police and probation services.

This book is concerned with the development of the public protection agenda and charts its rise to top billing among law and order issues. There is no doubting the primacy of public protection. Almost every public pronouncement and policy direction issued by ministers at the Home Office has emphasised the point that the law, and those who enforce it, have an overriding duty to work towards the prevention of harm to the public. In so doing, individual agencies are required to overcome their qualms about working with others and sharing confidential information, because protecting the public must come first and not be impeded by agencies operating in isolation. In particular, police and probation services have been given the primary task by government but can also be seen as having signed up enthusiastically for it. The focus on child sex offenders in particular has not only neutralised political debate but has also ensured that criminal justice agencies, and also those on the periphery, have been drawn into a process that may considerably impact upon the way in which they operate. One of the dangers in this process is that of conflation or net-widening. The mandate of public protection is both onerous and risky. Failure is likely to have very serious consequences and everyone is anxious to be seen to have done their best to reduce the risk of harm to vulnerable members of society. This leads to an inclusive rather than an exclusive policy which means that many offenders who may now acquire the 'dangerous' label might have been dealt with competently and safely in the past without it. There is therefore a danger of 'serious' being conflated into 'dangerous'. Alongside this risk is that which sees an even greater number of offenders sucked into more punitive measures because they are mentioned in the same breath as dangerous offenders. An example of this was Michael Howard's policy of 'prison works' extending to increase the levels of punishment on a range of offenders, including persistent offenders:

Prison is not, of course, the right response for all offenders. We have cautions for first time offenders and community sentences for less serious offenders. We are piloting tagging. But for the most persistent and dangerous criminals, prison is the only suitable punishment and the only means of ensuring that the public get the protection they deserve. (Howard, 1996)

Prison offers safety for the community and the mention of persistent offenders alongside dangerous people ensures that prison sentences are increased and more people receive those sentences at the expense of fines or community penalties. The whole process is taken up several notches so that community penalties become more regulatory and controlling and a range of public agencies merges, almost seamlessly, in crucial areas of practice. This book will attempt both to trace that process and assess the impact upon the agencies most concerned with it.

Chapter 1 reflects on the literature concerning dangerousness and revisits what is known as the 'dangerousness debate'. Although this debate took place some 28 or so years ago, much of it remains extremely relevant to today's discussions — or lack of them. The Britain of the late 1990s uses the terms 'danger' and 'dangerous' very loosely and invariably to support the introduction of measures to deal with reducing risk and working towards safety. Yet risk and danger is invariably defined in terms of individuals. Corporate and environmental dangers remain remarkably absent from the debate. Referring to a list of lethal white-collar violence committed by people who run America's corporate giants, Hills says:

toxic chemical dumps that have poisoned drinking supplies, caused leukemia in children, and destroyed entire communities; cover-ups of asbestos-induced cancer, and the gradual suffocation of workers from inhaling cotton dust; radioactive water leaking from improperly maintained nuclear reactors; mangled bodies and lives snuffed out in unsafe coal mines and steel mills. (Hills, 1987 in Geis, 1996)

Undoubtedly many of these situations are replicated in this country but it is usually only environmentalists who will use the terminology of dangerousness to describe the actions of large-scale businesses. Dangerousness remains sited in individuals and a plethora of legislation has been introduced to deal with it, to manage it and to reduce it. Despite the difficulties of assessment and prediction discussed in chapter 1, measures continue to be introduced to 'govern the dangerous', a section of the population constantly reinvented (Pratt, 1997). The rapid escalation of public protection issues in the mid to late 1990s made little mention of these difficulties, preferring to 'bureaucratise' the process of assessing and managing risk. Managerialism has been a key feature in recent criminal justice policy and may be viewed as positive and negative (James and Raine, 1998), but in the public protection agenda it has been crucial. It has embedded risk assessment and management into the working practices of police and probation officers, ensuring a degree of collaboration unthought of a few years ago. Unfortunately, many of the key theoretical and moral issues raised by the original dangerousness debate appear not to have resurfaced in the management-led agenda of the late 1990s.

Chapters 2 and 3 chart the rise of the more punitive climates associated with right-wing governments and in particular how the public protection issue drove criminal justice policy forward in an ever more rapid and upwards direction. However, it is the political use made of public protection issues, the play on the public fear of crime and the failure of politicians, and to a lesser extent professionals working in the criminal justice system, which is so lamentable. The way in which certain categories of offenders, in particular sexual and violent criminals, were singled out for 'special attention' by the criminal justice system is an important evolutionary stage in the public protection process. This process of 'bifurcation' (Bottoms, 1977) and later 'punitive bifurcation' (Cavadino and Dignan, 1997) enabled successive Conservative governments to appear to be seen as being tough on crime, whilst pursuing policies which in many cases were quite liberal. Although the government's intention in this may have been more financial than paternal, the undoubted influence of Home Office researchers and civil servants was apparent for a while. The political situation was, however, to dispel this apparent liberalism quickly and unleash a reign of crude, popular politics which was to have a tremendous impact upon the nature of criminal justice in this country (Dunbar and Langdon, 1998). The vehicle that was to be used in an attempt to put clear water between the Conservative government and the Labour opposition was the dangerous offender. The result was a range of legislation which represents a considerable incursion into a range of civil rights — the details of the legislation are included in chapter 4.

Chapter 5 traces how the police and probation services have managed to come together in such an emphatic way. Those who have worked in either of these organisations, or students of criminal justice more generally, will know that they have never been the best of allies. There has always been a substantial culture clash, especially at the lower levels of the organisations. Although much of this may have been misguided it remained a fact and, despite closer management co-operation, the two services never looked as if they would share much in the way of daily working practice (see, for example, Stephens and Becker, 1994). Although there have always been small amounts of joint working and collaboration this has generally been limited to specific projects. Even an issue such as crime prevention in its heyday failed to establish a common agenda between the police and probation service. The public protection agenda has, however, changed all that. Because it offers us all a prospect of security, especially those most vulnerable in society, it cannot be dissented from. Once it is set as a key organisational task, as it has been for both police and probation services, it demands a shared managerial approach. Not only is this a requirement for practice but it could be viewed as desirable by these organisations. The police service, under increasing fire for its failure to solve the crime problem, finds another agency with which to share the load. The probation service, also under fire for its social work offender focus, can gain increasing public credibility for its collaboration with the police, still popular with the public if less so with the government.

Chapters 6 and 7 examine how the public protection agenda has impacted upon the working practices of the police and probation services. The agreements or protocols between them, ostensibly concerning the sharing of information and joint assessment of risk, have ensured a tremendous depth of collaboration. The case conference style of working has spread rapidly around the country and is now established good practice. The problems experienced with this way of working in a child protection context, are re-examined and applied to what are frequently termed 'public protection panels', using the points raised by Stevenson (1989). The way in which dangerousness is considered tends to reflect an exclusionary model, that is the offender is usually not included and community involvement is limited. An alternative model which features in 'republican criminology' (Braithwaite, 1989), that of community conferences, is considered as a potentially more effective way of managing risk, although the limitations of this model are acknowledged. It is also suggested within these chapters that, although public protection began life with a focus on a wide definition of potential dangerousness, it has been increasingly driven by public fear of predatory paedophile offenders. For practitioners there are risks involved for their practice in being driven by a media, political and public agenda which is not always evidence led — to say the least. The potential to fall into the trap of ranking risk according to vulnerability of victim is considered, as well as the need to expand the definition again to consider the extent of violence within the home and within other relationships.

Chapter 8 returns to the issue of assessment and prediction initially raised in chapter 1. Despite the problems of accurate assessment which is acknowledged by all practitioners, it is evident that people other than clinicians will be involved in the assessment of risk. These people will need baselines for their evaluation and their managers will expect to be able to demonstrate that a thorough risk assessment has taken place. This increasingly points to the use of predictive tools which serve many purposes. They enable an agreed definition of risk and dangerousness to be used by several agencies, create a common language, attempt to eliminate subjectivity and also publicly signify that something is happening. Nonetheless, the ability of these tools to predict behaviour which tends to occur at the extremes is questionable, therefore the prospects of over caution, or net-widening, raised in chapter 1, are further explored. Several methods and devices are considered and it is suggested that the police, with their increasing development of offender profile information, used for detection purposes, could utilise this for prevention. Police officers will increasingly be asked to judge danger-ousness and risk in the context of a range of offending behaviour. Within this range, levels of seriousness will vary, as will the possible rate at which reoffending occurs. Profile information may assist police officers to differentiate and also make use of information which is increasingly at their disposal.

Chapter 9 considers the issues of rights, something which has taken a back seat in recent discussions. Much of the concern in the initial dangerousness debate was directed at the rights of the offender, in particular the right not to be punished for what they had not yet done. The issue for rights protagonists was whether offenders should lose rights in the future, because of what they had done in the past. In many ways this issue has been nullified by a discussion of competing rights

(Floud and Young, 1981), whereby people who commit heinous crimes lose many of the rights associated with citizenship. The issue is further simplified when it is cast in the crude context of the rights of children versus the rights of paedophiles. Although few would dispute the winner of such a contest it is nonetheless a simplified version of reality and serves the purpose of neutralising any discussion of rights and civil liberties. For the probation service in particular this may become an uncomfortable issue. Although it is increasingly being moved away from its social work origins it still retains values which amount to a concern for and respect of the individual, whatever they have done. The language of public protection virtually recasts this concern as being on the offender's side, a worrying situation for those who wish to see an ethical criminal justice process in Britain. This chapter also explores the development of community notification schemes, examining their growth in the USA and their implications for Britain. These schemes, now mandatory in the USA, are a clear example of competing rights with the winner being the community. Although the argument is unlikely to be changed when the subject is a child sex offender, the possibilities of such schemes being extended to other offenders is always there. The issue of rights then is one which must be viewed in the broadest sense and should not be allowed to be contained within the context of one range of offenders. The extension of the target group for 'three strikes' style legislation has already shown the potential for net-widening and the power of the government to demonise whomsoever it wishes. The rights debate is one which must be held, and held soon.

The very title of this book demonstrates the way in which the public protection agenda has come to dominate criminal justice policy making in recent years. Even a few years ago a book on the subject would not have cast these two organisations together. At the present time the British government is increasingly looking at greater collaboration between the prison and probation services, creating a seamless continuum of corrections. Yet without the type of formal review had by those two services, and with very little in the way of public announcement, police and probation officers have already come together to a considerable degree. Welcome to the age of the 'polibation officer'!

Part 1
Political and Policy Background

Chapter 1
Danger, Danger Everywhere

Dangerousness is a dangerous concept . . . It is difficult to define, yet very important decisions are based on it; there is as yet little reliable research in relation to it; it is a term which raises anxiety and which is therefore peculiarly open to abuse. (Scott, 1977, p. 127)

In the late 1990s we are again being told that we face the prospect of society being overrun with large numbers of dangerous offenders. The activities of paedophiles in particular have reached folk devil status and have been the subject of intense media scrutiny and political activity. Newspapers have taken the lead in 'outing' allegedly convicted paedophiles, although they have not always been accurate in the information that they have passed on to local communities (see Hebenton and Thomas, 1996). There has been a limited debate over the rights of individual offenders who have served their sentence or completed their punishment, but this has very much taken second place to the right of the public to be protected. A concerted media campaign has been taken up by politicians of all parties and in the last months of the Conservative government a series of punitive, protective measures had been set in motion which have not been overturned by the Labour government elected in May 1997, indeed more stringent measures have been introduced. These measures will be discussed in chapter 4, but here attention will focus upon the broad issues which underpin these recent developments. In particular this chapter will focus on the difficulties involved in the assessment and prediction of dangerous behaviour. The question of 'rights' inherent in this debate will be touched upon here but dealt with in greater detail in chapter 9. The effect that a renewed tough law and order emphasis, with the focus on public protection, has for law and order agencies, especially the police and probation services, will be the central theme of the remainder of this book.

DEFINING DANGER

We are never far away from the age of the so-called dangerous offender. It is simply a fact that they come to, or more accurately, are brought to public attention on some occasions more than others. However, the epithet is usually applied to particularly heinous crimes, for example the murder or sexual assault of children, or a murder which has been committed with more than necessary violence, or behaviour which is bizarre by 'normal' standards. If the behaviour falls into such categories then it is almost axiomatic that the offender becomes labelled as dangerous. In other words we tend to see the word used when behaviour is difficult to explain, when motivation cannot easily be identified or is something that 'no normal person' would do. We may even use the word 'evil' to describe such crimes, as was the case in the murder of James Bulger by two children. Inexplicable behaviour still requires a label. If we cannot explain it rationally we can view it as abnormal and therefore dangerous. Traditionally we differentiate by degree between murders and murderers. The person who kills his spouse in a fit of jealousy is rarely assessed by criminal justice practitioners as being as dangerous as the man who abducts and kills a child. This is reflected in both sentencing and release decisions, for example, see the imposition of a 200-hour community service order on a man in Scotland convicted of killing his wife with 11 stab wounds (*The Guardian*, 9 July 1997). Yet as Scott (1977) makes clear, pathological jealousy is a notoriously dangerous passion and, in the right circumstances, there is a consider-able risk of a second murder taking place. Therefore, the jealous murderer is a high risk case and if jealousy is the motivation for a 'domestic' killing, then that individual offers a strong probability of further, very serious offending.

If we can see a rationale for behaviour, no matter how unacceptable, we are less likely to regard the perpetrator as dangerous — a view apparently shared by the judge in the case cited above. Similarly, if we find it difficult to identify specific potential victims, more a diffuse community of risk, we are again less likely to predict dangerousness in our assessment. As Floud and Young (1981) indicate, 'fear converts risk into danger and it tends to be inversely proportional to time and distance' (p. 6). The recent media campaign focusing on sexual offenders has increased public fear and anxiety, indirectly leading to more offenders being viewed or classified as dangerous (and incidentally increasing the incidence of vigilante activity). The spread of the 'dangerous' tag has seen it move beyond the typologies briefly discussed above and applied more to a range of people who have committed particular crimes, rather than considering the nature of those crimes.

The heightened levels of public awareness and concern have had a considerable impact upon the agencies of criminal justice as dangerousness becomes a political issue when it is unquestionably a social policy issue. In particular, police services find targets set for them which aim to reduce the fear of crime in their communities, especially the fear generated by sexual and violent offenders. Such a target is less tangible than say one of increasing arrest rates for a certain offence category and probably much more difficult to achieve. All agencies, however, feel the pressure of public protection issues as a serious agenda item for their professional practice. Before we go on to consider contemporary approaches to potential dangerousness, and the way it has impacted upon police and probation work, it is worth revisiting the literature on dangerousness from another period when public fears led to consideration of what to do with dangerous offenders.

WHAT IS DANGEROUSNESS?

There are several adjectives which could be used in place of the word dangerous, the alternatives depending both on context and subject. If the dangerous label is applied to people, then we might substitute threatening, menacing or alarming; it would rarely be as straightforward a word as violent. If, however, we refer to situations, the choice might include hazardous, perilous, risky or unsafe. Now think of an antonym to dangerous in both of these contexts. Words such as safe or harmless come to mind, but the list is much shorter than for their opposites. Safe is a sound alternative within the situational context, but is harmless a reasonable antonym to dangerous when describing people? Harmlessness has its own subjective connotations within a people context, often used to describe a person suffering from a form of mental impairment but regarded as unlikely to cause any serious harm. The phrase, 'he's harmless' has slipped into common usage. Yet how does an offender move from being someone who might be safe, or harmless, to someone who might be labelled as dangerous? Is it a one step move or is there a progression? Conversely, can an offender labelled as dangerous make a one step move back to being harmless? If the label is not applied because, in effect, the person is assessed as harmless, does the whole mechanism of public protection cease? In the influential work of Floud and Young (1981) it was said, 'it is impossible to divide people sharply into the dangerous and the safe; dangerousness is a matter of degree and the spectrum is wide' (p. 25). Yet contemporary systems designed for the management of potentially dangerous offenders are frequently based on a binary decision of dangerous or not. Actions such as the development of community protection plans often depend upon the application of the label. In a similar vein it was the case that children were deemed to be at risk or not in child protection conferences, decisions which had tumultuous consequences in some cases. As Dale et al (1986) indicate, there are what they term 'dangerous professionals' whose decisions, or lack of them, increase the dangerousness of given situations. Chapters 6 and 7 of this book will examine the process by which professionals place people into one category or another and the results of that placement. Undoubtedly the label once applied is difficult to lose and it should not therefore be applied lightly. Equally a failure to apply it in the first place may have catastrophic results. The process of considering dangerousness needs to be rigorous, both in its application and in the process of de-labelling.

As we shall see below, many people argue that the dangerous offender forfeits certain rights and certain civil liberties. Naturally these rights should not be removed from a 'harmless' person or indeed categories of 'ordinary' offenders. Yet the transition from harmless to dangerous which triggers the loss of rights, may simply be the result of a label applied by professionals as a response to certain behaviour occurring within a specific personal and social context, behaviour which may not recur. Those professionals, however, may only think of applying the label when particular types of criminal behaviour have been carried out, in other words certain types of behaviour are excluded from even the basics of consideration whilst others trigger the process of public protection. The label of dangerous and the accompanying loss of rights therefore may only be considered in respect of a certain group of people, a relatively narrow band of the offender population. Yet dangerousness is likely to spread itself over a much wider behavioural base than one determined by, say, specific offence categories, the most common delineator used by professionals working within the criminal justice process. Scott (1977) would caution against such a simplification, 'The legal category, even murder, arson and rape, is not very useful in determining dangerousness' (p. 129). It is important for practitioners working within this complex area not to be pigeon-holed in their thought processes. The bottom line is that dangerousness can be a social and political construct and applied unevenly to categories of offenders. An over-reliance on offence classifications runs the risk of both over-inclusion and also missing out those people whose behaviour is dangerous but does not fit the required category.

In later chapters, recent developments in Britain will be discussed which have encouraged the joint working of a variety of agencies, but most notably the police and probation services, in the area of 'potential dangerousness'. Systems and processes have been established, under strong central government encouragement, to assess the capacity of certain offenders for potential dangerousness and exchange information about them. This decision-making process may apply a label which could remove significant civil liberties and indeed influence a considerable loss of personal liberty. On what basis is this decision reached? Are all parties to the decision agreed upon what constitutes dangerousness? How likely is the decision to be accurate and how would anyone be able to measure its effectiveness anyway? Indeed, is accuracy a concern when the safety of the public and usually its most vulnerable members is at stake? Underlying all of this is a fundamental question: can criminal justice practitioners really identify someone who we can predict with confidence will, in the future, commit what we understand as dangerous behaviour?

DANGEROUSNESS REVISITED

The literature on dangerousness is conclusive in one respect, that opinions on both the assessment and prediction of it are inconclusive.

maximum Finnish penalty outside a life sentence), on 17 counts of attempted manslaughter. In reaching its verdict the court clearly agreed that there was a deliberate attempt at infecting his partners and that they would eventually contract Aids and die (*The Observer*, 13 July 1997). The sentence is one based not only on what the defendant had done but what the outcome of that action might be in the future, again without certainty. It is an example of how the criminal law can be used to impose severe sentences partially based on possibility.

Assessment

So where should professionals in the business of assessing and predicting dangerousness begin, especially those who perhaps have not benefited from a clinical training in psychiatry? Rather like their assessment of a dangerous situation, many people will rely on a combination of personal and professional experience, education, train- ing and perhaps importantly, gut feeling. Hawkins (1983) describes aspects of this process as 'patterning and characterisation', attempting to predict the future by making sense of the past. Characterisation, he says, 'is a means of endowing individuals with attributes to make sense of them and to place them; it creates and organises expectations since it embodies a description and a prediction. Embedded in the notion of "the kind of person" is another of what the person is likely to do' (p. 119). In their assessments criminal justice and health professionals will not only look to their own previous experience but in particular what the previous behaviour of the subject tells them. In other words, to cite Kvaraceus's (1966) famous maxim, nothing predicts behaviour like behaviour. This is not simply a statistical operation however, as statistics in this area are notoriously unreliable. In creating a criminal and behavioural biography, practitioners re-examine the significance of present acts in the light of past behaviour and of course give new or added meaning to past behaviour in the light of the present (Hawkins, 1983, p. 122). Gunn, however, expresses a cynical attitude towards the use of retrospective data in predicting the future, 'In psychiatry a strange cliché; "nothing predicts violence like previous violence" has sprung up. Where does this notion come from? It is a misunderstanding of statistics. ... the myth that previous violence predicts violence is constantly reinforced by retrospective statistical data' (1996, p. 53). Yet as we shall see, for the professionals involved in the decision-making process of labelling a person as dangerous or not, previous behaviour remains a powerful indicator, especially when supported by a criminal record and penal sanction. It will inevitably be the trigger for almost all professional consideration and indeed this is enshrined in all the legislation governing this area of practice.

Such a notion should not, however, be entirely discounted according to Walker (1980). Although reluctant to accept dangerousness in people as a feature of character, he does believe that statistics on violent offending are good enough to suggest a reasonable probability of it being repeated. As soon as a person commits one act of violence, they have already moved into a different statistical group which sees the prospects of their repeating that behaviour enhanced to a reasonable degree. Of course, we shall see below that much of the debate in this area is concerned with depriving people of rights and liberty for something that they may do in the future of which there is no certainty. The question then becomes, how probable does it have to be to justify extraordinary measures? This is a question which has remained unanswered in the dangerousness debate, although it has perhaps been simplified by recent two and three strikes legislation in the USA and in Britain (Dunbar and Langdon, 1998, Pratt, 1997 and Schichor and Sechrest, 1996). In such legislation an estimate of probability is made redundant by the imposition of mandatory penalties on repeat offenders with specific criminal histories. In such cases the offender's individual circumstances are minimised, rather the opposite of sentencing in a dangerousness context, which has traditionally had a focus more precisely on the individual offender rather than the specific offence committed.

Probably Right?

The question of 'probability' will be further explored below but for the moment it is worth noting the words of Conrad (1982) who, in acknowledging that the public believes that there is a class of criminals who must be dangerous said, 'a recidivist violent offender falls into a group with chances approaching certainty that its members will commit new crimes as soon as they are at liberty to do so and it's even money that the new crimes will be violent' (p. 264). For practitioners, the issues remain the transition from violent to dangerous and accepting odds or evens as a justification for protective mechanisms and measures.

Actuarial approaches are becoming fashionable in court and probation service circles but, as Floud and Young point out, care needs to be taken in generalising from 'normal' to dangerous offender populations, 'The assessment of the risk he presents must rest not only on evidence of a propensity to cause wilful harm, but the evidence must be specific to him and this precludes the determination of dangerousness by purely actuarial methods whatever may be their advantages in other respects' (1981, p. 27). This view stands in sharp contrast to opinion recently emanating from America, where it has been claimed that, 'The field of violence prediction has advanced to the point where actuarial predictions about serious criminal violence by men who have already committed one violent offence can be made with considerable accuracy' (Rice, 1997, p. 421). However, it should be said that Rice has based her work on a very detailed application of a range of criteria building up to the Violence Risk Appraisal Guide, a combination of 12 variables including a psychopathy score. Such a detailed instrument is unlikely to form part of the assessment tools used by practitioners operating in a working environment where time is of the essence. Nonetheless the feeling remains that the extreme of human behaviour is unlikely to subject itself easily to quantified predictions, as Scott (1977) indicates; 'Dangerous behaviour lies at the extreme of the aggression parameter, and most standardised tests tend to become unreliable at both their extremities, yet it is in just these areas that the most important decisions lie' (p. 129).

Some years ago the author ran a training course on dangerousness involving experienced probation officers, during which the course members were asked to identify, in advance, what they considered to be the attributes of a dangerous offender. The list of replies included the following behavioural characteristics; volatile, blames the victim, unpredictable, shows no remorse, clever, verbally manipulative, obsessive and negative attitudes towards women, gets close to potential victims, abusive, talks of violence. Such a list describes the behaviour of a considerable percentage of the population at any given time and for a smaller percentage, a good deal of the time. So what changes the perception of the probation officer in such cases from what may be described as normal (if unacceptable) behaviour, to one of potential dangerousness? Often it will be because the previous behaviour of the person they are dealing with, previous convictions or perhaps less commonly, behaviour observed personally by the officer (including threats), will make present behaviour appear to have greater potential for danger. In many ways this may be a sensible course of action and would have been supported by much of the literature in this area. Kozol et al (1972), for example, say that no-one can predict dangerous behaviour in an individual with no history of dangerous acting out. One of the advantages of this approach is that the offender, who may lose rights and freedom as a result of the dangerous label being applied, is at least doing so as a result of their own previous behaviour — in other words they have already demonstrated the capacity to do serious harm to others. Yet is this sufficient to predict that they will carry out the same behaviour in the future? A parallel might be drawn with dogs that seriously injure people — usually children. Even if the dog has no history of aggressive behaviour it is invariably put down. Is this a punishment for what it has done, when there may have been provocation for example, or is it for what it might do in the future?

Unpredictable or Unacceptable Behaviour

So far two qualities of dangerousness have been hinted at, the likelihood of future serious harm and the unpredictability of behaviour. It is worth noting the context into which these features have been placed by previous authors and committees. The Floud Committee (1981) which, as we will see, reviewed the evidence for and against protective legislation in the form of preventive detention, said the following: 'There is no such psychological or medical entity as a dangerous person and that dangerousness is not an objective concept. Dangers are unacceptable risks' (p. 20). Floud's reconceptualising of the problem of dangerousness into one which concentrates on the acceptability or otherwise of risk will be discussed below, but it should be observed that others have been prepared to focus more on the behaviour of the individual in describing what makes an offender dangerous. For example, the Butler Committee (1975), established to consider the discharge and after care of the mentally abnormal offender, had suggested that, 'a propensity to cause serious physical or lasting psychological harm' was a characteristic of the dangerous offender. Of course the use of the word propensity still leaves us in the area of predicting likely future behaviour. In the same year, the Scottish Council on Crime gave a similar definition, 'The probability that he will inflict serious and irremediable personal injury in the future'. The late Peter Scott gives us an enhanced definition in his illuminating account (1977), 'An unpredictable and untreatable tendency to inflict or risk irreversible injury or destruction or induce others to do so' (p. 128). This definition expands the definition and perhaps in doing so narrows the band of offenders to whom it may be applied. The inclusion of the untreatable clause does suggest that a degree of mental disturbance is likely to be present of a specific kind which offers little hope for rehabilitation. The move towards seeing the dangerous offender as falling within the mental health field reflects the findings of the Scottish Council on Crime (1975) which had recommended that the evidence of two psychiatrists, a clinical psychologist and an experienced social worker would be needed to confirm the assessment of dangerousness for the courts. As we shall see, the types of systems presently being instituted for the assessment of potential dangerousness do not, in general, contain this degree of clinical experience, if at all. In attempting to tie down Dworkin's (1977) idea of vivid danger, Bottoms and Brownsword (1982) had suggested three elements to enhance the analysis; seriousness, temporality (frequency and immediacy) and certainty. Low scores on either seriousness or certainty would militate against an assessment of dangerousness. Yet again we are left with the view that modern-day practitioners need to take very great care, utilising all available information, in coming to their decisions.

Rare Behaviour — Great Fear

It is evident that there is not a clear definition of what constitutes dangerousness in people. The seriousness of potential — or likely — future harm is a key constituent: it should not simply be repeated acts of a minor nature. Most observers would include psychological as well as physical harm, this of course including sexual assault (however, domestic violence rarely makes it into the dangerousness category, despite the real and potential harm suffered by victims), but it is the degree of probability in its recurrence which causes most of the difficulties. Our probation officer group mentioned above would have had a very large number of individuals classified as dangerous if all the offenders known to them and showing their identified attributes were present. In the late 1990s, the media-induced moral panic over paedophiles suggested that society is increasingly at risk from people who, due to the rare and unusual nature of their behaviour, are dangerous. The implication of much press reporting was that numbers of these people were increasing at a fast rate. Yet expert opinion tells us that the number of dangerous offenders is very small, although of course the harm that they can potentially do is enormous. Prins (1988) said, 'At the outset it is important to stress that the population under consideration is very small in relation to the populations of offenders and psychiatric patients overall'. Indeed Prins went so far as to put an approximate figure of 300 on this offender group. In 1980, Brody and Tarling had suggested that, '... those whose aggressiveness is so repetitive or obsessive as to leave little room for doubt are rare', going on to say that predictions most likely result from a combination of inclination, opportunity and ill-luck, very similar to Scott's equation cited above. However, one of the issues here is clearly that of thresholds. The base levels of dangerousness used by these authors do not accord with those experienced by the public and indeed many practitioners. The likelihood is that, in the present climate, the lower levels will prevail.

Therefore a sense of low numbers and rarity does not coincide with the impression given out by the media and politicians in the late 1990s, the emphasis in press reports being very much upon the heightened state of risk in which society was said to be. The focus on serious sex offenders, especially paedophiles, led to the Sex Offenders Act 1997 which, among other things, established a registration scheme for sexual offenders. Clearly, explicit in this scheme is the sense of danger presented by these offenders. Calculations by the Home Office (1997b) indicate that, had the Act always been in force, 235,000 men would have been obliged to register, with 40,000 of these for life. This gives an impression of huge numbers of men presenting a continuing danger for a considerable period of time, yet the evidence suggests that a substantial proportion of these men would not offend again. The same Home Office research indicated that within its sample of men convicted for any type of sexual offence, 10% had a further such conviction within five years and another 12% were convicted of a violent offence. It therefore quickly becomes evident that if we apply dangerousness criteria and labels by offence categories alone, rather than concentrating on the individual offender, then the whole mechanism of public protection will collapse under sheer weight of numbers. A more detailed discussion of these issues is to be found in chapters 4 and 9.

Prediction

The definition of dangerousness includes a risk of a form of serious harm being inflicted on a person or people in the future, the key point then is

the basis of prediction which may result in the loss of those rights. The Young case mentioned above is an example of a 'false positive', that is a person considered no longer to be a danger who in fact turns out to be so. The Baxtrom case identifies the possibility of the converse, namely, false negatives, that is, people who continue to be detained on the assumption that they will present a future danger but, when released, by and large do not. The bottom line for many in this argument is that there is an even chance of being right or wrong, either the released person will offend again or the detained person would not have done so. The issue of course is to establish which is which, a decision which has to be made at all stages of the criminal justice system and clearly the likelihood is to err on the side of caution.

Conrad (1982) has already been cited as indicating that the chances of a recidivist violent offender offending in a violent way again will be about even. Can these odds be made any better? Over the long term the answer is probably not, although there is a degree of confidence between psychiatrists and psychologists that, in the short term, predictions of future serious harm may be reasonably accurate, rather like the weather forecast. Yet the implication behind much of the discussion which considers the application of severe measures to offenders, at least in the sentencing and release context, is that they will unleash serious harm on the community not in the near future, but in the long term, usually following release from a prison sentence. Many of the professionals involved in the discussions concerning dangerousness do not have a clinical background in psychiatry, although this would not prevent them engaging in what Scott (1977) described as painstaking social casework analysis of all the available evidence. Attention to detail is crucial. However, as we shall see, the types of conferencing system outlined in this book are not based on such a process and would not have the time to be so. Predictions of the future are then, to a large extent, based on an assessment of the past in relation to the present. The 'tools' may then become previous record, institutional and community reports, police and (possibly) psychiatric opinion. Undoubtedly such processes increasingly focus on the detail of offending behaviour and will determine odd or bizarre aspects. The process is one which therefore attempts to tip the scales in one direction or another: in other words, does the evidence favour a label of dangerous being applied or not?

Floud (1982) accepted that there was a huge gap in the accuracy of predictions. However, for that committee it was as important that the process was right and fair as it was that the judgment or outcome was correct or not. In the words of the committee, 'The correctness of a predictive judgment cannot depend on our being justifiably certain that an offender will actually reoffend ... it depends primarily on the soundness and reliability of an assessment of his disposition to inflict harm. Whether, if he is left at large, he will actually do harm is very much a matter of chance' (p. 57). This of course opens up the discussion which will be pursued in chapter 9, that is, the issue of rights. Floud is suggesting that the forfeiture of rights is reasonable if there is a thorough and detailed assessment behind any prediction. Walker (1980) suggests three rules to underwrite the assessment: that the behaviour should result in lasting psychological harm, disabling, disfiguring injury, rape, kidnapping and blackmail were also included; that there is a good reason to believe that the actions to which the first rule applies were not an isolated, out of character episode so far as the individual was concerned; and thirdly, if the circumstances which led to the offence no longer exist this should be taken into account (p. 102). This checklist is a wise prerequisite, although there is a danger of over simplification in its application. For example, many so-called domestic murderers are regarded as a safe bet for early release from a life sentence for the very reason that their spouse is dead and therefore the obvious victim is no longer at risk. The traditionally shorter life sentences served by men who have killed their partners bears testimony to this widespread belief. However, there is evidence that men who have previously murdered their wives have re-engineered a similar situation with a new partner and either killed, or nearly killed, again. Often it is partially a result of jealousy which, as we mentioned above, is regarded as extremely difficult to treat (Scott, 1977).

Mature Sense of the Past

As we shall see, police and probation officers involved in the assessment of dangerousness will frequently rely upon previous offending behaviour as their criterion for initial assessment, although increasingly risk of harm procedures, especially those employed by the probation service, offer a more informed judgment. Brooks (1984) suggested seven criteria which appear as relevant today in assessing dangerousness:

(1)   the nature of the harm involved;
(2)   its magnitude;

(3)   its imminence;
(4)   its frequency;
(5)   likelihood or unlikelihood that it will occur;
(6)   situational circumstances and conditions that affect the likelihood of harm occurring;
(7)   balancing alleged harm and the nature of society's intervention
(in Prins, 1988, p. 597).

The overwhelming view from the literature on dangerousness is that
the more detailed the assessment, the more likely is the prediction to be at
least reasonably accurate and at least fitting Floud's criteria of a just
application. Prins (1988) says that, if previous behaviour is to be a
dominant factor in assessment, it must meticulously re-examine all the
available information from as many sources as possible. Full details are
required of the main offence and other apparently less serious matters.
The danger of offence based criteria is that the significance of behaviour
from other offence categories can be missed. For example, the author is
aware of a man charged and convicted with domestic burglary who,
during his parole review, admitted that the real purpose of the burglary
was to assault the woman occupant, whom he had been watching over
time. The offender had been disturbed in the house and escaped with a
bag of stolen antiques, his 'cover story'. His ready admission of guilt to
the police who apprehended him near the scene was to a straightforward
burglary, followed by a three year prison sentence. Because he admitted
his crime the police investigation was curtailed as was the court hearing.
There was no need for police and probation officers to determine the real
motive for the crime, this only coming out some time later during the
parole review. The significance of this case is that many of the offences
not falling into what we regard as 'serious offence' categories, may
demonstrate behaviour which should at least provoke concerns in
professional minds. As we have already seen though, such cases may not
even be considered as they are regarded as run of the mill, especially if
there is a ready admission of guilt, too often perhaps taken as a sign of
remorse. This difficulty with offence based criteria is emphasised by the
omission of burglary with intent to rape from the list of sexual offences
invoking the 'dangerousness' criteria of the Criminal Justice Act 1991
(amended by the Criminal Justice and Public Order Act 1994).
    Prins (1988) suggests that a much more intrusive form of questioning
be used to get behind the bald facts of the offence, for example, what

kind of rape? why this victim and not another? what did the offender get out of the crime? what was their behaviour following the crime? In Prins's words, 'the painstaking assembling of facts and the checking of information from a variety of sources are essential' (p. 600). Supervisors in the community, especially probation officers, need to be aware of a range of indicators which might offer clues to potentially dangerous behaviour. These indicators would include employment, self-image, capacity for dealing with provocation and so on. What this does is to put the offender into his situation and focuses upon the situational components of dangerousness. There is a danger that the modern actuarial approach will be driven by a mechanistic application of factors which will not allow sufficient time to consider the way the whole picture comes together. Police officers have said the same on using the police computer package HOLMES (Home Office Large Major Enquiry System), which, in giving masses of detail and possible leads for officers, often does not allow for the instinct of the experienced officer to come through. Process driven enquiries, as with assessments of dangerousness, may lead to an efficient demonstration of outcomes but the outcome may be engaging in the process itself rather than effective practice.

SUMMARY

The focus of this book is essentially upon the process by which some offenders make a transition from being assessed as safe to dangerous and the effect this has on professional practice. Everything that has been said in this chapter has suggested that the evidence for assessment and prediction is inconclusive and yet practitioners have to operate in a climate of fear and high public expectation, making judgments in a short time and based on limited information. There is risk in making both the right and the wrong decision and of course a right decision for one agency may be wrong for the other. Naturally, the offender also may severely disagree with the assessment. Police and probation officers are really in a no win situation and as such are likely to err on the side of caution and operate within strict agency guidelines. These of course may be over-inclusive, especially if they operate on a previous offence baseline. The risk then becomes that familiarity breeds contempt and too many cases are excluded from consideration. These issues and problems for practice will be explored in subsequent chapters but this one will conclude with a few comments on the tension within the dangerousness debate for practitioners and sentencers, for example Hood and Shute (1996):

> In penal policy there is a perennial tension between the liberal principles of punishment, with their emphasis on certainty and proportionality, and the doctrine of social defence, with its emphasis on social danger and the mechanism of the indeterminate sentence ... the ability of prison personnel and other penal 'experts' to predict human behaviour remains far too fallible, and the possibilities for abuse far too tangible, for a liberal and just state to sanction a form of detention which, in the end, amounts to preventive punishment for what a person might do in the future (p. 799).

Undoubtedly the same issues will arise at all stages of the criminal justice process although, perhaps, the control which might be exercised in an open court setting will be absent from closed case conferences. In this case the need for a careful and just consideration must be of the essence. Those involved in the process of assessing and predicting dangerousness also perhaps need to stand back from the political context in which much of this work proceeds. Their determination of risk will be set within a state defined definition of danger (Pratt, 1997) and the use of a range of actuarial methods to back their judgment merely serves, according to Pratt, the political purpose:

> New calculations at work at the back door of the penal system; new criteria and specifications at its entrance: overall, these trends at both front and back are indicative of the attempt to govern the dangerous in this period in accordance with the tenets of neo-liberal political rationalities. This acknowledges that, like its welfare predecessor, the neo-liberal state must give its commitments to protection from the dangerous. But, having accepted this, it was also determined to break with its welfare antecedents and the nature and extent of the protection it had been prepared to give under that system of rule. Old risks from which the public had hitherto expected protection lost their dangerous qualities and were allowed to fade into oblivion, or were subjected to differing modalities of governance appropriate to their new status; against this, dangerousness became more specific over

this period and targeted those new risks that had come into existence (p. 177).

As risk and danger became more specified so the need arose to develop tools to match this specificity. For a variety of reasons this may be appropriate, but practitioners involved in their use should perhaps think more about the why than just the how.

Chapter 2
Punitive Climates and Protection

The academic activity which followed the Report of the Floud Committee in 1981, outlined in chapter 1, suggests a long history of concern over how the criminal justice and mental health systems should deal with serious and dangerous offenders. However there were few indicators, within that earlier dangerousness debate, to suggest that we would end up in the late 1990s with a degree of public and media concern which at times borders on the hysterical. For example, a comparison might be made between the media coverage of the trial of Mary Bell, convicted of killing two young boys in 1968, or the abduction and murder of Sharone Joseph in 1988, by a twelve-year-old, with that concerning the killers of James Bulger in 1993 (Thompson, 1998, p. 96). The mood of the public has shifted, or has been shifted, to a considerable degree in the past 20 years. This punitive mood is discernible not only in the United Kingdom but also in most countries around the world (Pratt, 1997), a mood which has led to a range of harsh sentencing policies which will be discussed below. It is beyond doubt that, during the early months of the first Labour government in nearly two decades, the protection of the public and concern with and fear of dangerous offenders, had reached the very top of the criminal justice agenda. As a result it has continued both to feed the public's fear of crime and fuel the cries for greater punishment and higher levels of protection.[1] In so doing it has not only dragged the whole criminal justice system up-tariff, but has also pulled in a range of non-criminal justice agencies, thereby making public protection a truly multi-agency issue. An example of this is the Chartered Institute of Housing which, in March 1998, issued guidelines to support housing workers in the difficult task of taking housing decisions in respect of convicted paedophiles. Part of the rationale for issuing the guidelines, according to the Institute, was to counter the knee-jerk response of the Labour government, amid growing fears that paedophiles would be driven underground (*The Guardian*, 3 March 1998). This chapter will trace the changing nature of the penal climate since 1979 and in particular focus on those aspects of it which relate to serious and dangerous offenders. This changing climate was not only to have significant impact upon sentencing practice and the prison population, but also on the working practices of the two agencies named in the title of this book. These changes will be discussed in detail in chapter 5.

PENAL POPULISM

The election of Margaret Thatcher as head of a Conservative government in 1979 signalled an increased emphasis on law and order issues, an emphasis which was to signal toughness and an increasing rejection of rehabilitation as a key task for many criminal justice practitioners. The government was elected on a populist agenda which included a hard and unforgiving attitude to crime, greater support for the police and the building of more prisons. The attitude of the new government was reflected in several sound bites from Margaret Thatcher. In the run up to her first electoral success in 1979 she made the position of her party clear:

> People have asked me whether I am going to make the fight against crime an issue at the next General Election. No, I am not going to make it an issue. It is the people of Britain who are going to make it an issue. (Brake and Hale, 1992, p. 15)

---

[1] The reduction in press reporting of so-called dangerous offenders has, in part, enabled the more progressive, evidence-based criminal justice agenda promised by Labour, to emerge just over a year into their term of office.

... the demand in the country will be for two things: less tax and more law and order (28 March 1979).

Never, ever, have you heard me say we will economise on law and order (10 August 1985). (Both in Savage, 1990, pp. 89–91)

A range of criminal justice measures was enacted by the early Conservative governments which were meant to reflect the new, tough approach and which have been commented on in great detail elsewhere (Savage, 1990, Nash and Savage, 1994, Savage and Nash, 1994, and Newburn, 1995), but our concern here is the development of measures aimed at serious and dangerous offenders in particular.

From an early stage in the history of the new Conservative government, there was a clear tension between its political rhetoric and its policy development, particularly in respect of Treasury-driven economic policy. That tension surrounded the financial costs of a strong law and order programme and the policy and political pledge to reduce public spending and with it to lower the cost of personal taxation. These competing aims are clearly a dilemma for any political party which has embraced so-called New Right ideals. The government is forced to make difficult financial and policy decisions, some of which may include serious moral issues. One such decision may be to replace current aims of public spending, e.g. higher education, with different aims, e.g. more police and prisons. This has been the recent solution in many American states, most notably California, but the public's fear of crime has provided support for these decisions (for a detailed study of the financial implications of harsh penal measures for other public expenditure budgets, see Greenwood et al, 1996). In this country similar choices have been made, and undoubtedly still are being made. Yet there was a way in which this dilemma was successfully tackled by successive Conservative governments and which was to hold political and economic sway from the early 1980s until its rapid erosion under Michael Howard in the mid-1980s. The way in which this dilemma was resolved was by adopting a policy which has been termed 'bifurcation' (Bottoms, 1980).

TWIN TRACKS LEADING TO THE SAME ROAD?

Bifurcation is in essence a relatively simple idea. Certain categories of offenders are selected by governments for 'special treatment' by the criminal justice system. This special treatment can span the entire range of the criminal justice process and might involve the following: more targeted policing of serious and high risk offenders (see comments in the concluding chapter), longer prison sentences, reduced or restricted early release opportunities, more restrictive release licence conditions or more stringent supervision in the community by the probation service. Parallel with this development of a tougher or more punitive approach towards certain categories of offenders, is one which sees others not regarded as a threat to public safety dealt with in the community, albeit under more controlling community sentences, in other words, two classes of criminals are created. Indeed the courts are encouraged to differentiate sharply between these two groups of offenders. Unfortunately confusion and difficulty can set in when dealing with persistent offenders who do not pose a threat to public safety, but who are clearly undeterred by more punitive community sentences.

The political rationale for a policy of bifurcation is also quite simple. It enables a government to declare war publicly on serious offenders, particularly those associated with vulnerable victims, whilst more subtly pursuing policies aimed at reducing the use of custody for the other — and much larger — group of offenders. Such a policy sits well with a perceived public fear of serious criminals and also has the effect of drawing opposition parties into support of those measures. It is very difficult for any opposition party strenuously to oppose a set of policies aimed at protecting vulnerable members of the community, even if they believe that the measures will not be effective or are unnecessary. Equally, they are likely to be attracted to the wider aims of reducing the costs of custody — although this invariably does not happen. Such policies are likely to be popular with what has been termed the 'red meat brigade' at the annual Conservative party conferences, and might allow other and more liberal policy change to slip through more or less unnoticed under cover of the tough policy focus. Indeed this is precisely what happened with the introduction of the 1991 Criminal Justice Act (which will be discussed in greater detail in chapter 4).

TOUGH TALK – TOUGH ACTION

As early as 1984, the Conservative government had signalled a tougher approach to certain types of crimes and criminals, with a substantial shift in the way that life sentence prisoners were reviewed and released and in particular the way in which tariffs (the recommended length of detention), were set. The Home Secretary, Leon Brittain, announced to the House of Commons in July 1984 that certain classes of life sentence prisoners would serve a minimum of 20 years in custody. The categories of lifers identified were sexual murderers, those who had killed children and murderers of police and prison officers. Alongside this policy was an indication to drugs and violent offenders serving five years or more that they were unlikely to be paroled until a few months before their remission date (Cavadino and Dignan, 1997, p. 187). This then could be seen as an early indicator that the criminal justice system was to be asked to make an example of certain crimes and that within the broad categories of crime, such as murder, certain people were to be marked out as deserving special punishment. The significance of the lifer policy review was added to by the overruling by the Home Secretary of release decisions already set in motion by the Parole Board. The Home Secretary's announcement to the House of Commons triggered the reversal of release decisions in the case of certain lifers who fell within the newly defined categories of those to serve a minimum of 20 years. Those who were progressing through the lifer system anticipating release, for example already located in open prisons or even pre-release hostels at the time, and therefore potentially within a year or so of possible release, were pulled back into the prison system and reallocated to a higher security classification. This meant that in cases where the risk upon release had been deemed acceptable by the experts employed within the prison system, and release therefore authorised by the Parole Board, the decision was reversed by a politician for political reasons. This was a bold reaffirmation by the Home Secretary of his powers to set the tariff for a life sentence prisoner, but exercised at a very unusual stage, that is in cases where release had already been agreed by those employed to assess risk and recommend release. Perhaps the greatest significance of this type of decision is the signalling of a move towards considering categories of crime rather than the individual circumstances of the criminal who committed it. Risk of reoffending, which should be heavily weighted to a thorough assessment of the lifer's personal and offending history and behaviour, is considered secondary to the instant offence when determining release. This way of making decisions has become an increasingly influential method in the 1990s and for example contributes to the moral panic concerning paedophiles which sees all sex offenders treated as social lepers. Individual case assessment is increasingly subjugated to blanket decision-making processes and policies. Professional experience and expertise is reduced as decisions become increasingly led by routinised processes often set by central government. There is little evidence that the professionals have got it badly wrong in considering release decisions for dangerous people, although they may be accused of overcaution. The decision to reduce their discretion is therefore much more a political one than one based on hard evidence.

This intervention by the Home Secretary is indicative of the more proactive stance which has been taken by successive Home Office ministers throughout the 1980s and 1990s. It is one, however, which has been increasingly questioned, none more so than in the case of the Home Secretary's involvement in the sentences passed on the killers of toddler James Bulger in 1993. In this case, the sentences passed on the two children, that of detention at Her Majesty's Pleasure, included a recommendation from the trial judge of a minimum tariff of eight years. This tariff was subsequently raised to ten years by the Lord Chief Justice. The Home Secretary of the day, Michael Howard, intervened to increase the tariff to fifteen years, in response he said to the mood of the public. It should also be noted that the decision followed a massive campaign in a tabloid newspaper to increase the tariff and the delivery of a 20,000 signature petition sponsored by the newspaper (this action undoubtedly reflects the down side of making life sentence tariffs public when they were once secret even from the prisoner, although a return to that situation is not advocated). That decision has since been questioned by the European Commission of Human Rights and it appears that the cases of the two children, Venables and Thompson, will be re-examined in the light of legal claims that they were subject to inhuman and degrading treatment in the way that they were tried, detained and sentenced. Alongside this it is anticipated that the Home Secretary will lose the power to set tariffs, a power not enjoyed by politicians elsewhere within Europe (*The Guardian*, 7 March 1998).

Incidents such as these emphasise the interplay between the political situation of the day and the use of the criminal justice agenda as a populist vote winner. The process of bifurcation can be seen as both a response to external pressures (party members, the media and the public) and internal pressures (the Treasury and perhaps, for a while, Home Office civil servants). The period under consideration throughout the remainder of this chapter will emphasise the shift away from a concern for the latter to an overriding concern with the former.

SWINGS AND ROUNDABOUTS

As suggested above, the 1980s had revealed the oscillations in Conservative law and order policy. The period had been marked by pledges to increase police pay, the numbers of police officers and their levels of equipment, especially that aimed at improving public order policing. An ambitious programme of prison building had been embarked upon with the stated view that there would always be enough prison places available for the courts to use. Yet it was the very scale of this expenditure which caused the tensions in government policy. It was evident from research, whilst the government still listened to research findings, that effectiveness in terms of reducing crime did not automatically follow on from greater spending on the main law and order budgets (rediscovered in July 1998, see Postscript at the end of this book). As we shall see, this was eventually to lead to considerable questions being asked about police effectiveness, to the extent that the government alienated many of its traditional supporters. It also caused a wobble in the government's belief in the power of greater punishment to act as a deterrent. Before this happened though, during the 1990s, the government attempted to reconcile its apparently conflicting aims by further developing the philosophy of bifurcation into practice. This policy was for a while to have a roller coaster effect on the prison population but was eventually to see it rise in a sustained fashion. It was to have a major impact upon other criminal justice agencies such as the probation service and ultimately, the police service as well.

It is evident that a criminal justice philosophy which is wedded to the idea of custody as the primary, or indeed only punishment in the minds of some people, and which also demonstrates a great belief in deterrence, is bound to be hugely expensive. To reduce the costs of the system it is therefore necessary either to reduce the amount of crime in society, which is a long-term solution, or to reduce the use of custody. This can be achieved in the short term by legislation or perhaps by persuasion and of course in the long term by achieving the first solution. It is certainly susceptible to influence by the public pronouncements of politicians who can quite easily foster a punitive climate without introducing new legislation. By the middle of the 1980s it was apparent that the Conservative government was coming round to the latter idea — although, as we shall see, it did look at the longer-term goals through the crime prevention agenda in particular.

The Conservative governments of the 1980s had been determined to be seen as tough on law and order issues and not to shrink from the use of custody. Their attraction to short prison sentences for their deterrent value was obvious with the embracing of the 'short, sharp, shock' slogan attached to two detention centre regimes in 1980. Yet quite quickly this particular populist initiative fell into disrepute for several reasons. Prison officers were of the view that the new short sentences, lasting days and weeks, were insufficient for deterrence or training purposes. Home Office research indicated no change in deterrent effects for the trainees or other young people in the areas near to the centres (Home Office, 1984) and it was evident that magistrates had no great desire to impose short sentences. They had instead been more attracted to their new powers of sending offenders into the old borstals, previously the preserve of judges in the Crown Court. For example, whereas 69 boys had been sentenced to borstal for every 100 sent to detention centres in 1982, in 1986 the corresponding figure was 168 (Cavadino and Dignan, 1997, p. 254). The government was therefore faced with the youth custody centres rapidly filling as detention centres emptied, despite provisions such as those contained in the Criminal Justice Act 1982 which demanded that courts seek alternatives to custody for young offenders wherever possible and state reasons for custodial sentences in open court. The government therefore faced the prospect of rising crime rates, an increasing public fear of crime, a massively increased law and order budget and a dent in its belief that custody would serve as a deterrence in most instances of criminal behaviour. Their flagship penal measure, the short, sharp, shock had also been revealed by all concerned as nothing more than hot air, containing little of punitive or rehabilitative value. It did however make trainees much fitter than before they entered!

The proposed solution to what was a developing crisis of confidence and policy, began to emerge in a government Green Paper, *Punishment, Custody and Community* (Home Office, 1988). The paper contains a very important statement:

Imprisonment is not the most effective punishment for most crime. Custody should be reserved as punishment for very serious offences (p. 2).

These words had been echoed elsewhere in the world at about the same time, for example in South Australia in the same year:

> there is the overriding interest of this government to ensure that the prisons of the state are reserved for real malefactors and the perpetrators of the more serious crimes. The government is confronted by the burgeoning problem of overcrowding in correctional institutions occasioned and exacerbated by the presence of offenders who ought not to have been there in the first instance (Pratt, 1997, p. 161).

The government's ideas were not therefore occurring in a vacuum but were part of an international trend, reflected in the aims of many 'New Right' style governments, to reduce the use of custody and thereby lower the financial costs of a policy based on incarceration. The direction in which the Green Paper was to lead, would mean a strengthened role for community sentences and with it for the probation service, giving the courts the confidence to impose 'alternative to custody' disposals. The subsequent White Paper, *Crime, Justice and Protecting the Public* (Home Office, 1990), which followed a very extensive period of consultation, considerably fleshed-out the government's proposals and also introduced the notion of public protection into the public debate about the aims of the criminal justice system.[2] This was to be an astute move, which attempted both to marry together the desire to be tough on law and order whilst at the same time restraining public expenditure by encouraging sentencers to make less frequent use of custody, or to do so for shorter periods. In prefacing the Criminal Justice Act 1991, the White Paper had an explicit purpose: to encourage a reduction in the use of custody by the courts without being seen to interfere with judicial freedom and discretion. The method of achieving this difficult goal was to be carried out in several ways according to the White Paper. Foremost among the new measures was the decision substantially to upgrade community disposals in terms of their punitive element and also introduce extensive national standards for the

---

[2] In what many regarded as a 'liberal' Act, the introduction of public protection in the Criminal Justice Act 1991 could be regarded as an 'illiberal' measure. It is argued here that its use was quite specific in that it acted almost as a camouflage for the more liberal measures contained in the Act which might not have been acceptable to the government's supporters.

probation service. These measures would ensure compliance with the new sentences, thereby giving the courts confidence that offenders would not be 'let off' by probation officers. This entailed a considerable reduction in the professional autonomy of probation officers (see Worrall, 1997 and Brownlee, 1998).

For our purposes the question must be put: how could a Conservative government, committed to the idea of a tough law and order policy, propose the introduction of an Act which was aimed at reducing the prison population? This express purpose was denied by the Home Secretary, David Waddington, when he said, 'If the end result is a fall in the prison population I will be very glad, but that is not the prime objective' (Wasik and Taylor, 1994, p. 2), although it is evident that this was an underlying but central aim of the Act. The Act was described as one of the most enlightened of the century (*The Times*, 27 August 1992). It set out to achieve its dual objectives by developing an advanced process of bifurcation, dubbed 'punitive bifurcation' by Cavadino and Dignan (1997). The 1991 Act would encourage a reduction in the use of custody by the introduction of a range of sentencing principles designed to structure decision-making in the courts. By basing the sentencing process on a policy of 'just deserts', or of proportionality, where the seriousness of crime determines the level of punishment, it was intended that custody would be reserved for the most serious offenders. These offenders would in the main be those committing offences of violence, sex or drugs. These were offenders who were viewed as most likely to put the public at risk. The intention was that other offenders, even those who were persistent in their behaviour, should be sentenced within the context of just deserts, hence the very important provision to reduce the practice of sentencing based upon previous record (section 29, Criminal Justice Act 1991). The government was therefore quite clear in its attempt to reduce the use of custody by the courts, although it stopped short of legislation which might have reduced sentencing discretion more directly.

POLITICS AND THE EMERGENCE OF PUBLIC PROTECTION

The immediate effect of the Act appeared to be one of achieving its aim. The prison population of the country fell to approximately 40,000 in the period following the Act's implementation in October 1992, accompanied by a rise in the use of community penalties (Home Office, 1993). However, this 'success' was to be short-lived and many of the more liberal measures intended by the Act were reversed by the Criminal Justice Act 1993, less than twelve months following implementation. Any success was however to be relegated to a need to keep a political lead over the opposition, as Brownlee (1998) indicates:

> It cannot be coincidental that the announcement of this first reverse in policy came shortly after a humiliating by-election defeat and within days of a national opinion poll in which, for the first time ever, the main opposition party had taken a lead over the Conservative government on the issue of law and order (p. 26).

Once again the government was to alter policy in a way which was presented as a shift in direction, rather than a reversal or a U-turn. The renewed emphasis of the criminal justice system was to be that of public protection, taken out of the White Paper, dusted down and placed at the top of the agenda. There was to be no doubting that public protection would be moved from its previously camouflaged role to one which would drive the agenda from the front. In so doing a punitive climate was to be unleashed which was not only to lead to a prison population outstripping all official forecasts, but also a conflationary effect on community penalties and therefore the probation service. The White Paper made the re-emphasised role of the probation service crystal clear:

> Preventing reoffending and protecting the public from serious harm should be the objectives of the probation service, whether they are supervising offenders who are carrying out community penalties or offenders released from custody (Home Office, 1990, p. 2).

Until this time, the role of the probation service had been geared more towards the prevention of reoffending than public protection from serious offenders. The government had added public protection to the list of probation service tasks in an upfront way by linking it with the prevention of offending, itself a traditional function. It therefore made this new emphasis less contentious and more in line with traditional roles. Public protection at this time was not linked to the concept of dangerousness to the extent that it is now. Indeed the White Paper indicates that probation supervision was likely to be of less serious offenders than those receiving custody, thereby making supervision in the community linked with prevention of crime (a traditional police function of course):

> The protection of the public must be the first thought in the supervising officer's mind, particularly when supervising offenders released from custody ... Offenders sentenced to community penalties are likely to have committed less serious offences than those sentenced to custody, but it is still important to protect the public against reoffending during the period of supervision under a community penalty (p. 35).

It should be clear however that the release arrangements of the Criminal Justice Act 1991 meant that more serious offenders would be released on licence to the probation service than would have been the case under the old parole arrangements.

The White Paper raised the public protection profile of the probation service and, in so doing, set members of the service firmly in the law and order camp, which had become the home of the public protection protagonists. This clearly had important implications. It was important for the continued survival of the probation service that it was seen to be moving away from its traditional association with social work as a discipline and more towards a correctional organisation (for more on this, see chapter 3). The White Paper and subsequent Criminal Justice Act 1991 had placed the probation service centre stage in delivering the government's criminal justice policy, the policy of bifurcation. The trade-off therefore, for a social work based service, was to be placed in a slightly different camp and certainly one which initially was not regarded with total enthusiasm by the rank and file of probation officers (Harris, 1992, Worrall, 1997). The gap between a management increasingly wedded to new public management ideals and the delivery of punishment in the community, and a workforce (perhaps mistakenly) retaining its social work values and ideals, was to lead to tension for several years. It could be argued and indeed has been by many commentators, that this was a short-sighted management strategy which would inevitably lead to the decline of the probation service as we have known it in this country:

Having consciously adopted the 'high-risk' strategy of focusing on 'high-risk' offenders and having conceded the right of central government to dictate its priorities, it was bound to become vulnerable if the penal climate were to get any colder ... (Worrall, 1997, p. 76).

Changing penal climates and, in particular, changing Home Office ministers, were to see the probation service lose its centre-stage role. Its focus on serious offenders, which saw it become a much more controlling organisation, was to see it lose its way to a certain extent as its client group became fodder for the 'prison works' strategy which was soon to be unleashed by Michael Howard. Once this process had begun, the opportunity for reduced budgets and even financial cuts was evident. Indeed this was to be the future of the probation service until one happy day in July 1998 (see chapter 10).

There will be more discussion of the changing role of the probation service in the next chapter but for the moment it is important to signal another issue raised by the White Paper. This entailed a re-emphasis on partnership and multi-agency working, notably in the field of public protection. For the probation service, close co-operation with the police was stressed in both the White Paper and another document, *'Supervision and Punishment in the Community'* (Home Office, 1990b). Both of these documents can be seen as early indications of a changing role for police and probation services under the mantle of the public protection agenda. The Criminal Justice Act 1991 had been passed through a parliament which saw stress laid upon its public protection sections rather than those which were aimed at reducing the use of custody. Although it could be said that the 'punitive bifurcation' (Cavadino and Dignan, 1997) elements of the Criminal Justice Act 1991 were to have far-reaching implications for probation service practice, the absorption of the service into the public protection area was possibly the road to far more significant change.

The policy of public protection focused primarily on serious sexual and violent offenders. The Criminal Justice Act 1991 was clear in its emphasis by stating, as one of its sentencing principles, that, 'a clear distinction should be drawn between offences against the person and offences against property'. This was carried out in various ways, from quite simple means such as lowering the maximum penalty for non-domestic burglary to 10 years whilst retaining it at 14 years for burglary of the home, to the more important return to the notion of dangerousness in its provision for sentencing offenders from whom the public should be protected (von Hirsch and Ashworth, 1996). Included within the Act were provisions (sections 2(2)(b)), which would allow the court to pass a sentence longer than the sentence which would be appropriate under a strict application of the 'just deserts' policy on an offender who posed a threat of a serious risk of harm to the public. This was a significant departure from the overall 'just deserts' philosophy of the Act, a philosophy which meant that penalty severity was directly associated with offence seriousness. These provisions in the Criminal Justice Act 1991 again raised the vexed question of predicting dangerousness which was discussed in chapter 1. The issue for the courts was one of predicting the likelihood of an offender causing serious harm to the public in the future and, if coming to that judgment, imposing a penalty which was longer than that merited by the instant offence, up to the legal maximum for the crime. In simple terms, two like offences committed by different offenders could receive completely different sentences due to the court being persuaded that future serious harm was likely to follow from one of them. There has been much debate over these provisions, particularly from a legal perspective (see von Hirsch and Ashworth, 1996). However it is also important to emphasise the political context in which the legislation was passed. As indicated above, there was a need in government to reduce the use of custody by the courts so as to meet public expenditure targets. To do so by appearing soft on crime was of course politically unacceptable. To attempt to do so whilst making a stand against offenders for whom there would be little public sympathy made the task much easier. The Criminal Justice Act 1991 was therefore a landmark piece of legislation in many ways, although our discussion is concerned with the focus on serious offenders and the public protection agenda. It did single out these offenders for special attention because of the crimes they had committed, but also, very importantly, singled them out as individuals. The Act was very much an offence-focused piece of legislation, true 'just deserts'. Yet in considering potential dangerousness, the courts could ignore the instant offence in terms of its seriousness, although it still needed to be a violent or sexual crime, and focus on the individual, departing from the just deserts philosophy. It could be argued that this was one of the early signs that certain offenders were to be isolated within the criminal justice system for special attention, a process which has continued with quite astounding implications not only for sentencing but also for the practice of all criminal justice agencies.

COLD WINDS FROM AMERICA

However, before we focus on the measures aimed at these offenders it is important to understand the increasingly punitive climate in which they began to flourish. To do so it is necessary to examine developments in the United States of America, from where so many of the recent initiatives in UK criminal justice have emanated. Having conducted research in America, the Prison Reform Trust (PRT) was able to conclude:

> During the 1970s American sentencing policy underwent a dramatic change. Individual states, as well as the federal government, began to look towards a system of determinate sentencing, as elected officials were no longer to defer to judicial expertise on sentencing matters (PRT, 1997).

Although this change in attitude was put down to a concern with disparity and discrimination, it could equally be viewed as the politicians looking for votes. Nonetheless, a series of reports and academic publications during the 1970s had seen a move away from treatment as a major feature of the criminal justice system, towards a model of determinate sentencing (Dunbar and Langdon, 1998). Beginning in 1971 with the *Struggle for Justice* (American Friends Service Committee) and then, in the same year, the National Crime Commission's report, a move began which aimed to counter disparities in sentencing and parole decisions. But it was a report prepared by Judge Marvin Frankel in 1972, *Criminal Sentences: Law without Order*, which really began the push towards controlling the discretionary powers of the judiciary and putting sentencing guidelines in the hands of a commission, or similar body. These bodies existed in 25 American states by 1996 and reflected the transfer of power from the judiciary to prosecutors and indeed the members of the sentencing commission. In attempting to limit the discretion of the judge, however, it should be noted that the potential to pass sentence having taken account of the offender's circumstances, is very much reduced. As the PRT noted:

But there is equally no doubt that many guidelines were too rigid and complex. They turned judges into nothing more than calculators at the sentencing stage. This has been particularly noticeable at the federal level, where mathematical formulae are used to calculate the punishment for federal crimes. Guidelines have effectively neutralised judges in some jurisdictions... (p. 2).

In the UK a sentencing commission has not materialised despite being frequently talked about by the Labour Party in opposition. (Section 81 of the Crime and Disorder Act 1998, establishes a Sentencing Advisory Panel (planned for 1999). This Panel could be viewed as a watered-down commission.) However there has been a gradual erosion of the 'individualised' nature of criminal justice and an increasing focus on a just deserts, offence-focused sentencing philosophy. Dunbar and Langdon (1998) believe that those American states that have set up a form of sentencing commission have managed political turmoil and avoided politically-driven extremes better than those states without (p. 49). Yet they also caution against a belief that a commission will be moderate and free from interference, citing the US Sentencing Guidelines Commission, established in 1984, as an example of producing a harsh and complex sentencing structure. The sentencing principles contained within the Criminal Justice Act 1991 can perhaps be seen as a watered down attempt to control judicial discretion in the sentencing context. However, even in this limited attempt the government quickly backtracked, abolishing the more liberal reforms in the light of judicial criticism in particular (although it should be noted that much political capital was made out of this situation which again was not an accurate reflection of the merits and demerits of the Act).

Two other American developments have begun to influence sentencing in this country by way of fuelling the retributive climate, these are mandatory sentences and in particular 'three strikes and you're out'. Both these forms of sentencing virtually eliminate discretion and the ability of the judge to sentence the individual based on his circumstances as well as for the crime he has committed. Three strikes legislation means, as in the baseball terminology, that the third strike (or offence) means that you are out (or in prison for a minimum of 25 years in some cases, or indeed for life). In some American states such as California, although the first two strikes must be for serious felonies, the third can be triggered for any felony, often leading to a life sentence for a relatively minor crime. Federal law, however, and the law in many other states, concentrates the intention of the legislation on violent, sexual and drugs offences. Few members of the public, or indeed politicians, find it easy to argue against the logic of incapacitation. Once people have succumbed to the arguments in favour of incapacitation, however, discussion of the potential for reform and rehabilitation is sidelined. This is despite the move from 'nothing works' to 'what works?' in recent years.

The answer to the question of 'what works?' is that 'prison works', at least prison worked according to the then Home Secretary, Michael Howard, in 1993. It was his appointment which was to see the real importation of American criminal justice ideas into the UK environment. The importation was more or less wholesale, with little allowance for a British context. The three strikes ideology was adopted and suddenly everyone on this side of the Atlantic became familiar with the game of baseball. The Crime (Sentences) Bill, published by Howard in 1996, carried very similar proposals to American federal provision. Automatic life sentences were to be imposed for those convicted of a second serious violent or sexual offence and mandatory minimum sentences of seven years for persistent drug dealers. A third provision, imposing a mandatory three year sentence on persistent burglars, was not to be enacted by the incoming Labour government in 1997 (this measure was resurrected by Home Secretary Jack Straw in January 1999), nor were proposals concerning the reduction of parole eligibility. The focus on serious criminals of this nature was not likely to provoke a significant defence of judicial discretion, indeed the opposite was likely in view of the widespread myths about judges' 'over-leniency' in sentencing serious cases.

The details of legislation aimed at dangerous offender populations are described in greater detail in chapter 4. This chapter has briefly sought to describe the changing nature of the penal climate as reflected in predominantly new right criminal justice policies which were seen in jurisdictions around the world. The development of just deserts which, it could be argued, was an attempt to eliminate disparities in sentencing, was a perfect vehicle for delivering the economic goals of governments committed to reducing the cost to the public purse. Ashworth (1989) noted that,

> across the common law world and elsewhere, new sentencing systems
> are being introduced or recommended. For example, Sweden, the US

federal jurisdictions and several American states have already begun to operate new sentencing schemes. ... and it is at this stage that the just deserts approach has been influential (p. 340).

This move to just deserts at the end of the 1980s and beginning of the 1990s was undoubtedly a real attempt by governments to reduce the use of custodial sentences. The effect of these measures was a general toughening-up in the nature of community penalties and also increased prison sentences for certain classes of offenders. This has been described by Pratt (1997) as the redefinition of dangerousness by neo-liberal governments and was eventually to lead to a range of ever harsher penalties being applied to that newly defined group of offenders. Much of this process took place in distinctive political circumstances which will be described in the following chapter.

SUMMARY

Public protection became an increasing feature of criminal justice policy in the 1980s. It was presented as a response to a growing public fear of serious crime, yet much of the evidence from around the world did not really support this fear. Governments did little to reduce that fear as public protection itself became a useful political tool. It could be used both to put distance between any government and its opposition and also to alter the shape and direction of criminal justice policy and agency practice. It neatly fitted in with the general attack on professional autonomy within the public sector and the probation service in particular.

Punitive climates are cold climates and have an effect which spreads throughout the criminal justice system. None of the criminal justice agencies has been immune from a hardening of attitudes and it has been necessary for them to adapt and adopt some of the practices associated with these attitudes in order to survive. Harsh climates are relatively easy to create and will often fly in the face of real evidence to the contrary. The reversal of many of the provisions contained in the Criminal Justice Act 1991 was in direct contrast to the real gains achieved by that Act, one of the very few Criminal Justice Acts to make such gains. The lessons from America are the same. Despite the evidence of an overall fall in the levels of crime (with the exception of murder), that country embarked upon a massive hardening-up of its criminal justice system, because the *fear* of crime was increasing. A report in *The Independent* (19 May 1994) suggested that Americans need to have something to worry about. As the perceived threat from the USSR diminished and as the economy recovered, so crime emerged as the main worry. The article suggested that it was not only the introduction of mandatory life penalties for non-serious offenders that was worrying, but wider trends such as the more adult treatment of juveniles and the increased use of the death penalty. It is clear that once the punitive bandwagon starts rolling, it is difficult to stop it. As *The Independent* reported:

> Maybe the panic will pass. Now though, the agitation over crime is a strange mirror of America's other current obsession, reform of the health system. Both are fixated on exterminating disease and its consequences, either by expensive treatment or expensive punishment. Neither is overly concerned with prevention, to keep people out of hospitals and would-be criminals out of the dock.

This is the pursuance of the clean and safe society, achieved by the exclusion and expulsion of undesirables. Through the criminal justice system, the 'dangerous' become the means of achieving this aim — the political context of this developing agenda will now be discussed.

Chapter 3
Protection as Politics

One of the major arguments of this book is that the issue of protecting
the public has shaped and manipulated the criminal justice agenda to an
ever greater degree in recent years. This is true not only in this country
but also in the United States, Canada and Australia, each country
developing the agenda to suit its own unique political situation (Pratt,
1997). The spread of a harsher, more punitive sentencing climate has
already been discussed, although during the early history of this
development, public protection from dangerous offenders was not the
only issue. This has come much more to the fore during the 1990s, as
witnessed by Home Secretary Jack Straw's speech to the House of
Commons (30 July 1997) when he mentioned 'protecting the public'
four times in a brief speech (James and Raine, 1998, p. 105). This
chapter will therefore examine the political context in which public
protection has become such a significant political issue and the next
chapter will examine the impact of this agenda on policy formation and
implementation.

The policy of bifurcation described in the previous chapter makes
clear the intention of a government to clamp down on serious offenders,
generally those people who commit the type of crimes that engender
fear in the minds of the public. These crimes would most obviously
include sexual and violent crimes offences, although it should be noted
that the early bifurcatory measures tended to include drugs offences as

well, and even, in their early manifestations, repeat or habitual offenders of any description (Pratt, 1997). Drugs offences remain a priority for most governments and remain subject to special legislation, such as the seven year mandatory minimum sentences contained in the Crime (Sentences) Act 1997. However, it is the fear of violent crime and sexual crime in particular that has dominated the agenda in recent years. As such it has become an uncontentious political issue, each main political party doing its very best to be seen as offering the public more protection than its opponents, or even in the case of some bold promises, a guarantee or right to protection from crime:

> A primary responsibility of any government at home is to take action to protect people from crime ... the guarantee of law and order is essential to the British way of life (John Major, 9 September 1994).

PROTECTING THE PUBLIC

Public protection has become a serious political issue. Although the evidence for the degree of public concern alleged is almost impossible to isolate and identify, politicians do, however, continue to claim that they reflect public concerns. The lack of a real debate around this issue and the reticence by key politicians and practitioners to elucidate the real facts of the situation are suggestive of a willingness to allow the public to believe that they are at greater risk than they really are. This suggests that politics has won out over professionalism, a potentially dangerous situation in itself.

Protection of the public has itself been a shifting policy. It is fair to say that protecting the public from reoffending by known criminals has long been a feature of criminal justice policy and special provision has invariably been made in respect of recidivists. Prevention of reoffending is a key element of probation supervision and was a rationale for practice long before the national standards introduced with the Criminal Justice Act 1991 set it as a priority. Probation supervision, in any form, is about changing the offending behaviour of the supervisee in the hope that it will not recur in the future. This has not changed over time, although the means by which it might be achieved and demonstrated certainly has, not least as a result of the growth of managerialism within the service (May, 1991, Brownlee, 1998). As was seen in the last chapter, protection of the public did begin to move into a new phase with the publication of the 1990 White Paper, *Crime, Justice and Protecting the Public*. This document not only saw prevention of reoffending as a key objective for criminal justice agencies, but also really began the focus on special categories of offenders. This focus was gradually to shape the way in which agencies were to operate. The 1990 White Paper made this message clear from the beginning:

> People's attitudes to crime and punishment seem to vary with the passage of time. Today, people are quite rightly much less tolerant of violence than they were and they expect violent crimes to be punished more severely. On the other hand, there is a growing awareness that prison is usually not the best way of dealing with many less serious property crimes (para. 1.3).

This is a clear expression of the policy of bifurcation, although the evidence for the claims of public tolerance and intolerance is not substantiated within the paper. The reference to the views of the public was, however, important and reflects the development of what James and Raine (1998) refer to as the 'public voice' and its effect on criminal justice policy. The next paragraph of the White Paper suggested that sentencers are mindful of public attitudes in sentencing, with the implication being that this is a good thing. More recently, however, a speech by the Lord Chief Justice would appear to contradict this view especially when the attitudes of the public have been framed by the media and vote-catching politicians:

> The tenor of political rhetoric has strongly favoured the imposition of severe sentences; this rhetoric has been faithfully reflected in certain elements of the media; and judges accused of passing lenient sentences have found themselves routinely castigated in some newspapers ... The increase in the prison population is not explained by any recent increase in sentencing powers, and I have no doubt that it is related to pressure of public opinion (Bingham, 1997).

In a White Paper dedicated (unofficially perhaps) to reducing the prison population, there was a particular emphasis on crimes of violence but not the hysterical concern with sex offenders that was to surface a few years later. The role of the police service with serious offenders, and the duty of the court to protect the public by imposing longer sentences was made clear:

The police give priority to detecting the most serious crimes, since the public need protecting from them. Long prison sentences are the right punishment for these offences. Some violent offenders pose a threat to public safety; and the legislation which the Government proposes will allow the Crown Court to send them to custody for longer than would otherwise be justified by the seriousness of the offences they have committed, *if this is necessary to protect the public* (para.1.8). (*emphasis added*)

The document makes frequent references to public concerns over certain types of crime, for example rape and sexual abuse of children. However, it also points out, at a time when policy announcements were perhaps more rational than of late, that increases in recorded rates for these crimes were probably a result of increased reporting rates rather than real increases in numbers of offences. Indeed, the focus on violent crimes appeared to be more a concern with alcohol-related violence among young men (see Field's research, Home Office, 1990), than with the type of predatory dangerousness which was to come to dominate the agenda later. This issue was dealt with in one paragraph (3.13) where it was explained that the proportionality principle could be overruled if there was a need for public protection from certain persistent violent and sexual offenders. It is interesting to note the use of the persistent criteria and how this disappears by the time we reach the 'two strikes' legislation of 1997, unless of course persistent becomes more than once! The attention to dangerous offenders was therefore limited in a paper which proposed to protect the public. This issue had not yet come to dominate the criminal justice agenda and the overriding aim of the Criminal Justice Act 1991 was to remain an attempt to reduce the use of custody by the courts and an encouragement to make greater use of community penalties.

In a chapter on supervision the White Paper made the role of the probation service very clear in terms of the public protection agenda:

The protection of the public must be the first thought in the supervising officer's mind, particularly when supervising offenders released from custody ... (para. 7.4).

Notwithstanding this public protection focus, much of the rest of the chapter refers to what may be viewed as traditional social work functions concerning reintegration and focused, planned intervention.

Furthermore, in talking about the supervisory function of probation officers, reference was made to the unlikelihood of their being successful if working alone, reminiscent of similar references increasingly made about the police service. Yet, in 1990, the potential 'partners' of the probation service were listed as employment organisations, voluntary organisations, the health service, mediation schemes and other, what might loosely be termed, 'helping organisations'. Conspicuous by its absence from this list of potential partners is the police service. This absence makes the growth of joint working between the two services in the period following the Criminal Justice Act 1991 all the more remarkable, as will be seen in the next chapter.

JUSTIFIED PANIC?

Although remaining the framework for legislation to the present day, the Criminal Justice Act 1991 was substantially revised within twelve months of its enactment. The climate had changed due to a series of perhaps unrelated events some of which will now be discussed. However it is quite clear that since 1993 it has been extremely difficult to detect many of the liberal minded influences within the criminal justice system that were so apparent in the Act. In the growing politicisation of the criminal justice agenda, 1993 is therefore a key year when, among many notable events, Michael Howard was appointed as Home Secretary. It was a year in which many of the Criminal Justice Act 1991 provisions were repealed without substantial opposition. The previous year had seen the election of a fourth successive Conservative government and a campaign in which law and order issues had been a relatively one-sided affair. The Labour party effectively sought to neutralise the issue, perhaps thinking that it could not challenge the government effectively in one of its traditionally strong areas (Downes and Morgan, 1997), having tried and failed to do so in previous elections.

Yet law and order was quickly destined to become a major political issue again and one which was increasingly to crystallise around the issue of dangerous offenders and public protection. The defeat of the Labour Party in 1992 can be seen as a watershed in its political and position approach to law and order. The appointment of Tony Blair as shadow Home Secretary saw a significant repositioning of the party's position, not least with his celebrated 'tough on crime, tough on the causes of crime' speech (Dunbar and Langdon, 1998, p. 101). This

position statement was hugely significant as it moved the party away
from a stance where it could be branded as an apologist for crime, or
'soft on crime', according to the Conservatives election campaign in
1992. By joining with the government in condemning antisocial
behaviour it became easier to attack the Tory record. Their polices had
failed, so a long-term social approach to crime prevention, alongside a
tough stance on criminal behaviour should be attempted according to
the Labour Party. For the first time in a long while it was able to talk
openly about crime with less fear than in the past. This process was to
result eventually in a true political neutralisation of the subject during
the 1997 election campaign. Blair's intervention had come about at a
time when the Home Secretary, Kenneth Clarke, had been discussing
measures aimed at young offenders 'whom the law could not reach'.
Within a month of Blair's new message the killing of James Bulger was
to alter the whole debate radically and set in train a punitive climate
which has not yet abated.

It is not necessary to go into the details of the Bulger case here,
although for an interesting perspective Young (1996) is recommended.
For our purposes, the significance of the case was the sense of moral
panic that it unleashed, not only concerning children who kill, but of a
deeper social malaise, of a society going wrong, and one increasingly
marked by a sense of insecurity and fear. For Britain, this case acted as
that unique catalyst which enabled the public protection debate to
develop the focus that it did. Much has been written about risk as a
feature of (post) modern society (Beck, 1992) and this is often linked
with cultures of anxiety and fear of crime (Hollway and Jefferson,
1997). Risk culture is about an attempt to reduce or eliminate risk, to
turn uncertainty into certainty. We shall see in chapters 5 and 9 that a
managerial approach to risk, 'risk management', offers the public the
prospect of certainty in an uncertain world, itself a dangerous idea
perhaps. The demand for certainty and with it safety, finds a degree of
security in blaming and naming. This applies to professionals as well as
criminals. Due to the pervasive nature of anxiety, it can find a base
anywhere and therefore perhaps needs to be located and 'managed', as
Hollway and Jefferson (1997) indicate:

> In other words, because we have no means of being sure where risk
> and safety lie, nothing can be trusted and anxiety, therefore,
> potentially finds a location in any area of daily life (p. 261).

They cite Douglas (1986) and her view on moral concern and real blaming; 'the belief that any misfortune must have a cause, a perpetrator to blame, from whom to exact compensation' (p. 16). This climate is one in which not only does crime occur but also in which it is not prevented, indeed this latter point may be a far more important indicator of success or failure. When that crime is serious then the real blaming can be laid at the feet of the very people charged with preventing it. One of the more skilful manoeuvres of governments in recent years has been to ensure that the blame for crimes is diverted from themselves to the public and the professions. As we shall see, the police service has increasingly been given a larger share of that blame.

Fear and Anxiety

Fear of crime is not the only contributor to a climate of anxiety and risk, although it is significant. Although not really quantifiable it is presented as if it can be quantified and therefore 'managed'. Risk reducing strategies aim in part to reduce the fear, and performance indicators aim to measure that fear reduction. Resources can be directed against it, or those parts which instil most fear and anxiety, and an attempt can be made to demonstrate that something is being done. Yet the realist position would have to be that the chances of being victimised by one of these very serious crimes are extremely low and that government shares a responsibility to downplay the risk, whereas reflecting an apparent fear of crime may have the opposite effect. However, we know that this is not usually the case, that even in the face of hard facts, the fear of crime is talked up if the political situation demands and if it serves other purposes:

> In an age of uncertainty, discourses that appear to promise a resolution to ambivalence by producing identifiable victims and blameable villains are likely to figure prominently in the State's ceaseless attempts to impose social order. Thus the figure of the 'criminal' becomes a convenient folk devil and the fear of crime discourse a satisfying location for anxieties generated more widely (Hollway and Jefferson, 1997, p. 265).

Hollway and Jefferson's point is also that such fears and anxieties are heavily dependent upon the unique biographies of individuals and their ability to handle uncertainties in their lives. This comment may be as true for the public as for the practitioners charged with the task of reducing the risk and needs to be allowed for in all the arenas in which the public protection discourse is an issue.

If we are living in late modern society which is characterised by feelings of being at risk and of uncertainty, then it is clear that the political situation in the 1990s has done little to allay those fears. The Bulger case did cause a significant shock to the nation's conscience, stirring up fears for the future if children could commit such an horrendous crime. The media did its very best to build on this fear, although it has been questioned whether or not this really constituted a moral panic (for a full discussion on both the use of the term and its 'reappraisal' see Thompson, 1998). Undoubtedly the media handling of the incident oscillated wildly, varying between calls for a rational debate on education, parenting and moral values, to the spread of evil throughout our society. If we consider the basic ingredients of a moral panic, it is clear that many were indeed present following the Bulger incident:

(1)   Something or someone is defined as a threat to values or interests.

(2)   This threat is depicted in an easily recognisable form by the media.

(3)   There is a rapid build-up of public concern.

(4)   There is a response from authorities or opinion-makers.

(5)   The panic recedes or results in social changes.

(Thompson, 1998, p. 8.)

Whether or not the Bulger incident constituted a moral panic may be debatable, but what is not debatable is the unleashing of the moral crusade which followed, epitomised by John Major's statement that society should, 'understand a little less and condemn a little more'. In other words, the public's fear of serious crime was not to be put to rest, but kept simmering. The political climate was to lead to an ever-increasing punitiveness and the well of public fear and unease was to be tapped when the issue of predatory paedophiles was brought out into the open both during and after the 1997 election campaign.

TOUGH TALK – TOUGH POLICIES

It could be argued, however, that the raising of the law and order stakes had less to do with public fear of spectacular and unusual crimes than the rapidly changing political landscape. Undoubtedly, Tony Blair had managed, as shadow Home Secretary, to steal many of the Conservatives' clothes, whilst just about retaining something of the Labour Party heritage of social crime prevention. By the end of September 1993, a MORI poll found the Conservative lead at 2% over Labour, down from 14% before the election (Dunbar and Langdon, 1998, p. 114). Michael Howard's appointment as Home Secretary in May 1993 was to unleash a competition between the two parties to win the law and order vote which had served the Conservatives so well in their previous victories. This competition was to become so fierce that by the time of the general election in 1997 there would be nothing left to argue over: it became a non-issue in the campaign.

The speech by Howard at the annual Party Conference in October 1993 has been much debated and it is unnecessary to go over that ground again. It is enough to say that the theme of 'prison works' was to become one of those issues which it was almost impossible to argue against if you were a politician. Howard has to be viewed as a very skilful manipulator of the law and order agenda as he forced the Labour Party to meet and at times raise the punitive stakes. Although the speech covered some 27 points, it was the message concerning prison which made the most impact. That message was that, in future, success in criminal justice terms would no longer be measured by the numbers kept out of prison, but by those inside, a message in direct contrast to that espoused by former Home Secretary Waddington, noted in chapter 2. The most vocal opposition to this policy came not from the Labour benches, but from the senior judiciary, with Lords Woolf, Taylor and Ackner prominent among them. Howard was not phased by criticism from the judiciary, however, indeed he probably viewed it as reinforcing his populist position. He announced that, 'thousands of dangerous criminals are prevented from attacking the community while they are inside' (*The Times*, 15 October 1993). How could anyone argue with the logic of such a statement, despite the clear exaggeration of the claim and the conflation in terms of dangerousness? Following on from Howard's conference speech, Prime Minister John Major launched his own moral crusade, his so-called 'back to basics' campaign. The political battle was therefore joined. The growing political consensus was no longer around the notion of liberal reform but around the value of punishment and incarceration. The rational presentation of evidence was to become a thing of the past as each party sought to establish the lead on the platform which it believed would win it the next election.

Howard's 27 points were to be turned into his flagship piece of legislation, the Criminal Justice and Public Order Act 1994. The reader may question why this book, with its focus on public protection from dangerous offenders, should discuss this Act in particular. It did not really contain any measures aimed at this class of offender, indeed the Criminal Justice Act 1991 had gone much further. What it did do though was to keep the political pot and plot simmering. The Criminal Justice and Public Order Act 1994 was wide-ranging in its scope, encompassing matters such as contracting-out in the prison service, measures aimed at young offenders including new secure training orders for 12–14 year olds, redefinition of some sexual offences, bail and committal matters. However, it was new proposals in two key areas which really provoked most opposition. One was the interference with suspects' right of silence and the other a raft of measures aimed at public order. The measures aimed at allowing the court to take a negative inference from a suspect's silence under police questioning were part of Howard's attempt to shift the balance away from what he viewed as being in favour of the criminal. Detailed discussion concerning this measure is unnecessary here, the reader can find an excellent summary in Wasik and Taylor (1994). However, it should be noted that the Labour Party chose not to declare its opposition to these measures publicly on the floor of the House of Commons, preferring instead to challenge the Bill clause by clause in committee stage. The public image of the Labour Party offered from the floor of the House of Commons was one of supporting many of the measures proposed by Howard. The public order measures provoked a more widespread and public opposition. In proposing measures to tackle ravers, squatters, protesters, travellers and gypsies, Howard effectively created a new breed of folk devils. He did so in such a way that indicated he was wanting to protect innocent victims, law-abiding people whose rights were affected by the actions of these new-age villains. In many ways the 1994 Act reflects a fundamental attack on a range of civil liberties and in the light of this the opposition to it, short-lived and vocal though it was, can be seen as relatively muted. The political climate was such that opposition could too easily be redefined as support for the criminal. The Criminal Justice and Public Order Act 1994 did therefore continue to stoke the law and order fires. It did so not only by enabling the government to cast itself in the role of dealing with all those issues which people felt 'needed to be dealt with', but also by pulling along the Labour Party every step of the way.

Unfortunately for Michael Howard, his proposals did not have the political impact he would have wished. Despite, or because of, an absence of opposition from the Labour Party, the Conservatives found that by June 1994, public opinion polls placed them behind Labour on law and order issues. This was of course unprecedented for a Conservative government. The effect was to stoke the fires even further, with senior Conservative politicians joining Howard in the crusade against crime. The subsequent history of criminal justice 'debate' leading up to the 1997 election can be viewed as an attempt by the government to raise the stakes so high that the Labour Party would eventually pull out. So many of Howard's measures were to become crude populism that he must have thought that the Opposition would have faltered. That they did not falter reflects the political stakes of the time and their determination not to be cast in the clothes of the 'criminal's friend'.

LOOKING WEST

A hint of the shape of things to come can be gleaned from an article in *The Independent* on 19 May 1994. In this, Rupert Corwell reported the developments in American criminal justice, fuelled and supported by a nation obsessed with crime. Opposition to the extreme measures proposed, including mandatory penalties and an extension of the death penalty, was described as 'the merest hint of being soft on crime is a political death sentence on its own'. However, it was the reported developments in the state of Oregon which were to be indicative of policy changes to take place here in the following years:

> In Oregon, residents are pressing for the baseball variant to beat them all: the 'grand slam', which scores four runs. Alarmed that draconian measures in neighbouring Washington state and California might send the criminal classes scurrying their way, Oregon has devised a four-pronged response: stricter conditions in prison, less probation, immutable prison terms and mandatory minimum sentences for violent offenders.

This is an extreme case of not-in-my-backyard and leads to the question, where did the Home Secretary spend his holidays in 1994? It is also a reflection of the total approach to crime, an approach which decrees that all agencies take on the same goals in the war against crime.

There are many other examples of Howard's scatter gun approach to criminal justice during 1994 and 1995. In November 1994 he announced that in future victims would be consulted before the temporary or paroled release of prison inmates. A telephone hotline would ensure that the views of victims would be given to the governor of the prison considering the release. Complaints ensued that, aside from being impractical, the proposed scheme was a breach of natural justice, not that such an attack was likely to bother the Home Secretary. He was busily involved politicising the issue of victims, not least because of his alienation of the victim movement. In proposing a new tariff-based scheme of compensation he was clearly hoping to cut costs. The measure had been declared illegal by the Court of Appeal (*R* v *Secretary of State for the Home Department, ex parte Fire Brigades Union and others* [1995] 1 All ER 888 (CA), [1995] 2 All ER 244 (HL)), but nonetheless was to result in the Criminal Injuries Compensation Act 1995 (Zedner, 1997, p. 604). The government also announced a pilot of the use of Victim Impact Statements in court proceedings, a measure widely practised in America. Despite many reservations expressed by American and English legal experts (Ashworth, 1993), the scheme was piloted in six police force areas following a working group set up by the Director of Public Prosecutions in 1995 (Zedner, 1997, p. 602).

The message on victims,[1] one which purportedly sought to increase the attention paid to their views and needs, was accompanied by one of clamping down on prisoners' privileges and the first official pronouncement that some life sentence prisoners would never be released. The list of lifers included names that would have been expected, such as Ian Brady, Myra Hindley, Dennis Nielsen and Peter Sutcliffe. The Home Secretary had tried to introduce a whole life sentence in the Criminal Justice and Public Order Act 1994 but was defeated by cabinet members. His new announcement has therefore been viewed as attempting to do the same by the back door (*The Independent*, 17 December 1994). Once again, although these measures were attacked by the judiciary, there was little evidence of Labour Party opposition. Michael Howard was doing an effective job in cranking up the law and order agenda. Widespread disillusionment with his performance, manifesting itself not only in constant judicial criticism and reversal of

---

[1] As with the public protection agenda, the message on victims was one which potentially represented an opportunity for liberal-progressive policy development, but which was again, it could be argued, hijacked for political purposes.

his decisions but also in the reported lack of faith by Conservative Party chairmen, seemed only to spur Howard on.

I'm Right, You're Wrong

However, it was to be late 1995 when the law and order stakes were at their highest. In the weeks leading up to the annual Conservative Party conference, leading government figures began to criticise the judiciary openly, not least for their lack of accounting for public opinion. The proposals offered at the conference were to trigger a fierce exchange between senior legal figures and the government, although not between the government and the opposition. These proposals were an English form of the American models which had become such a major political issue in that country. The attack was a two-pronged affair, although both were to lead to the same outcome, a massively increased prison population. The two principal themes were based on sentences passed and time served and related to notions of honesty and consistency, aping the American 'truth in sentencing'. The intention was to make prisoners serve longer, in other words to reduce the amount of time earned in remission or other forms of early release (the American 'good time' credit). As ever, Howard had a soundbite to accompany his measures, in this case it was, 'no more half-time sentences for full-time crime'. His other measures were to introduce mandatory minimum penalties for certain offenders, the American 'three strikes' legislation, the accompanying slogan this time being; 'If you don't want to do the time, don't do the crime'. Undoubtedly, the not so hidden agenda here was an attempt to put clear water between the government and the Labour Party. In the event this did not happen and indeed, to all intents and purposes, the escalation of the debate resulted in the issue becoming nullified. As suggested, the legal opposition to these proposals was fierce, with Lord Chief Justice Taylor leading the way, arguing predominantly that mandatory penalties would limit judicial discretion and were not in the interests of justice. Lord Ackner, a former law lord, suggested in December 1995 that Howard was 'playing politics with the administration of justice', describing his measures as a 'yaa-boo — I'm tougher than you' approach. He also predicted that the measures would not get through Cabinet, or both Houses of Parliament, before the general election in 1997 — in this he was to be very wrong (*The Guardian*, 2 December 1996).

In a speech to the House of Lords in January 1997, Lord Ackner skilfully dissected Howard's proposals with constant comparison between the considered approach of the Criminal Justice Act 1991 and that of the Crime (Sentences) Bill. His conclusion was telling:

> In my respectful submission, the Home Secretary is putting forward proposals in a manner which shows a degree of irresponsibility that I would not expect to go with that office. There is a growing belief that he is exploiting for party political gain the misapprehension of the public that judges are too soft on crime, which I accept is a commonly held view ... as the noble and learned Lord, Lord Nolan, pointed out, the Court of Appeal can increase sentences that are excessively lenient. Indeed the Attorney-General has a duty to bring such cases to its attention. But the Court of Appeal spends far more time having to reduce sentences when judges have been too severe ... the vast majority of sentences are not appealed against or questioned at all. All this the Home Secretary must know but, as was recently stated in a national newspaper, he has 'an unerring populist streak' which sadly the Opposition seem now to wish to emulate (Hansard, HL, 27 January 1997, col. 1013).

The detailed provisions of what became the Crime (Sentences) Act 1997, will be discussed in chapter 4 but before moving on it is worth noting some of the comments made about it since. The highly respected academic David Thomas produced a damning criticism in a recent article (1997):

> The Crime (Sentences) Act represents a low point in the development of English sentencing legislation. It is difficult to think of any legislation in the field of criminal justice enacted during the present century which has so little to do with the improvement of the administration of criminal justice. It is equally difficult to think of any legislation which has been greeted with such hostility by those who have the responsibility of superintending its operation (p. 83).

Thomas went on to state that, in his opinion, the effect of the Act will be minimal and that its importance lies more in symbolism. He understood why a failing Conservative government would have introduced the Bill and he equally understood why the Labour Party left the opposition to it to others. However, he failed to understand why a newly elected government needed to introduce the greater part of the Act at all and that the whole episode was one of politics rather than practical application. A few of Thomas's detailed comments on the Act will be considered in the next chapter but for now his summary of the situation will be offered, 'Sadly, the decision to implement this legislation seems to imply that the Labour Government intends to continue the process of piecemeal and often ill-considered legislation which has produced the quagmire into which our sentencing legislation has sunk' (p. 83).

The punitive climate is therefore one in which politics wins out over reason, where rhetoric wins out over evidence. The 1990s had seen an ever increasing amount of legislation drafted which aimed to prove that the government of the day were going to win the war against crime. Fear and anxiety had been regarded as increasing throughout this period but neither government nor opposition did much to allay those fears. Indeed, the measures proposed appeared to have had the opposite effect. Only when the climate appeared to be less anxious did the Labour government seize an opportunity to reveal its more progressive community safety agenda.

SEX OFFENDERS — A CASE STUDY OF HOW A PUNITIVE CLIMATE CAN AFFECT CRIMINAL JUSTICE AGENCIES

The generally punitive climate had already led to increases in detention for sex offenders, belying the popular myth that the courts were soft on dangerous offenders and even perhaps the widely held prison myth that sex offenders ('nonces') were always paroled ahead of 'normal' offenders. Hebenton and Thomas (1996) note that in 1979, 20% of sex offenders were sent into prison and that by 1989 that percentage had increased to 33. By 1992, 39% of sex offenders went into custody accompanying a consequent drop in those receiving fines from 39% to 17%. Worrall (1997) states that the numbers of sex offenders placed on probation has remained low, averaging between 12 and 15% of all those convicted and only 2% of all offenders placed on probation (p. 119).

Lessons for the Probation Service?

However, it is Worrall's description of the way in which the probation service now works with sex offenders which most reflects the changing climate in which the service operates:

The change of public and governmental attitude towards sex
offenders has forced the probation service to examine the value base
of its work. Under attack have been the key concepts of social work
value discourse which have traditionally governed the attitudes of
probation officers. It is no longer deemed appropriate to exhibit
'acceptance', 'empathy' or a 'non-judgmental attitude' in relation to
sex offenders. Indeed, the sex offender is no longer regarded as the
'client' ... (p. 118).

Worrall proceeds to argue that the 'new' way of working with sex
offenders assumes that the subject is lying, has offended more frequently
than he admits and that not even mitigation such as his own previous
abuse can excuse or account for his behaviour. This language of
confrontation fits well with the penal rhetoric of recent years, a rhetoric
which both denounces and blames, as well as seeking ways in which to
manage the problem. Much of the work described by Worrall takes place
in cognitive behaviour groups, both in prison and in the community.
These groups attempt to shift what are regarded as the distorted thoughts
and urges of the offender and replace them with more rewarding and
legal activities. Worrall notes that there is some evidence that those
treated within these groups have lower recidivism rates than those who
are untreated (p. 123) but that careful selection is necessary and that
some groups of offenders, such as child sex offenders, may be more
responsive than rapists for example. She also raises some of the
criticisms that have been levelled at these groups, ranging from a lack
of training and support for staff through to a belief that many group
members still retain unacceptable views about women and children and
have simply learned to give the required responses (p. 124).

In managing the problem of sex offenders the probation service has
followed what appears to be at least partially successful schemes
developed in North America (Gendrea 1995). However, it is important
that process does not outweigh outcomes in assessing the effectiveness
of this style of work. Worrall's concerns are justified if probation staff
believe that completion of the programme is, of itself, an indicator of
success, which it may be reduced to by managerial performance
indicators. Success, though, should be measured in terms of fundamental attitudinal shift which may begin within the group process but may
come more to fruition within an individual relationship with an
experienced probation officer. The language of confrontation and

challenge, of non-acceptance and disbelief, must not become the language of exclusion. Attendance at sex offender treatment programmes is increasingly a feature of pre-custodial release decisions or of an inclusion in a release licence. It is seen by multi-agency dangerousness panels as a means by which the 'risk might be managed', or even reduced. All of this may be entirely right and justified but it is important for the probation service to keep in mind that it has a much longer tradition of working with offenders, many of whom have also posed significant risk to the public. It must not run away with the idea that a programme of group work is a panacea (not that it appears to be doing so), or allow such a belief to become too widespread. Offenders are notoriously good at quickly working out what is required of them in certain situations and delivering accordingly. The good probation officer who develops a close relationship with an offender may well be in a better position to spot the trigger signs of potential danger than a colleague whose task has a slightly different emphasis. There is still life in individual supervision and in the dangerousness field it is almost certainly a key ingredient of good public protection practice.

Writing in *NAPO News* (July/August 1998), Helen Schofield expressed similar concerns about the 'what works?' approach which has been heavily biased towards group work so far. She wondered what she had been doing for 20 years in practice if much of what had gone before had been deemed as not working. However, she did feel that a conference sponsored by the Home Office in February 1998 had been useful in promoting the 'first genuinely supervision-based initiative for reducing offending in the community that has met with both political and Home Office approval for several years' (p. 13). Her view was that the criteria set for effective practice, e.g. the prioritisation of dynamic crimogenic factors over non-crimogenic factors, of matching individuals to programmes (responsivity), and that outputs and outcomes should be applied consistently, should be applied to one-to-one work as well as group programmes. Her overriding message was of course an attempt to restore commitment to alternatives to imprisonment, without, however, abandoning those areas of difficulty and need experienced by offenders with which the Probation Service has unrivalled expertise in dealing.

The probation service also perhaps needs to keep remembering that its business has always been about rehabilitation and returning offenders to the community. Sex offenders may present a more difficult challenge to this ideal but should not be excluded from it because of the political hype which has surrounded this group in recent years. As Worrall (1997) very well summarises:

> The debate on working with sex offenders in the community has been virtually foreclosed. The field of intervention has been exploited to its maximum but, despite evaluation studies that indicate grounds for cautious optimism (Barker 1995), official government discourse now rejects the language of rehabilitation in favour of the language of surveillance and control through information. The probation service has no alternative discourse with which to challenge this shift because it has itself accepted the official construction of the sex offender. It has sacrificed its better judgment about why people offend and what makes them stop, based on decades of accumulated wisdom, but has found that it no longer matters (to the public, the media or the government) whether or not it delivers in terms of preventing recidivism. The sex offender has been constructed as irredeemable. It is no longer his crimes that are unacceptable; he himself is unacceptable as a member of the community. He is forever non-reintegratable (p. 125).

SUMMARY

The most recent pronouncements from the Home Office (see concluding chapter) suggest the possibility of a slight change in the attitude described by Worrall. The rediscovery of 'what works?' is a good sign for the probation service yet, within that, Worrall's message remains important as well, that it should retain elements of the professional practice which has probably been more successful than some of the recent research suggests. 'What works?' suits a managerial agenda very well, but effective practice cannot always be judged in managerial terms. The strength of the political agenda has guaranteed compliance by the professions involved in public protection, yet that political influence has invariably been based on a populist agenda rather than quality research into outcomes. Perhaps agencies such as the probation service should now be more assertive in their claims of their own effectiveness. Work such as that carried out by Coker and Martin (1985) does suggest a key role in preventing reoffending which does not have to rely on an excessively bureaucratic process. Perhaps the assertiveness gained from working more closely with the police service will develop greater probation service confidence, although it is to be hoped that such a close association will not compromise traditional skills.

Chapter 4
Legislating for Protection

Earlier chapters have charted the politicised nature of the public protection debate. The focus on predatory paedophile sex offenders in particular served the purpose of raising the punitive stakes not only in Britain but elsewhere around the world, almost as if they had become a political necessity. The knock-on effects for both civil liberties and the working practices of criminal justice agencies have been considerable, yet have provoked relatively little debate. Legislation has been used to drive policy through, enshrining public protection as the number one priority for judges throughout the world. This chapter will examine legislation passed in the UK in recent years and also explore the way in which this mirrors legislation passed in other countries. Most of this legislation is aimed at so-called dangerous offenders but, in reality, its primary focus has been child sex offenders. The flagship legislation in the UK has been the Crime (Sentences) Act 1997, the Sex Offenders Act 1997 and many of the provisions contained in the Crime and Disorder Act 1998. The Sexual Offences (Conspiracy and Incitement) Act 1996 was aimed specifically at the activities of those involved in the 'sex tourism' industry so will not be dealt with here. However, before considering these recent developments it is necessary to revisit the Criminal Justice Act 1991 and examine its place in the history of dangerousness legislation.

THE CRIMINAL JUSTICE ACT 1991 AND DANGEROUSNESS

As mentioned previously, the Criminal Justice Act 1991 can be seen as setting out the means by which certain types of serious offenders, namely violent and sexual criminals, could be taken outside of the sentencing framework established by that Act. In other words, the principle of proportionality or just deserts, established for the so-called 'normal' offender population, could be deviated from if the offender was assessed by the court as posing a risk of serious harm to the public. The focus here was clearly on the offender rather than the offence, although, of course, the instant offence triggered the initial departure from proportionality. Those instant offences are sexual or violent crimes and section 1(2)(b) of the Act permits the imposition of a custodial sentence, where 'only such a sentence would be adequate to protect the public from serious harm', even though custody may not be merited by the seriousness of the offence. This departure from offence seriousness and proportionality is further emphasised in section 2(2)(b), where courts are empowered to impose a custodial sentence which is longer than that commensurate with the seriousness of the offence, again with the proviso that it is where necessary to protect the public from serious harm from the offender. The definition of serious harm is contained in section 31(3) and is one which has found its way into many of the multi-agency protocols established to protect the public: 'protecting the public from death or serious personal injury, whether physical or psychological, occasioned by further such offences committed by the [defendant]' (von Hirsch and Ashworth, 1996). These authors, however, challenge the rationale for a departure from proportionality, partly on the basis of the difficulty of assessment and prediction (see chapter 1) and partly on the absence of censure based on blameworthiness: 'Since punishment involves censure, its amount should fairly reflect *how wrong* the conduct is — that is, how serious it is. Proportionate sentences are designed to reflect the conduct's blameworthiness, whereas sentences based on prediction have no such foundation' (p. 176).

Where the Act did depart from proportionality, it was concerned with the seriousness of possible or potential harm, rather than the seriousness of the more general risk of reoffending. However, in *R* v *Creasey* (1994) 15 Cr App R(S) 671:

The trial judge fell, perhaps understandably in the light of the reports, into the trap of assessing the seriousness of the risk rather than the seriousness of the harm, which is what the statute requires (von Hirsch and Ashworth, 1996, p. 179).

This distinction in sentencing is equally a crucial one to be made in the decisions of public protection panel meetings, although, as with judges, the trap of a concern with the risk of offending, rather than the risk of serious harm, is an easy one to fall into. Further definition occurred in *R v Fawcett* (1995) 16 Cr App R(S) 55, in that previous offences of themselves were deemed insufficient to invoke the sub-section which departs from proportionality, but those previous offences must have demonstrated evidence of behaviour which posed a risk of serious harm occurring in the future. In his review of selective incapacitation after the Criminal Justice Act 1991, Dingwall (1998) noted that the history of extended sentencing, established by the Criminal Justice Act 1967, was marked by a failure to hit the right target. By this he meant that it was property offenders who had been the major recipients of extended sentences, with only 16% of extended sentences between 1974 and 1976 being imposed for crimes against the person. Von Hirsch and Ashworth (1996) conclude that there should be a review of protective sentences on the basis that there are compelling empirical and ethical difficulties, but the evidence of the years since their article was written would suggest that their plea has gone unheard.

The Criminal Justice Act 1991 added further sections which can be seen as offering protection to the public whilst at the same time continuing the separation and segregation of sex offenders from the rest of the offender population. These sections involved the probation service and were a further indication of that agency's developing role in public protection. Section 44 of the Act stipulated that, at the time of sentence and in the case of sex offenders only, the court could order supervision until the completion of the full term of the imposed prison sentence, rather than that prescribed by the Act's normal release arrangements. Furthermore it also stipulated that some sex offenders could be dealt with more appropriately in the community, perhaps one of the last references to this by any government. The intention was that the stricter and more 'time consuming' form of supervision available in probation centres, should be made available for sex offenders for the entire duration of their order (up to three years), rather than the customary 60 days (Powers of Criminal Courts Act 1973, sch. 1A, para. 4). The net effect of both of these measures was to be a substantial increase in the number of sex offenders supervised by the probation service and an increased desire on its part to demonstrate that it was working towards achieving its public protection goals.

AN INTERNATIONAL PROBLEM

The Criminal Justice Act 1991 was therefore a combination of proportionality and protection, a clear manifestation of the stated ideals of the Conservative government. However, this twin track or bifurcated approach (Bottoms, 1980), was not confined to Britain and there is ample evidence of jurisdictions around the world extending the range and severity of punishments handed out to the 'dangerous' at about the same time as the Criminal Justice Act 1991 was introduced, indeed the whole history of protective sentences is a long and chequered one. The term 'dangerousness' in itself should not be so simply stated, according to Pratt (1997). He charts the changing nature of the concept of the dangerous offender, in particular its transition from a judicially defined class of habitual offenders, to a state defined class of offences and offenders within that group of offenders. He quotes the New Zealand parliamentary debates (NZPD) for 1985 and these show a clear resemblance to the eventual provisions of the Criminal Justice Act 1991:

> ... the Bill enhances the protection of the public in a number of ways. It targets violent and sexual offenders for long periods of imprisonment, and for long periods of supervision on their eventual release in the community (p. 158).

This type of legislation, according to Pratt, was in stark contrast to discussions held in many jurisdictions during the 1970s, when ideas of preventive detention fell out of favour, although, as Pratt notes, many remained on the statute books. At this time rehabilitation enjoyed greater prominence, particularly in the United States where treatment was a key criminal justice objective. In 1989 Ashworth had noted the spread of new sentencing systems across the world which had been informed and influenced by the just deserts approach. Pratt (1997) comments that, at this time, 'it was anticipated that the indeterminate prison sentence would be driven out of modern penal systems altogether — as, by the same token, would the concept of dangerousness' (p. 168). Quoting a Western Australian judgment, he summarises what he sees as a dominant theme of the time:

> ... it is now firmly established that our common law does not sanction preventive detention. The fundamental principle of proportionality does not permit the increase of a sentence of imprisonment beyond what is proportional to the crime merely for the purpose of extending the protection of society from the recidivism of the offender (quoted in Pratt, 1997, p. 168).

Pratt saw a tension between just deserts and the right of the public to protection. This tension cut across a just deserts aim which was to give power back to judges and remove it from welfare experts and what he terms 'psy' professionals. He also saw that neo-liberal governments were undercutting judicial autonomy, especially in relation to the dangerous offender population, which it redefined rather than abolished. Prescribed sentences with a newly defined group of dangerous offenders severely reduced the opportunities for individualised sentencing.

Sentencing for dangerous offenders can take two principal forms. The first is an extended period of detention for certain offenders within certain offence categories, with the Criminal Justice Act 1991 in England and Wales being a good example of this. The second is where continued detention is allowed for at the end of the original and lawful period of custody, an idea which is now under discussion in this country for first time sex offenders (*The Guardian*, 14 March 1998). The following are examples of the latter and are all taken from a review of world-wide legislation undertaken by the John Howard Society of Alberta (JHSA) in 1995, as part of its briefing to the Canadian government. Undoubtedly, much of the legislation crosses the boundary into the mental health field and continued or extended periods of detention frequently rely upon psychiatric diagnosis. This is in itself interesting as the clinical ability to predict dangerousness has certainly taken something of a back seat in court proceedings, but appears to retain a considerable degree of importance at the other end of the criminal justice process, that is in release from custody decisions. The JHSA review noted a long history of preventive detention within

European jurisdictions, Norway, as an example, having had dangerous offender provisions since 1902. These provisions allow for continued detention at the end of the prison term if the prisoner is assessed as posing a threat to community safety. The review noted similar provisions across central Europe and Scandinavia since the 1930s, providing indeterminate confinement for recidivist, mentally ill, dangerous offenders.

An Australian example of introducing dangerous offender legislation is very similar to the discussion which took place in 1997 and 1998 in England concerning the release of convicted paedophile killers Sidney Cooke and Robert Oliver. In 1990 a dangerous sexual offender was due for release from a Victoria prison. The prisoner had a long history of violent offences and was known to have made plans for further offences upon release. Although diagnosed as suffering from an anti-social personality, he could not be held under mental health legislation because that disorder is not classified as a mental illness. The Victorian government enacted the Community Protection Act, making it clear that it applied to this one offender exclusively. The Act allowed the Supreme Court to put the offender into preventive detention if he posed a serious risk to the community. The Act allowed for a six month period of detention which was renewable. Four years later the Community Protection Act was passed to include all similar cases. The criteria for inclusion were: the offender's history must include one serious offence and at least one involuntary psychiatric confinement; an assessment by a team of two psychiatrists who must suggest that the offender suffers from a violent personality disorder and that there is a serious risk that he or she will commit one of the enumerated offences (JHSA, 1995, pp. 8, 9). This affords an example of how one or two individual cases can drive legislation, particularly if public concern and fear is aroused. This point could certainly be made in respect of the proposed sex offender orders contained in the Crime and Disorder Act (see below).

A similar response to public concern can be seen in the Labour government's proposals to detain first-time sex offenders at the end of their prison sentence if they are adjudged to be dangerous (*The Guardian*, 14 March 1998). Public anger had been reported over the release within two years of six violent paedophiles, who it was believed were still dangerous and would not be under any form of supervision. These men had been sentenced before the Criminal Justice Act 1991 and were therefore not subject to a mandatory licence. In denying them parole, on the basis that they were too dangerous, they were released at their normal time without supervision. It should be noted in passing that one of the more enduring prisoner myths is that sex offenders are treated more leniently than 'normal' criminals and have a higher parole rate. The element of truth in this is that, in many cases, local review committees and the Parole Board were anxious to ensure at least a minimum period of supervision for prisoners considered as posing a risk if unsupervised and not monitored. Undoubtedly, if measures such as this are enacted then the prospect will be for a good deal of legal challenge to the basis of the dangerousness assessment. It is with this in mind that many American psychiatrists do not become involved in these proceedings.

An interesting, and some might argue a worrying development, has recently taken place in the United States. Within Washington's Community Protection Act is contained the Sexually Violent Predator's Law, passed as a result of the release of prisoners considered dangerous but at the end of their lawful custodial period. The main target of the legislation were those offenders with a history of mental illness or sexual offences. Such persons, either at the end of their sentence or even already in the community, can be called to a hearing to determine if they are sexually violent predators (SVPs). There is no set time in which the application has to be made. If 'reasonable' grounds are found then the offender is sent to a clinical facility for assessment. The assessment is to determine if the offender has a disorder or abnormality which renders them likely to engage in violent acts. If this assessment is positive, the SVP can be detained indefinitely until the Health Services Secretary authorises release. Even then a further hearing is called to determine the status of the SVP and if the label is removed the community is still notified that an SVP is moving into their area. In Kansas, a similar measure has become known as 'Stephanie's Law', after the murder of 19-year-old student Stephanie Schmidt by a man on parole for an offence of rape. The Kansas Sexually Violent Predator Law allows for the involuntary commitment of convicted sex offenders who have served their sentence if they are declared 'mentally abnormal' and are considered likely to commit predatory acts of sexual violence. The Act was upheld by the Supreme Court in a challenge by a 30-year-old paedophile. A jury had found that he met the criteria for civil confinement, a decision which he challenged on the basis that it violated his constitutional rights. The court found that his rights had not been violated and that it was not a situation of double jeopardy in that the Act does not establish criminal proceedings and involuntary commitment under it is not a punishment' (Family Research Council, 1997). Similar laws are being enacted across the United States, although civil libertarians have expressed concern. The same article refers to the views of the New York Civil Liberties Union, '[this ruling] . . . opens the door to people being civilly committed solely because the government believes they are likely to commit a crime'. Quite clearly, the idea that a person may be detained for something that the state believes he or she *might* do is truly alarming, not least because the evidence for the application of serious offender laws in the United States suggests that it is usually applied to the non-dangerous population (Shichor and Sechrest, 1996).

Extended detention on the basis of an assessment of dangerousness is a key feature of the community protection model of dangerous offender legislation. It is a model which seeks to redress an alleged imbalance between offender and community/victim rights. It is also undoubtedly a model which is concerned with naming, notification and, if the voices of many are to be believed, exclusion. If the criminal justice system is seen as 'failing' the public by releasing a dangerous individual, then the public will at least know the whereabouts of that person. It is of course a possible flaw in the original sentences of potentially dangerous offenders which triggers the initial problem. In the case of Sidney Cooke and Robert Oliver, the sentences served were approximately eight years for the manslaughter of a 14-year-old, a killing preceded by abduction and buggery. The problems arising upon the release of these two, and others, is the relatively short period served for such serious crimes, indeed crimes for which the discretionary life sentence had been available. It is undoubtedly cases such as these, as well as a mind to public opinion, that led the last Conservative government to introduce mandatory life sentences for certain repeat offenders. In Maricopa County, Arizona, another way of tackling this problem has been attempted. There, as a condition for release, incarcerated offenders must agree to a lifetime of probation supervision, attend weekly counselling sessions and submit to routine lie detector tests and unannounced home inspections by surveillance officers. Those running the programme claim that in its five year history, only 1.5% of the participants have committed further sex crimes, at a 10% financial cost of what would have been the prison bill for continued detention.

There may yet come a time when financial figures such as this feature more heavily in criminal justice policy making.

Another variant of this attempt to reduce the post-release risk posed by certain offenders is to be found in British Columbia (John Howard Society, 1997a). On the basis that, '... community notification laws neither support or reintegrate sex offenders back into society', the article emphasises the responsibility of the community to assist the offender in making a transition back into society. It describes a scheme known as the Community Reintegration or Circles of Support project. The scheme takes on sex offenders from federal institutions who will be released without community supervision, with high needs and little if any community support. A circle of six volunteers is formed for each offender. The offender must agree to live by the consensus of the circle, participate in counselling sessions and identify and address any substance abuse problems. Circle members assist with the offender's daily living needs, maintain open and honest communication and mediate between the offender and the community. In its first two years the project claimed not to have one single relapse (JHSA, 1997b).

MANDATORY SENTENCING

The political background to two and three strikes legislation in the United States and the United Kingdom has already been discussed in chapters 2 and 3. According to Pratt (1997), the neo-liberal state had already redefined dangerousness along a continuum of state-self protection. Dangerous criminals had moved from being 'habitual' to become a clearly defined group of (usually) sexual and violent offenders. Yet the move to the two and three strikes legislation of the 1990s actually saw the group identified for extra punishment widened beyond these specific offence categories and is in a sense a return to the old habitual offender laws, themselves having a much longer history. Zeigler and Del Carmen (1996) identify forerunners of three strikes legislation occurring in Virginia in 1796. The state that has driven much American legislation in recent years, California, had forerunner three strikes legislation in 1927 as did 11 other states, all of which offered life sentences for third time non-violent offenders. Much of Zeigler and Del Carmen's review concerns the constitutional issue of 'cruel and unusual punishment', an idea taken from the English Bill of Rights of 1689 and yet remarkably absent from debates in this country, except from the mouths of a few distinguished judges. A good deal of American research is already in place regarding three strikes style legislation but we have yet to see it discussed in any meaningful way in this country.

The rationale for the policy of breaking from proportionality — and individualised sentencing — was that the public gained insufficient protection from the courts in the case of violent and sexual offenders and persistent offenders. The door was therefore open to a growth in the use of longer prison sentences and with it, the usual associated conflation of all other disposals throughout the criminal justice system. This can happen in two ways. The first is that the target group is extended from so-called dangerous offenders to others such as property offenders — some of whom may well be dangerous but would generally be excluded from dangerousness provisions. The second is that crimes which are not necessarily as serious as those which preceded them may be dealt with in a way which is beyond the seriousness they merit under proportionality rules. Consequently the whole tariff is raised as a result of the focus on special classes of offenders. In America it was recognised early on that this would be the result:

> California's law defines the first two strikes as violent and serious felonies. The third strike is any felony. In some California counties more than half of the 'third strike' cases have involved such non violent offences as shoplifting and auto burglary, theft of cigarettes and in one Los Angeles case — theft of a pizza (Skolnick, 1995 p. 5).

In this country, the Crime (Sentences) Act 1997 has introduced a combination of two strikes and three strikes legislation. During the early discussions on the Bill, the proposal included mandatory life sentences for certain classes of second time serious offenders, and minimum mandatory sentences for third time drug dealers and burglars. The final category was eventually left out of the legislation by the incoming Labour government but of course the opportunity remains to extend the provision to this and other groups of offenders (this measure was resurrected by Home Secretary Jack Straw in January 1999): 'A Home Secretary who has brought these provisions into force will find it difficult to resist pressure for mandatory sentences in other contexts' (Thomas, 1998, p. 83). The Act itself already includes a quite extensive list of offenders who could receive the mandatory life sentence, namely those who are convicted of the following offences:

- attempt, conspiracy or incitement to murder;
- offence under section 4 of the Offences Against the Person Act 1861 (soliciting murder);
- manslaughter;
- an offence under section 18 of the Offences Against the Person Act 1861 (wounding, or causing grievous bodily harm, with intent);
- rape or an attempt to commit rape;
- an offence under section 5 of the Sexual Offences Act 1956 (intercourse with a girl under 13);
- an offence under section 16 (possession of a firearm with intent to injure), section 17 (use of a firearm to resist arrest) or section 18 (carrying a firearm with criminal intent) of the Firearms Act 1968;
- robbery where, at some time during the commission of the offence, the offender had in his possession a firearm or imitation firearm within the meaning of the Firearms Act 1968.

The Act also requires the passing of a mandatory minimum seven year sentence for any person convicted of a class A drug trafficking offence where that person has two other convictions for the same offence.

The Home Office White Paper (1996), in spelling out these proposals, made clear the then government's intention to target the violent and sexual offender in order to protect the public:

> ... too often in the past, those who have shown a propensity to commit serious or violent sexual offences have served their sentences and been released only to offend again ... Too often, victims have paid the price when the offender has repeated the same offences. The government is determined that the public should receive proper protection from persistent violent and sexual offenders (p. 48).

It is interesting to note here that persistence is actually only the second instance of such behaviour. This means that perhaps greater flexibility might be allowed for other offenders but for those offences mentioned in the Act, persistence is only the third such instance of that behaviour. In many cases your first chance is your last chance. What had now happened was that the definition of dangerousness had again been broadened, by and large ending judicial discretion with only poorly defined 'exceptional' reasons enabling a judge to deviate from the mandatory penalty. The intention to impose mandatory minimum penalties on domestic burglars almost appeared to be an attempt to punish those offenders who were caught more severely in lieu of the large numbers who were not caught, or who had previously undetected offences. The belief in deterrence, virtually abandoned for this type of offender in the Criminal Justice Act 1991, resurfaced here with a vengeance:

> Research shows that most burglars are highly persistent offenders . . . it also shows that the penalties imposed on those convicted of burglary, even if they have numerous previous convictions, are not a sufficient deterrent . . . In too many cases, a short spell in prison has become an acceptable risk (Home Office, 1996, pp. 51, 52).

The sentencing climate was then set to escalate in terms of punitiveness. As mandatory minimum penalties are introduced for offenders with a fixed number of previous convictions, so it is likely that they will increase for other offenders further down the scale. The result is inevitably going to be a rise in the prison population although not necessarily a drop in the number of crimes. In March 1998, prison governors urged the Home Secretary to halt the overuse of prison sentences which was leading to severe prison overcrowding. At the Prison Governor Association's annual conference the chairman, Chris Scott, called for new sentencing guidelines to be issued to courts to ensure that imprisonment is used only for the most persistent and serious offenders. At the same time, the Police Superintendents' Association called for the robust policy to continue. This plea was based upon a fall in the numbers of reported crimes by half a million during the four year period which had seen the increased prison population (*The Guardian*, 10 March 1998). Of course, the rise in the prison population is not necessarily made up of persistent or serious offenders and the claims for the drop in reported crimes is naturally open to a variety of interpretations. Suffice it to say that reported crimes of violence and sex have risen in the past few years, during that same period of general downturn alluded to by the Police Superintendents' Association.

PROTECTIVE LEGISLATION

Although the sentencing bedrock was in place, the Labour Party did not fall into the 'elephant trap' set for them by Michael Howard (Dunbar and Langdon, 1998) and instead, as was seen in chapter 3, decided to escalate the race to be seen as the party most committed to protecting the public (although it might be argued that the race was to develop in slightly different terms). The results of this race can best be seen in the final measures proposed in the Sex Offenders Act 1997 which, among other things, established the sex offenders' register. The register is closely linked with the idea of community notification schemes described in detail in chapter 9, and places an onus on the police service to assess and manage risk. It has also extended the scope of offences beyond what some people might regard as a 'dangerous' list to include the following: rape, intercourse with a girl under 13, intercourse with a girl between 13 and 16, incest by a man, buggery, indecency between men, indecent assault on a woman, indecent assault on a man (both of these offences do not qualify if the victim was aged over 18 years), assault with intent to commit buggery, causing or encouraging prostitution of, or intercourse with, or indecent assault on a girl under 16 (all contrary to the Sexual Offences Act 1956). Added to these offences are indecent conduct towards a young child, inciting a girl under 16 to have incestuous sexual intercourse and taking indecent photographs of children. The original rationale for the introduction of the register was to monitor the activities of paedophile sex offenders in particular but a glance at this list of offences shows that the scope of the register has been widened considerably. The criteria for registration are not only a conviction for one of these offences, but also a caution (or a finding of not guilty by reason of insanity). The inclusion of the caution, although understandable, is a little worrying. There is evidence of people admitting crimes to gain a caution rather than face court proceedings, even if the evidence against them is not particularly strong (Gillespie, 1998). To do so with the additional sanction of a register could lead to a double injustice or, alternatively, a reduction in the number of people prepared to admit guilt at the caution stage and therefore take the risk of court proceedings.

The register does, however, have much greater implications for the police service than simply its administration, which in itself will be an onerous task. It is seen by the government as a proactive device, in that it provides the police service with information to assist in the protection

of children and other vulnerable persons. Speaking at a Home Office conference in 1997, a speaker from the police service made it clear that the expectation on the police was to undertake risk assessment in partnership with other agencies in order to protect the vulnerable. This assessment of risk was an ongoing task on a case by case basis, balancing operational considerations, human rights and the protection of the public (Home Office, 1997a, p. 16). For the police service this more proactive assessment role was a new departure and one in which they would seek the expertise of other agencies. The speaker, Helen Skelton, from the West Midlands police noted a three tier approach to risk assessment as a means of sifting information to identify high risk offenders, on the basis that all those included on the register would not pose a risk of serious harm to the public. The three tier approach identified was as follows. The first level was the sifting of information normally available to the police service. The second involved identification of serious risk which would probably involve obtaining information from other agencies. The third level was the resulting management of risk, the responsibility of multi-agency collaboration and agreements. Obviously an issue in this arrangement would be the need for greater agreement on what constitutes danger.

The register itself began on 1 September 1997, and in the end was a rather rapid piece of policy implementation. Probation officers for example, who were given a key role in the referring process to the police, claimed to have been told of the start date by *The Times* on 13 August 1997 (*NAPO News*, September 1997). The period of registration was to be determined by the sentence passed for the qualifying offence, as follows:

- A person who has been sentenced to life or for more than 30 months, will be registered for an indefinite period.
- A person who has been admitted to hospital subject to a restriction order, will be registered for an indefinite period.
- A person who has been sentenced to more than 6 months but less than 30 months, will be registered for a period of 10 years beginning with the relevant date.
- A person who has been sentenced to less than 6 months, will be registered for a period of 7 years beginning with that date.
- A person who has been admitted to a hospital without being subject to a restriction order, will be registered for a period of 7 years beginning with that date.

- A person of any other description will be registered for a period of 5 years beginning with that date.

This last category of course includes all those offenders subject to community penalties for qualifying offences and would also include the group cautioned by police officers. The registration requirement was not, however, to be retrospective and calculations made at the time suggested that the majority of the 110,000 convicted paedophile offenders in England and Wales would not be eligible for registration. The Home Office estimated that the number would be approximately 6,000, increasing by roughly 3,000 each year. In a thoughtful analysis on the effect of the register, Soothill and Francis (1997) come to a conclusion which can perhaps be suitably applied to a great deal of legislation in the area of sex offenders:

> Any assumption that the scheme 'captures' the most active sexual offenders is untrue. . . . there seems no criminological rationale to the determination of the periods of registration. The varying periods under different conditions seems more akin to continuing the punishment of sex offenders rather than representing appropriate measures to protect the public. While it may be a laudable aim to try to keep those most likely to be serious sexual recidivists under surveillance, we suggest that this Act fails to identify such persons in a systematic manner. The public remains equally at risk from those sexual offenders not covered by the provisions of the Sex Offenders Act as well as continuing to be at risk from offenders outside the period of registration. In brief, the Act seems to be a political gesture which is probably misleading, potentially mischievous and almost certainly mistaken (p. 1325).

The key issues here are those offenders who are included and excluded, the degree of risk assessment which takes place, the arbitrary nature of the registration periods, the drain on police resources (the register was supposed to be a nil cost option) and the nature of proactiveness taken by the police over the information obtained.

Absent from the Register!

Although there was widespread public and professional support for the sex offenders register, or at least not widespread opposition, there were

doubts expressed about its ability to offer greater protection to the public. Both Chief Police and Chief Probation Officers' Associations warned that the public should not rely too much on the registers for protection. Public and media concern in particular centred on all those paedophile offenders not required to register and the government moved quickly to re-establish its public protection credentials in the form of new legislation aimed at plugging these loopholes wherever possible. These new measures appeared in the proposals contained in the Crime and Disorder Act 1998. The debate has perhaps been conducted in less frenzied terms than previously seen on this issue, but has nevertheless continued the rapid escalation of punitive measures and further intrusion into the area of human rights.

Because the sex offenders register was promoted as a measure to protect the public from harm, it naturally followed that those offenders not required to register would continue to pose a serious risk to vulnerable members of the community. The primary measure aimed at closing what was regarded as a loophole started life as a community protection order but quickly became known as a sex offender order. The consultation paper, issued in November 1997, made clear the government's intention:

... more must be done to protect society from sex offenders who pose a continuing risk. In particular, sex offenders who fall outside the provisions of the Sex Offenders Act 1997, because they were no longer in prison, or under supervision when the Act came into force ... for whatever reason, are not subject to adequate supervision in the community, and whose behaviour gives rise to cause for concern are not, at present, subject to safeguards sufficient to protect the community.

In announcing similar measures for Scotland, Home Affairs Minister Henry McLeish said that, 'we do not expect that large numbers of Orders will be necessary. But every one that is made will increase the protection we are giving our children and should reduce the risk of further offending' (Scottish Office press release, 14 December 1997).

The measure was aimed at protecting the public from offenders with a qualifying previous conviction (as outlined in the Sex Offenders Act 1997) and whose behaviour gave rise to a concern that there was a current risk to the community. It was to apply to the same group of

offenders as those targeted by the Sex Offenders Act 1997 and
this included those cautioned for qualifying offences. As with
the register, concerns have to be raised about including this group
within this new measure. This point was commented upon by Gillespie
(1998) when he stated the general principle that cautions do not
contain punitive elements, because there has been no opportunity to
test the evidence. He argues that, unlike with 'normal' cautions
which expire after two years, this will not be the case for sex
offenders and they should be so warned by police and legal
advisers: 'The offence of breaching the order, would mean that
the person would be punished for acts that do not amount to an
offence (save for breach of the order) which seems contrary to the
aims of a caution' (p. 3).

An example of someone thought likely to come within the terms of
the legislation was described as a person with a previous conviction for
harming children in or near school grounds, who was again seen
loitering in such a vicinity. The assessment of risk would follow
discussion between the police service and other experts (probation
officers, psychiatrists, housing officials, or social workers) but it would
be the police service who made the application to the relevant court. The
government intends that the order should last for a minimum period of
five years, after which application can be made for discharge. An earlier
discharge is to be regarded as exceptional and would require the
agreement of all parties. The effect of an order is similar to an injunction,
that is, if the conditions were complied with, the offender would be
untouched by it (except of course in terms of freedom of movement).
The order was not to be a sentence of the court or stand as a conviction,
it was a civil order. Alongside the injunction-style conditions of an order
would be a requirement that every person subject to a sex offender order
would also have to register under the provisions of the Sex Offenders
Act 1997. Breach of the order was, however, to be a criminal offence
and the discussion paper suggested a maximum penalty for this of five
years' imprisonment.

The order itself can be described as a 'restraining order' (Gillespie,
1998). He saw similar examples in Australia and Canada. However, he
believed that the legislation in those countries was drafted more tightly
than that proposed for this country and as a result would be more
effective. The Canadian legislation means that an offender against
children may be prohibited from:

- attending a public park or public swimming area where persons under the age of 14 are present or could reasonably be expected to be present;
- seeking, obtaining or continuing any employment or voluntary position which involves children under 14.

The South Australian 'paedophile restraining order' stipulates that if the offender has been seen loitering around children and has within the previous five years been convicted or released from prison for a child sexual offence, he will be restrained from: loitering in the vicinity of a school, public toilet or place at which children are regularly present; *and* children are present at that place at the time of the loitering. Gillespie argues that where the penalty for breach is so considerable, the certainty of the Canadian and Australian legislation is preferable to the more loosely drafted British version. Either way, it is evident that the measures proposed by the present government are not unique and it is to be hoped that the costs as well as the benefits of such measures have been examined in these other jurisdictions.

Despite a good deal of debate in Parliament (see Hansard, 15 May 1998), there is to be no additional element of supervision by the probation service included in the orders, as they remain a civil measure (albeit moved from the civil courts to the magistrates' courts in terms of jurisdiction) and cannot therefore contain punitive or coercive elements. Alun Michael, responding to an amendment (House of Commons Standing Committee B) calling for the creation of a sex offender supervision order, stated that this additional element of criminal punishment could not be part of a civil measure, but that, 'close working between the probation service and the police to ensure that the public are reassured that things are being done to protect children is at the top of our agenda'.

The sex offender order is clearly aimed at curbing the behaviour of people who, it can be seen, by their actions in association with their previous criminal behaviour, pose a risk of harm to the community, and children in particular. In some ways this is an improvement on the usual discussion concerning dangerousness which often takes place in an institutional vacuum, and is frequently of little use when transposed to the community context. At least these orders call for demonstrable evidence in terms of observed behaviour to be presented to and accepted by the magistrates' courts.

The Crime and Disorder Act 1998 provides for periods of extended supervision at the end of a custodial sentence where a court considers that the period of licence would not be adequate for the purpose of preventing the commission of further offences. Qualifying offences for these purposes are sexual and violent crimes and, in the case of a violent crime, the penalty must be at least four years before the provisions can be imposed, although there is no such minimum for sexual offences. The maximum period of the 'extension' is ten years for a sexual offence and five years for a violent offence, up to the maximum permitted for the offence.

Both the current Labour government and its Conservative predecessor have been moved to legislate for protection. Each time an incident has arisen, the media and public call has come for new legislation to plug the gap and increase the feeling of safety. The result, however, may be that in responding, the public sense of anxiety is increased. The evidence for most of the measures proposed is flimsy to say the least and out of proportion to the scale of the problem. Yet this is an area of criminal justice policy where even one case going wrong is one too many and where all the good work of police and probation officers is instantly forgotten in the face of one mistake — even if it could not have been foreseen. As with much recent Labour policy, ideas come out of government with a rush and usually accompanied by reviews and committees. Thus concern at a loophole in the provisions concerning sex offenders working with children resulted in an inter-departmental working group being established to consider the issue. The group was to consider the establishment of a central register of people deemed unsuitable to work with children and the creation of a new criminal offence for anyone on that list who seeks work with children. The then Home Office Minister Alun Michael said in announcing the new group that, 'we must work together to make sure that there are no loopholes. This is why we have set up a working group to ensure that our children are given the protection they deserve' (Home Office press release, 4 June 1998). However, by using terms such as 'no loopholes' and 'ensure protection', the government is almost setting itself up to fail. Complete protection is as impossible as the completely safe community. A further review was announced of all sex offences to reform and bring the laws up to date (Home Office press release, 15 June 1998). Once again it was Alun Michael making the announcement, suggesting that the government would, 'ensure that the courts have the powers they need to deal with the offenders who appear before them. We take that responsibility very seriously'. This turn of phrase could have come from any of the Conservative Home Secretaries from the four previous governments. The range of measures already available to the court appears to most people to be quite up to the task of public protection. It is perhaps more a matter of consistent application and meaningful, well resourced attempts to change the behaviour of those offenders assessed as capable of reform. A continual upgrading of sentences and closing loopholes sounds very much like closing the stable door after the horse has bolted. A government committed to tackling the causes of crime should make as many pronouncements about preventive measures with sex offenders as it does expanding the range of protective and restrictive measures available to the courts.

SUMMARY

Legislating for protection has been a process which has served several purposes. The dangerousness provisions contained in the Criminal Justice Act 1991 enabled a government keen to maintain its tough law and order focus to pursue other, more liberal policies in terms of prison number reduction. It also served to mark a significant departure from the just deserts philosophy of offence focus and reintroduced an offender focus. This is significant as it has signalled a quite concerted attempt within the legislation to identify certain offenders for a different approach. However, this approach has not been consistent and has oscillated between an individual and an offence-based focus but always with a certain category of offences triggering the initial consideration. Thus the Criminal Justice Act 1991 determined that the court had to be convinced that individual offenders posed a threat of serious harm to the public, but only if they came within sexual and violent offence categories. The introduction of mandatory fixed penalties eliminates the need for this consideration, dangerousness here determined by the act of repetition.

Other legislation appears to be a combination of offering a sense of public security, such as the sex offenders' register, or of plugging loopholes which have been brought to public notice, such as the sex offender orders. Much of this legislation has already been tried in other countries and has generated a combination of legal and civil rights concerns. The debates in this country have been more muted, not least because much of the debate became a political battle ground. Perhaps now that the Labour government has had a period of time to settle in and with such a large majority it will begin to examine the issues in a more rational manner. There are signs of this happening but as yet they remain limited.

Chapter 5
Protection as Policy

The previous chapter described how the issue of public protection was increasingly used to fuel a punitive, retributive penal climate. It can be seen that the debate was marked by a good deal of cynical politics and an absence of reasoned debate and opposition, except from the senior judiciary and the House of Lords. The cheapening of political debate and the resulting changes in legislation had a serious knock-on effect for the agencies operating within the criminal justice sector. Clearly the prison service was to be the main 'beneficiary' of this more populist political climate. Rising prison numbers were to outstrip all forecasts, both official and unofficial, as the 1990s wore on. The positive effects of the Criminal Justice Act 1991, which resulted in a fairly rapid fall in the prison, were to be very short-lived, lasting no more than twelve months after the Act became law. However, there were to be other effects, much more long-term in nature, although perhaps not so publicly obvious, for other criminal justice agencies. The police and probation services in particular were to feel these effects as the 1990s produced an ever more populist criminal justice climate. This chapter will explore the slow coming together of these two unlikely bedfellows, resulting in a degree of collaboration which perhaps even the government had not quite intended, although the outcome is one which would now need a great deal of reversing if that was desired.

It has already been established that an agenda of 'public protection', especially protection of the vulnerable, is one which cannot be dissented from. If it is political suicide, it is also professional suicide. Any agency which distances itself from a public protection mandate, especially under a punitive-minded government, is likely to find itself facing extreme criticism and undoubtedly a refocusing of its role by outside scrutiny. The Conservative government had not been slow to reform the public sector by central direction if it showed a reluctance to move in the required direction. The fact that both Conservative and Labour politicians had signed up so willingly to the protection agenda suggested that agencies had to take a long-term view. The issue was not likely to recede if a new government were to be elected — indeed quite the reverse as we now know. Yet at the beginning of the Conservatives' time in office in 1979, there was little to suggest that police and probation services were to converge to the extent that they had at the end of that term, and at the beginning of a new government. A very brief synopsis of the development of the 'crime prevention' role of each service, and its transformation into the wider community safety and ultimately public protection role, will help to explain the shared practice and managerial agenda which has evolved in the late 1990s.

POLICE, PROBATION AND CRIME PREVENTION

Since the formation of the modern police in 1829, the prevention of crime has been a central feature of the philosophy of policing, although not always a priority of practice or of resource allocation (Gilling, 1997). Prevention in this sense meant the obvious, preventing something from happening, not responding once it had. In other words, prevention rather than detection was meant to be the key element of effective policing. It is not for this book to chart the development of the police crime prevention role, this has been very well covered elsewhere (Reiner, 1992). However, it should be noted that, although crime prevention is a key function of the police, the priority and resources allocated to it varied over time. There was a fairly constant tension between management and front-line officers (Weatheritt, 1986), the former being more vocal in their support of prevention as a key task, many of the latter seeing it as a fringe activity for older officers or those who should really have been social workers — it was something of a

Cinderella role in its early stages (Reiner, 1992, p. 99). There was a similar debate about the role of crime prevention in the probation service, although for that organisation the focus was slightly different. For probation officers the debate about a crime prevention role took many years to surface and was not such a major issue as it had been for the police, reflecting the lower priority given to it. As it was not such an upfront function, the nature of its being practised was a less important issue. Probation officers traditionally worked with offenders on a one-to-one basis with a focus on psychoanalytic casework methods (see McWilliams, 1985, 1986). The aim of such intervention was of course to change the offender's behaviour so that future offending would be avoided, in other words, a form of crime prevention. However, the work of the service was never really articulated in this way and for years probation officers were tagged with the label of being 'on the criminal's side', showing little concern for the victim of the crime or the community more widely. Matters were to change in the 1970s, however, with the developing idea that this form of traditional probation intervention was not really effective, or did not work (a slight misconstruction but see Martinson, 1974 and Brody, 1976).

Gilling (1997) sets the developing debate on crime prevention within the probation service as one which was closely linked with its response to the 'collapse of the rehabilitative ideal (Bottoms and McWilliams, 1979), or the belief that nothing worked. The changing political and penal climate, which regarded crime as a matter of personal choice on the part of the individual, not as something determined by external and internal factors beyond their control, also caused a reconceptualisation of role. Readers are referred to Gilling's work for an account of the crime prevention debate within the probation service but a few key points are relevant here for the purpose of charting the rise of the protection agenda. The early debate focused on the extent to which the service should be more widely and actively involved in community crime prevention initiatives, or should more simply be represented on local committees and lend support, what might be termed as a difference between active and passive support. This author recalls hearing a speech from a senior Home Office civil servant in the early 1980s imploring probation officers to get out from behind their desks and begin working actively in the community, and this at a time when the service was becoming increasingly office based. In other words the service was being asked to work in ways which had steadily moved away from its quest for professional status. The probation service was offender-focused in its crime prevention work and many did not wish to lose this role (NAPO, 1994). This role was also one which was relatively discrete and lacking in public accountability. Community crime prevention was a much more public activity and was not felt to require the professional skills of probation officers. Crime prevention, especially the new rhetoric of 'situational crime prevention', was felt best left to others with greater expertise. However, in an article which merited wider circulation, Laycock and Pease (1985) suggested another approach, and a very radical one for the time, for the probation service role in crime prevention. This involved obtaining information from offenders known to the service and passing it on to other agencies better suited to make use of it for physical security purposes. This would undoubtedly have been viewed as a breach of professional confidence and was not supported by the National Association of Probation Officers (NAPO). A similar argument has been put for the idea of community policing, described as a covert and insidious way of penetrating communities to obtain information (Reiner, 1992, p. 100). Sampson and Smith (1992) in their research in London and a northern city found police officers supportive of the probation service not becoming too closely involved with them:

> We shouldn't have liaison with probation; it would make their job impossible ... Clients wouldn't be able to trust a probation officer who had dealings with the police (p. 108).

However, this notion has reappeared in the late 1990s in a much more coherent form as part of management expectations of good professional practice. The idea of trust and confidentiality has taken something of a back seat in the public protection setting. As we shall see, information sharing between the agencies has reached new levels of sophistication but, under the public protection agenda, has provoked virtually no opposition from practitioners or professional associations. The power of the public protection philosophy to neutralise debate is worrying, to say the least.

THE SHIFTING OF THE PROBATION SERVICE

Gilling (1997) suggests that the development of the crime prevention role into one of community safety made the issue one which was more palatable to probation staff:

Developments in the later half of the 1980s and beyond, when a narrow version of crime prevention has gradually given way to a more integrated notion of community safety, have generally benefitted the service, by bringing national policy more into line with the preference and values of those within the service who have supported the social side of crime prevention (p. 123).

The internal probation debate very much focused on the extent to which probation officers should actually be 'doing work' in and with the community, or bringing their own unique experience to bear in a multi-agency forum. This was certainly the view of the Association of Chief Officers of Probation (ACOP) and its newly-formed crime prevention subcommittee established in 1987. The chair of that committee was able to say in 1989 that crime prevention thus becomes, 'a major opportunity to present some traditional probation service objectives in a way which commands widespread public support' (Bryant, 1989, in Gilling, 1997, p. 124). This view of a more public working style offering a platform for probation practice, is one which could equally be applied to the public protection panels described below, but that opportunity still appears to be one which has yet to be fully taken. Similar thoughts had been expressed by Harris (1992) in a very prescient comment on the crime prevention role of the probation service (p. 84):

Government is increasingly concerned that the probation service should see itself not primarily as a provider of services but as working in a more integrated way with local criminal justice networks. Such networks will almost certainly be in place long before the 1990s are out, and it is inevitable that much of their focus will be on crime prevention. It would be highly desirable for the service to determine what contribution it should make to those discussions and what roles in crime prevention it could properly play.

By pursuing opportunities for their own practice, probation officers are likely to enter into a tension with other agencies. This is inevitable when roles and expectations, let alone cultures, are some way apart. If that tension is absent it could mean that the agenda is agreed and shared, or that one of the agencies has succumbed to the dominant ethos of another. Sampson and Smith (1992) spoke of a 'fundamental set of structural conflicts. ... which reflects their different and not always compatible aims, interests and priorities ... and this should not be regarded as unequivocally a bad thing' (p. 106). For Sampson and Smith the whole point of inter-agency working would be lost if agencies' views became indistinguishable from one another (p. 113)

The government was, however, to advance the community protection agenda with the publication of the Green and White Papers which prefaced the Criminal Justice Act 1991. When seen alongside developments within the police service it is possible to begin to identify the process of merging areas of interest between police and probation services, in a way which is little different from that envisaged by Bryant (1989). *Crime, Justice and Protecting the Public* (Home Office, 1990), is an important document in the evolution of the probation service. It spelt out what was to be the way forward for a number of years, although the emphasis within the various component parts was to change over time. In so doing it offered a guaranteed future and a hint of growth, a significant incentive for an organisation which might have feared for its future under populist Conservative governments:

> Preventing re-offending and protecting the public from serious harm should be the objectives of the probation service, whether they are supervising offenders who are carrying out community penalties or offenders released from custody. Offenders should be helped to acquire the habits of a stable and useful citizenship under supervision. Improved arrangements for supervising released prisoners are an essential part of the stricter parole system which will replace the present arrangements. Voluntary organisations, as well as the probation service, can help in preventing further crime (para. 1.9, pp. 2, 3).

This paragraph contains the essential elements of the new probation practice as the government saw it. There was the clear emphasis on public protection, the role which was to grow considerably in importance towards the end of the decade, the prevention of reoffending, a traditional role but now very much given greater public notice, the focus on a new style of supervision and of course the mention of the role of the voluntary service. This last point is important as probation services are now required to allocate 5% of their budgets to working with the voluntary sector. Overall, the message given to the probation service was that it had to be more accountable and more disciplined in its exercise of community supervision. The creation of the 'graduated restriction of liberty concept' meant that probation-led penalties were now part of a continuum of punishment and were therefore something that the courts should have confidence in: 'The discipline exerted by these orders on offenders may extend over many months. These orders intrude on normal freedom, and the court should be satisfied that this is justified' (Home Office, 1990, p. 18). Despite moving the probation service into a more controlling role, there was not a great deal of emphasis on police and probation collaboration, although the role of the police in protecting the public from serious offenders was mentioned in the White Paper. What was therefore emerging was a sharper, more focused role for the probation service, one in which the beginnings of the 'corrections' ideology is evident, as is the gradual move away from social work origins. This move would ultimately facilitate the convergence of police and probation objectives but, in 1991, this was still a little way off.

For some time an effort had been made in official documentation to stress that the police service could not tackle the crime problem alone. Much of the early focus of these documents was on the idea of the active citizen and the watchful community (Brake and Hale, 1992), or closer collaboration with local authorities or manufacturers of desirable goods such as motor cars. Opportunity reduction by target hardening was a key focus of police crime prevention policy. However, in the police service's work with serious and dangerous offenders little had previously been made of other agencies becoming involved. The inclusion of the probation service in the public protection camp was therefore a significant development for both services, although the impact of this development was not really to be felt until the mid-1990s. The culture of both of these organisations at the time was not one which saw close working with the other as part of their daily operational practice, although the table had been laid in readiness by the government.

The generally liberal tone of the White Paper, for example, 'Nobody now regards imprisonment, in itself, as an effective means of reform' (p. 6), and 'reforming offenders is always best if it can be achieved' which ran alongside a general critique of the principle of deterrence as being an issue for the majority of offenders, was somewhat offset by the focus on just deserts and public protection. Undoubtedly this allowed the main reforming elements to go through a Conservative dominated House of Commons, but it was cast in suitably tough language to leave

the door open for the type of criminal justice policies which were to
follow. It was the tough, public protection sections of the Act which
were to become the most prominent, rather than those which aimed at a
reduction in the use of custody. For example, in the chapter on
supervision, the White Paper made clear the role of the probation officer:

- protection of the public;
- prevention of reoffending;
- successful reintegration of the offender in the community.

Leaving aside the earlier discussion of what constitutes 'community' for
the probation service (dealing as its members do with people generally
excluded from what most people regard as community), the focus on
public protection in the document was paramount. 'The protection of
the public must be the first thought in the supervising officer's mind'
(p. 35). This is a very long way from 'advise, assist and befriend', the
original basis and ethos of probation intervention. Of course, protection
of the public may indeed be obtained by those early goals, but they were
unlikely to have been cited as best practice in 1990. Instead the emphasis
was one of consistency and firmness and the new discovery, 'restriction
of liberty'. As with the police, the probation service was cited as an
agency which, to work effectively, had to work in partnership with
others. The White Paper suggested a list of suitable agencies, such as
job centres, the health service, education projects and of course a range
of voluntary organisations such as the Citizens' Advice Bureau. This
list does not include the police service and, it is true to say at this time,
the police service in its partnerships was not looking too closely at the
probation service. This list is still suggestive of a largely rehabilitative
role for the probation service, albeit seeing it move more towards a
facilitative function. Police and probation as a collaborative unit was
still a little way off, but further policy development was to bring it closer
together.

POLICE UNDER SCRUTINY

The focus in this chapter will now switch to policy development within
the police service and its response to a growing, critical scrutiny by the
government as it was cast into the role of an apparently failing crime

fighting force. In 1993 the Audit Commission, the agency which was so influential in shaping the direction of public sector organisations under successive Conservative governments, published a report entitled, *Helping with Enquiries: Tackling Crime Effectively*. Naturally, with the Audit Commission's focus of interest, the main feature of the report was a scrutiny and evaluation of efficiency and effectiveness measures which could be adopted by the police service. However, for the purposes of this book, there were two important messages contained in the report. One was the need to be more proactive by making greater use of intelligence, to be achieved primarily by making more effective and extensive use of informants. The second was that the police service should work with other agencies to increase the amount of information at its disposal. The use of good intelligence was central to an efficient crime prevention and detection role and the police service was advised to make much greater use of information held by other agencies. It was further stressed again that the police service could not operate alone in tackling crime effectively, especially with its focus on serious and prolific criminals. That focus has also been highlighted by the Home Secretary's targets for the police service, set nationally and transmitted into local policing plans. These targets make a priority of reducing both the fear of crime and the maintaining or increasing the number of detections for violent crime in each area. As indicated, however, success in these tasks cannot be left to the police service operating alone and indeed the aforementioned policing plans also point towards greater working with other agencies.

This sharing of tasks and resulting sharing of knowledge leads us to the view that members of the police service are increasingly becoming 'expert advisers on security' (Ericson, 1994) and that (p. 159):

> The contemporary police officer spends most of her time in the production and distribution of technologically-mediated and bureau-cratically-formatted communications *for other security institutions* and coterminously, *taps into the already-processed knowledge of these other institutions* to help fulfil the security mandates of her own organisation. (*emphasis supplied*)

This exchange of information undoubtedly occurs in a variety of settings although is likely to happen less at the lower levels of any organisation where there may still be a tendency to guard knowledge as power

(Johnston, 1997). The 'policy lag' between management and workers was noted with regard to crime prevention policies above and will be seen in respect of dangerous offender policy later. Information-sharing often takes place in formal settings at management level with those at a lower rank in the organisation perhaps sharing on a basis of personal trust and respect rather than formally agreed management protocols. The media and political attention given to serious sexual offenders in the last two years or so has made the need both to obtain and to share information greater than ever. For agencies charged with the duty of protecting the public, the need to share the task and manage the problem, and to be seen to be doing it, is essential in the currently sensitive climate of fear which has developed, or been constructed. For all agencies it is likely that significant changes will take place and perhaps the agency most likely to be affected will be the probation service. The 'risk society' will have far reaching implications (Beck, 1992).

A range of other inquiries and reports published in the early 1990s was to put the police service in the position of looking for allies, and both to reaffirm and perhaps redefine its role, before this was done for it. As the Conservative government became increasingly keen to deflect blame from itself for an increasing crime problem, it looked for others to pass the blame onto. This blame culture had traditionally excluded the police, with social workers, teachers and the church being the preferred targets. However, the huge increase in police expenditure, seemingly without the service being able to demonstrate any significant success in reducing rates of crime or public fear of crime, something soon to be added to by the government, meant that eyes were increasingly cast upon its efficiency and effectiveness. Several reviews took place in the early 1990s:

(1)   Inquiry into Police Responsibilities and Rewards (Sheehy Inquiry, 1993);
(2)   White Paper on Police Reform (1993);
(3)   Police and Magistrates' Courts Act (1994);
(4)   Home Office Review of Police Core and Ancillary Tasks (the Posen Inquiry, 1995).

Although the immediate impact of this examination of policing was patchy (see Leishman et al, 1996), it did serve to awaken police awareness to their position of potential vulnerability and also pushed them to re-emphasise the local nature of service delivery as they saw it, despite much evidence to the contrary. These years also saw to it that effective policing was to become an increasingly politicised issue, not least with the rapid development of management agendas and a 'results or performance culture', which many saw as several steps removed from the real aim of police work. As Butler (1996) commented (p. 227):

> There appears a very real danger that the future direction of policing will be overly influenced by the pursuit of 'success' defined by a narrow set of performance indicators.

United We Stand ...

Therefore two agencies working within the criminal justice sector, not often considered as being in similar positions, found themselves under a good deal of public and government scrutiny in the early years of the 1990s. These two agencies were not noted for close working relationships, although of course pockets of inter-agency working were in evidence. These generally centred around areas such as child protection committees, intermediate treatment schemes, especially those aimed at motoring offenders and other, specific activity based schemes. For some time it had been considered good practice for probation officers to speak with the 'officer in the case' when preparing reports for the court. This was, however, patchy in reality and the quality of the information received often depended upon the personal relationships involved. The language of social work and the language of policing did not always sit together easily. The author remembers that several colleagues had joined the probation service after serving for many years in the armed forces. These officers appeared to form easier working relationships with police officers, perhaps due to a common command structure background. Undoubtedly there was a greater managerial interest in developing shared agendas but, it is fair to say, the troops came some way behind the generals, on both sides of the lines.

At the same time that the amount of external scrutiny was increasing, so internal responses to perceived threat and change also grew, responses which in part aimed to anticipate government intrusion into practice but also sought to implement policy changes initiated by the Home Office and Inspectorate. An example of this is the joint ACPO, Police Federation and Superintendents' Association Quality of Service

Initiative in 1990. This attempted to redefine not only the purpose of policing but also police–community relations, perhaps in anticipation of the government doing it for them. Another example, from 1993, the undertaking of a trawl by the Association of Chief Officers of Probation (ACOP), of probation areas with the aim of assessing policy and practice development concerning work with high-risk and serious offenders and it was to be the resulting document in particular that really began the push towards police and probation collaboration. The review was said to be a response to the requirements contained within the provisions of the Criminal Justice Act 1991, and spelt out its expectations quite clearly:

> In the light of current expectations of probation services, particularly those arising from the Criminal Justice Act 1991 and National Standards, the working group consider there is a *need for a culture shift within services to a more active recognition of responsibility for assessing the risk to the public and its subsequent management* (ACOP, 1993, emphasis in the original).

The resulting ACOP guidelines go on to emphasise the prevention of reoffending and protection of the public as key tasks for the service under national standards, as well as citing the guidance to the parole board which said that a 'small risk of violent offending is to be treated as more serious than a large risk of non-violent offending'. Risk assessment was to become a significant element of probation practice. There was a clear and obvious concern that potentially dangerous offenders who might not have been released under the old parole scheme would now become a statutory responsibility under the new early release arrangements. This is undoubtedly true but probation officers had previously supervised potentially dangerous offenders, on life licence or upon discharge from special hospital, and done so very effectively (Shaw, 1996 and Coker and Martin, 1985). What was happening was not so much a change in role as perhaps the public being made much more aware of the role. Also changing was the means by which managers could be sure that effective supervision of the dangerous was taking place, in other words systematising the process of supervision and risk management. Once this happened, and the government had highlighted the role in the Criminal Justice Act 1991, then it became an urgent matter for probation managers to be seen to be doing something to meet those expectations, and perhaps more importantly, to be able to demonstrate it. Hence a managerial agenda for managing risk evolved, very quickly, within probation services, and soon incorporated police services as their responsibilities for sex offenders in the community became more pronounced. It is to be hoped though, that as a result of putting together a managerial agenda on risk, the good work of officers pre-1991 is not forgotten. The service has a good record and should have perhaps been stating it more loudly than it did (see Coker and Martin, 1985, for example). That said, the new emphasis on shared information was to be applauded. Working with serious and high-risk offenders is clearly a business which demands a range of special skills rather than just those of any one agency. The ACOP guidelines stressed the need for close liaison with other agencies and full and accurate information. One significant point was made on page 4 of the guidelines, 'Being prepared to learn the language of the other agency is an important part of effective inter-agency communication'. This comment was to prove prophetic as we shall see when examining the language of the service as it developed during the late 1990s. It could be said that the die had therefore been cast. The management of the probation service had responded to the raised profile of the public protection agenda by recommending a culture shift in the service and by an introduction of the types of systems which will be considered later. The stress was on consistency in practice, the establishment of information systems and a full integration of risk assessment into everyday practice as a matter of routine.

The ACOP guidelines reviewed a range of documentation from other agencies such as those issued by the Department of Health, and from probation areas which had already established systems for risk reduction and management. However, in its own accompanying notes, the police service was mentioned just once, in stark contrast to the amount of collaboration which was to develop in the subsequent five years. As already noted, the 1993 Audit Commission report had also stressed the need for the police service to work with other agencies to obtain new information so that better efforts could be made towards proactive policing. Better crime pattern analysis and better use of intelligence were essential to effective crime prevention and detection. Yet, nowhere in that document is there mention of the one other agency that knew offenders as well, if not better, than the police service, that is the probation service. This reflects the fact that, until later work by the Audit

Commission, effectiveness had been measured in terms of single agency working. Despite the growing convergence of police and probation agendas, particularly in respect of public protection and, to a lesser extent, crime prevention, each appeared not to see the other, at least in 1993, as a natural ally. The managerial agendas were beginning to merge but for the time being practice remained relatively separate.

THE BEGINNINGS OF CONVERGENCE

By 1995, however, matters had changed considerably. That year saw the publication of what was to become one of the most widely published reports from Her Majesty's Inspectorate of Probation (HMIP), *Dealing with Dangerous People: the Probation Service and Public Protection.* Report of a Thematic Inspection (Home Office, 1995), and undoubtedly one of its most influential. The report was described as the first report on the probation service's role in contributing to public protection through work with potentially dangerous people. It stated, 'The inspection took place at a time of considerable public concern at the level of violence in our society' (p. 9). The statistics quoted were 295,000 crimes of violence in 1993, an increase of 11,000 over 1992, or in percentage terms, just under 4%. Whether or not such an increase would, in normal political circumstances, engender such public concern is debatable. The report went on to say that of this total number of violent crimes, 205,000 were 'against the person', of which some 90% did not involve danger to life. The reality then is that approximately 20,500 violent offences involved a danger to life. This is undoubtedly 20,500 offences too many, but in the context of the population at large hardly appears to represent violence running out of control. Yet over the next few years little was to be done to correct the media-driven image of an increasingly violent and risky society. The inspection was to concern itself with assessing the probation service's responsibilities, policies and practice in relation to dangerous persons with whom it has contact and defined these as individuals who pose a threat of serious harm to the public and others, including probation staff. It was the publication of this report which led Baroness Blatch, then Home Office minister, to decare that public protection was the first priority of the probation service. Such a clear pointer to the future work of the service therefore deserves full consideration, so the report will be examined in detail.

Inspecting Developments

The report describes areas of good practice and reassuring quality but, as explained by the Chief Inspector of Probation in the introduction, 'parts of this report will make uncomfortable reading'. Key recommendations were, in brief:

- reports written by probation staff must deal more adequately with public protection issues (interestingly suggesting that consideration be given to the imposition of custody if required to protect the public);
- risk assessment must be carried out in every case;
- staff must record and respond to indicators of dangerousness;
- identification of potential dangerousness is a corporate responsibility;
- national standards must be complied with;
- information must flow more freely between agencies and organisations dealing with potentially dangerous offenders.

Key principles also emerged in the report, such as suggesting that the probation service should work at all times to reduce the risk of serious physical or psychological harm to the public, that officers had a personal responsibility in relation to public protection and that confidentiality took second place to protecting the public. The report stressed many examples of good probation practice which will be briefly discussed below, but for the purposes of this book it is important to pick up on the sections dealing with inter-agency co-operation. It has already been noted that, in official crime prevention documents up to 1993, little indication had been given of a greater police and probation collaboration. This report, however, put the issue into clear perspective. Reiterating a familiar line of, 'The responsibility for public protection does not rest with any one agency' (p. 24), it went on to say that:

- joint policies, procedures and strategies should be agreed with other agencies (particularly the police but also social services, health providers, special hospitals, prisons and voluntary agencies);
- there should be regular liaison to ensure that policies are being implemented;

- there should be open exchange of information between agencies about individual cases (governed by protocols); and
- a case conference style of information sharing and decision-making is recommended.

It is interesting to note that, although the task was a newly prioritised one, the police service had now assumed the mantle of principal partner and the voluntary sector had been relegated to last place, although this is understandable given the nature of the task. It was to be the development of protocols governing case conferences and the sharing of information which was to become a major task for both services and lead to collaboration on an unheard of scale in the mid to late 1990s, most notably when the public fear of paedophile offenders hit new heights of frenzy during 1997 and 1998.

The inspection noted a seedbed of goodwill between agencies and a growing recognition of shared aims in respect of public protection. The report stressed the need for chief officers to lead in this area. Police and probation service relationships were singled out for special attention, as appearing to have developed particularly well in the last five years, 'with a growing appreciation on both sides that they were in the same business' (p. 55). The issue of developing trust was raised for effective joint work, especially among middle managers and service deliverers. The importance of personal contact was highlighted by those involved in the inspection. However, the need for an additional impetus for sharing information, beyond that brought about by personal relation-ships, was a key feature of the report's findings. The barrier to effective information sharing was identified as the issue of confidentiality, 'Many probation services and agencies were more concerned about this issue than any other aspect of joint working' (p. 57). Whilst observing that probation areas recognised the need to pool information, it was felt that the reality of practice did not always match the ideal:

It followed therefore, that agencies needed to pool their information but this was not always reflected in policy statements and practice guidance adopted by individual agencies. A number of probation services appeared reluctant to share information with the police. One chief officer was openly sceptical whether the police would use information discreetly. In other services, chief officers see sharing between police and probation as desirable but exceedingly difficult to achieve. In contrast, services appeared more willing to exchange information with social service departments. Such a situation, given the role of the police service in providing public protection, must be a matter for concern (p. 57).

Even a quick reading of the protocols developed since this report was written would reveal a very substantial turn around in the whole situation of information sharing (see chapter 6). The report had noted that there were examples of information exchange, both formal and informal, and in parts of the country there were good examples of multi-agency working across a range of issues. The West Yorkshire model was noted as the most well developed observed by the inspection team. Here, it was noted that information was 'shared unreservedly' but amongst a limited number of staff and in a tightly monitored policy. The case conference style of information sharing was recommended in paragraph 7.13 of the report and has since become the model for most police and probation services around the country, although with various refinements added as they arise out of experience.

Effective work on protecting the public was therefore to consist of two essential elements. One was a more effective and open partnership with key agencies, especially the police service, and the second was greater rigour in the internal arrangements of the probation service. This was to involve a range of issues from probation officer practice through to management monitoring and support. Public protection was to be written into the daily practice of probation staff and the assessment of risk was to take place in all parts of its activity, from court reports through to supervision at the end of a prison sentence. However, although not always complimentary of probation practice, the report also did not really highlight any serious shortcomings which had resulted in the sort of calamity with which the dangerousness debate usually concerns itself. For example, 80% of case records indicated whether or not the offender posed a risk to the public, with 20% of those inspected giving no indication at all, a percentage which was considered too high (p. 41). Supervision plans, required under national standards, were assessed as covering the aspect of risk adequately in 31% of cases; inadequately in 38% of cases, and not at all in 20%. In 10% of cases the offender had been assessed as posing no risk. Perhaps more damning were the levels of supervision contact identified in those cases assessed by the supervising officer as posing a threat to public safety:

It was alarming to discover that in 16 cases (27%) of the sub-sample (those assessed as posing a risk to the public), the supervising officer was intending to see the offender, on average, less than once a fortnight despite regarding him or her as a current risk to the public (p. 43).

As well as the frequency of contact, the quality of that contact is crucial to the assessment and management of risk. In the sample, HMIP noted that supervision was good in 58% of cases, adequate in another 22% and the remaining 20% was poorly supervised. The report cited research into the supervision of life sentence prisoners as indicating the importance of regular contact:

> ... the PO may forestall some offences by activating recall or some type of intervention ... supervision was not expected to be able to prevent all further offending. It was intended as a mechanism to alert the Home Office, through the supervising officer, to the possible risk of further serious crime (Coker and Martin, 1985, in Home Office, 1995, p. 45).

Regular contact in this context must also be quality contact. The supervising officer needs to know the offender, and be in a position to recognise the trigger signals of potentially dangerous behaviour. To do this the officer needs to know what to look for, which of course implies both basic and post-qualification experience and training, as well as a set of finely tuned antennae. Despite these elements of criticism, the HMIP report did not discover any glaring errors in practice which could have led to the occurrence of a serious incident. In reading records held at C6 division at the Home Office, HMIP noted 19 cases reported over the preceding 12 months in which a serious incident had occurred and had been committed by an offender under supervision. In these incidents one involved a breach of licence, one a serious injury to a child and 18 deaths (p. 46). However, in a telling comment, it was noted that any change to supervision practice was unlikely to have altered the outcome, 'There were no examples in the cases examined of an offender *showing recognisable signs that he or she might be about to commit a violent offence*' (p. 47, emphasis supplied). There were examples of officers not taking appropriate action when the offender had failed to comply with the requirements of their order or licence, but this was not in any way linked with the serious incidents which followed. This could be used as an argument to counter the 'intensive, intrusive, surveillance' style of supervision which is being talked about at public protection panel meetings around the country. The agencies involved in this area of work need to be sure that they are not going overboard in the systems they establish and the demands of servicing placed upon their staff, particularly those doing the face-to-face work with high risk offenders. The reality of the situation should have been given greater emphasis than that contained in the following paragraph:

> Only a very small number of offenders under supervision had committed serious violent offences in the probation areas involved in the inspection. In the last 10 years, three Chief Probation Officers could recall no such incidents, three could recall one and, elsewhere, there had been two or three in each area. Of the 138 cases in the sample examined, eight were known to have been convicted of a further violent offence during the course of the supervision ranging from arson and robbery to assault occasioning actual bodily harm (p. 47).

ALMOST THERE

By 1998, much of what HMIP had been looking for in terms of policy development in 1995 appeared to be falling into place. A thematic inspection on work with sex offenders revealed, even in its title, the direction in which the probation service had moved, *Exercising Constant Vigilance: The Role of the Probation Service in Protecting the Public from Sex Offenders* (Home Office, 1998a). The title is expressive of the ongoing watching and protective brief now given to the probation service. In his foreword to the report, the chief HMI says:

> Sex offenders are currently the group of offenders most frequently and extensively discussed in the media. The harm they cause is rightly a matter of major public concern. The government has given priority to introducing a range of legislation designed to extend to the public a greater level of protection. The probation service has an important part to play in protecting the public through accurately assessing and taking steps to reduce the risk posed by sex offenders.

Once again, although rightly acknowledging public concern with sex offenders, there is no attempt, even in the foreword, to differentiate between degrees of harm posed by different types of offenders. By going along with the conflation of all such offenders this official document does little to reduce public concern, even though much of the report concerns good practice on the part of the probation service.

The 1995 report on dangerous offenders had expressed concern that there was a reluctance within the probation service to work collaboratively with the police service. By 1998, significant advances appeared to have been made in this respect:

> collaborative work was extensive and increasing. Some excellent examples were seen of representatives from different agencies pooling their knowledge and expertise to tackle sexual offending and to protect potential victims more effectively. *In particular, close and effective working relationships existed between the probation and police services in many areas. The exchange of sensitive information on individual offenders had led on to the development of jointly undertaken strategies to reduce the risk posed by dangerous offenders* (Home Office, 1998, p. 10, emphasis supplied).

A few of the commendable aspects of probation service work with sex offenders were identified as follows:

- protection of the public was unambiguously identified as its central purpose;
- recognition of the distress and harm experienced by victims was its prime focus;
- a high level of vigilance was being exercised;
- a high priority was allocated to the supervision of sex offenders, despite them representing a very small proportion of the caseload of probation services.

This last point is important as it is an example of how a publicly conceived problem can determine patterns of work for public agencies which are really out of proportion both to the extent and degree of risk posed. For example, the report noted that there were approximately 9,000 sexual offenders on the caseloads of probation services at the end of 1996, 4,753 in the community and 4,338 in prison. This represents a total of 3% of the total court order caseload and 9% of the throughcare caseload (p. 31). Figures estimated for the number of pre-sentence reports prepared on sex offenders in any one year amounted to 4,000 to 4,500 (within the smaller sample scrutinised, this amounted to 1.9%). Overall the report calculated that there had been a 27% increase in the number of sex offenders on the probation service caseload since a survey was conducted in 1995. However, rather than representing any serious increase in sexual offending, this increase was likely to be due to the extension of post-release (and of course longer periods of) supervision following the implementation of the Criminal Justice Act 1991. The largest category of offender was that of 'indecent assault on a person under 16' at 1,946 out of 9,012. The next largest category was for 'indecent exposure' at 1,594, however, it should be noted that over 3,000 were in the 'other' category due to a lack of specificity in coding before 1996. Of all the sex offenders on the probation caseload at the end of 1996, approximately 39% were on court orders, whilst 61% were either in detention (approximately 72% of all) or on post-detention licence or supervision (approximately 28% of all). It is clear that this post-release supervision caseload will continue to grow whilst the present climate towards sex offenders is maintained.

As indicated above, much of the report contained examples of good practice identified according to the principles established by HMIP. An illustration of this, and perhaps the new realism of probation officers, can be seen in a quoted conclusion to a pre-sentence report:

Mr X has been left in no doubt about the seriousness of his actions and the expectation of a custodial sentence today. Indeed, in view of his behaviour and lack of cooperation, I would have difficulty in considering other options. With a high risk of reoffending, not only by virtue of the offences committed but Mr X's lack of expressed remorse or insight, the court may wish to consider the imposition of an extended period of supervision at the conclusion of his sentence pursuant to section 44 of the Criminal Justice Act 1991 (p. 58).

During the inspection, the views of judges were canvassed as to the quality of PSRs prepared on sex offenders. The consensus was that reports on sex offenders were better than the average and more clearly focused (p. 121). In particular, judges appreciated the directness with which report writers tackled issues such as risk to the public and the straightforward acknowledgment that only a custodial sentence was appropriate. They also observed more challenge by defence barristers to the reports' contents, inevitable they thought as more realism and objectivity were included. Another interesting point raised by judges was, however, one which has been touched upon in this book several times already, and that is the risk of conflation. They believed that risk assessments on all sex offenders produced a blanket assessment of high risk so that probation officers would be able to defend themselves against accusations of underestimating the danger an individual presented (p. 121). Judges were not calling for less risk assessment but a more differentiated method, a task that they thought was more than one officer's job. This issue will be discussed in greater detail in chapter 8 but it is one of significance not only for probation officers in their court reports but for police officers in their assessment of risk.

SUMMARY

This 1998 HMIP report is one which contains many references to the developing and improving way in which the probation service works with sex offenders. For our purposes it also highlights the considerable development in partnership working with the police and undoubtedly this will increase with the requirements of the Sex Offenders Act 1997 in mind. The seeds of coming together which were identified at the beginning of this chapter, now appear to be very close to fruition. The process has involved a substantial realigning of the work of the probation service and rather less in the case of the police service. For both organisations, however, there has been a very considerable culture shift to enable closer working relationships to develop.

It is the shift from a crime prevention brief towards one of public protection which has facilitated the organisational, moves and un- doubtedly the government's new emphasis on community safety will firmly underwrite multi-agency working and will involve the prison service alongside local authorities and other services. Historically, the probation service never appeared to be comfortable with the wider crime prevention brief, finding it did not sit easily with its focus on individual offenders. Although their task has always been about crime prevention, through the prevention of reoffending work with individuals and groups, this did not fit in with terms such as target hardening and situational crime prevention. Social crime prevention was something that did sit more easily with probation officers but more often than not was rebranded under other terms such as casework, group work or community work. The police service itself, although a key crime prevention agency, often preferred to let others do the running as it concentrated its efforts on detection. Both organisations, however, felt the winds of change blowing in from central government and sought to anticipate and perhaps even divert this from being imposed upon them. In this the police service might be viewed as having been the more successful. The probation service has undoubtedly undergone the greatest transformation which is not yet finished. Its evolution may yet result in a completely new organisation along the lines discussed in the conclusion to this book. The public protection agenda has succeeded where others have failed — it only remains to ask if this was the intention of the government all along.

Chapter 6
Working Together?

The rising public protection agenda has, it is argued, had a significant impact upon criminal justice agencies, and the police and probation services in particular. The success of their working relationship was likely to determine the effectiveness of the public protection initiatives. The previous chapter identified that recent Home Office policy had indicated that the 'case conference' style of information sharing, especially between police and probation services, was the most effective way for agencies to work towards the protection of the public. There is already a history of such an approach which is best seen in multi-agency child protection case conferences, where police and probation services constitute core members. Yet that history is not one which has always been marked by openness and trust, and certainly not by a free flow of information. For the probation service to avoid the pitfalls of early collaboration found by social services departments, it was important that shared goals and agendas were agreed. The protection of the public was to be the common ground, as child protection was. That said, there was not always evidence that police and social services departments had agreed upon the most effective means of securing the child protection goals, so a need for formal inter-agency agreements was essential for success.

THE CHILD PROTECTION MODEL

It is perhaps worth briefly revisiting the history of police involvement with social workers in the field of child protection to see what lessons can be offered for the probation service. In their review of some of the literature, Fielding and Conroy (1994) note an uneasy alliance, marked by power differentials (Thomas, 1988), role conflict (Blagg and Stubbs, 1988) and different recruitment patterns (Cornick, 1988) and of course, overall different working cultures. As already noted with the HMIP document on working with dangerous offenders (Home Office, 1995), joint training was seen as something of a panacea and important within that training was an understanding and appreciation of the 'other's role'. In gaining trust, respect and acceptance, however, how much did the less powerful agency have to concede? To what extent would it have to assume the dominant values of the more powerful organisation? If it failed to do this, would trust still ensue and if it did, would it any longer be the agency that it started as? Furthermore, to what extent would the dominant agency set the agenda and the focus of any multi-agency working? These questions are very important to the newly established public protection panels, or potentially dangerous offender conferences which have recently developed around the country. The purpose of multi-agency working is to bring together a range of professional perspectives, so answers to some of the questions posed in this chapter are important.

Stevenson (1989) offered a list of dimensions along which inter-professional and inter-agency co-operation can be examined. Her criteria constitute a document for good practice based on many of the major child abuse inquiries of the 1970s and 1980s. This list offers a useful framework in which to examine probation and police collaboration in a multi-agency, conference style arrangement. Her list included:

- structures and systems;
- relative status and perceived power of the parties;
- role identifications;
- professional and organisational priorities;
- the extent to which co-operation is perceived as mutually beneficial and in which ways;
- the dynamics of case conferences;
- differing attitudes towards, and values concerning, child abuse and the family.

Some of these points will be discussed further relating to of the developing police-probation protocols in respect of potentially dangerous offenders. They will be set alongside the author's observations at actual conferences and a reading of a range of documentation concerning this issue from police and probation services around the country.

Structures and Systems

Stevenson (1989) refers to the findings of the Cleveland Report (1988) which recommended the development of specialist (multi-agency) assessment teams, in particular so as to help with difficulties arising from individual cases. Another reason for this as she saw it was a need to pool and share knowledge, rather than have it spread among a number of staff operating more as individuals than as team members. In terms of working with dangerous offenders the probation service has gone through many stages of evolution, frequently oscillating between specialist (by function) teams and teams of officers carrying a generic caseload. It was felt by Stevenson that specialist teams might also increase the amount of knowledge of others due to a more frequent exchange with other agencies. In one area observed by the author, a combination of specialist and generic teams was in operation, although the most likely 'source' of offenders regarded as potentially dangerous was a resettlement team which dealt with those released from custody and was of course involved throughout their sentence. That team had developed a good deal of expertise in both the assessment and management of potentially dangerous offenders and, as a result of a pilot protocol with the police service, worked very closely with it throughout the trial period. The results of that collaboration will be discussed later but one interesting point emerged from the pilot study. Throughout the six month period of the review only one referral was made to the potentially dangerous offender (PDO) conferences by a probation officer from outside of that specialist team. Obviously most of those considered to be likely to present a risk were already on the resettlement team's books, but it is doubtful that other offenders within the area had not at least demonstrated signs of seriously risky behaviour. The concentration of task and specialism may have led to a false sense of security among other staff members or a pigeon-holing of offender history and sentence as an indicator of dangerousness, rather than a more holistic approach: '... these factors are neither the only, nor absolute, indicators of risk and such an approach was, therefore, unsatisfactory' (Home Office, 1995, p. 33). This is not to say that officers in other teams were not alive to the risk and public protection issues possibly shown by offenders under their supervision. But it is possible that, despite the advantages of specialism, it may have the effect of others thinking it is not their responsibility. The HMIP stress on risk assessment in every case therefore becomes extremely significant.

Relative Status and Perceived Power of the Parties

Stevenson (1989) is particularly concerned with relative power within a health context, although her observations have a wider application: 'It is now widely understood that inter-agency and inter-professional working is affected by the ways the parties see each other' (p. 184). Conferences aimed at discussing potentially dangerous offenders afford an opportunity for a range of perceptions to be expressed. Within the perception of 'the other' could be a variety of issues which could impact upon decision-making. An example of this different perception might be gender, for example. There are proportionately many fewer female police officers than female probation officers, and despite efforts at eliminating discrimination in the police service there remain entrenched views about male and female officers' work. In the multi-agency setting, police officers will work with a probation service whose members are at least 50% female — and protection is often viewed as 'man's business' (but see Nash, 1995). Differing gender-based perspectives on risk and danger should enhance the multi-agency process, not hinder it, and conference leaders should be alive to this issue.

Importance of Task

Here the issues could be clouded by old style perceptions of key tasks such as detection and of 'letting-off'. Undoubtedly these perceptions are shifting as well as the distinctive nature of task, but nevertheless the opportunity remains for disagreement. The tension inherent in agency role and task should be healthy and in seeking to reduce possibilities for disagreement, professionals should ensure that they do not compromise their specific expertise.

Status and Rank

The significance of the public protection task has been indicated by the rank of staff allocated to the task, so this should not be a major issue between the key agencies (although it may pose a problem for 'visiting' agencies). There will, however, be many basic grade probation officers working with middle and senior ranking police officers. Protocols should aim to ensure harmonious and equal working relationships between them — agency status may be less important than individual status although, in his observations to date, the author has not seen this as a problem.

Power is of course relative and can be balanced to a certain extent by legislation and policy. The shared nature of the public protection agenda overcomes one hurdle in terms of agreeing the task, the agenda has already been forcibly set by the government. Yet, public protection has a much longer history for the police service and its role has traditionally attempted to fulfil this purpose. As already noted, for the probation service the role is relatively new, at least in terms of it being made a public priority. The danger would then be that the newcomer signs up to an agenda already set by the incumbent. However, it should be noted that the real thrust for co-operation in the dangerous offender field came from the HMIP report and it was therefore the probation service, in many parts of the country, which took a lead role in establishing the joint agenda. The issue of status within the conferences is not likely to be such a drawback as that identified by Stevenson (1989, p. 186). Observations of protocols and discussions with practitioners around the country suggests that middle to senior managers have been mostly involved in potentially dangerous offender (PDO) conferences (assistant chief probation officers, senior probation officers, police superintendents, chief inspectors, inspectors and sergeants). Supervising probation officers are invariably present although there may be less consistent attendance from police constable ranks, unless in a detective or other specialist role. In some areas it is always the probation service which chairs the conference, whilst in other areas the responsibility is rotated. Some split the task depending upon the offence under consideration; thus sexual offences lead to the police service chairing and violent offences to the probation service chairing, to reflect police responsibilities under the Sex Offenders Act 1997.

Role Identifications

This area perhaps offers one of the greatest challenges to effective collaboration between police and probation officers working with dangerous offenders. Naturally the recruitment and training of the two organisations has been completely different. Until the abolition in 1995 of the requirement for a probation officer to hold a professional social work qualification, that had been the professional basis of the service. Those social work roots were long-established and perhaps were those most likely to offer a culture clash with police officers. Yet, it is argued here that this issue appears to have caused minimal difficulty among those staff who already held the social work qualification. What struck the author was the common use of shared language by both police and probation staff, a common language of public protection which frequently contained little which an outsider might regard as 'traditional social work speak'. An example of this can be found in a questionnaire sent out to people who attended a conference set up to precede the formal piloting of a PDO conferencing system. In reply to a question asking what respondents thought would be the main purpose of conferences concentrating on potentially dangerous offenders, the police respondents suggested the following summarised points:

- to share information and evaluate risk;
- to identify potentially dangerous people and where they live;
- to protect the vulnerable;
- to establish a common goal of public protection;
- to flag concerns and devise action plans.

This is the type of police agenda which might be expected, suggesting a combination of prevention and detection measures, with a key focus on the use of information or, as the police might call it, intelligence. The probation service response was as follows:

- to reduce the risk of harm;
- to share information;
- to pool information;
- to plan case management and maximise information;
- to test out perceptions on other agencies.

This is an agenda which does not mention that traditional focus of probation work, namely concern for the individual offender, but has a wider, more proactive focus in keeping with those traditionally expressed by the police service.

In talking with people involved in the conferences, the close nature of respective roles and working relationships is even more apparent. Reproduced below are comments from both police and probation officers concerning their feelings about trust within the conference process.

'If we have information that can assist the police then I believe we are duty bound to share it.' (probation)

'There was no noticeable holding back in the conferences that I attended. I was extremely impressed by the openness on both sides. I think that we gave them a vast amount of information about how we saw things and I think they were very open with us, both about attitudes and about accessing information . . .' (probation)

'There was a sharing of information which I was heartened by. I was a little concerned that maybe the probation service wouldn't release their intelligence but they did — in fact, quite the contrary, they opened up.' (police)

'The police have actually given us more confidence in tackling dangerous offenders, very high risk dangerous offenders.' (probation)

'The traditional (police) view is still out there — we catch them and you nurse them . . . we're more upfront about public protection now and that has helped.' (probation)

These comments reflect a few of the traditional role differences but on the whole show quite considerable culture shifts within both organisations. The suggestion here is that role identification, at least in the area of working with dangerous offenders, is not one of difference but of similarity and a sense of shared task. The question is, of course, is this coming together shared by both the police and probation services more widely, or does it remain a feature of small numbers of staff working in a discrete area? A key task for both police and probation managers will be to implant these ideas more generally into their respective organisations and not leave it to a few specialist staff. Public protection in the fullest sense will require the whole organisation to be committed to shared working, not just discrete elements of it.

Professional and Organisational Priorities

Any one who has attended multi-agency conferences will know that they are extremely time consuming. Obtaining agreements for action plans across a range of professional areas is never easy as there may well be competing professional interests as well as personal perceptions of risk. In contrast to the amount of time taken up by these conferences is the need very often for swift decision-making. The type of danger discussed by multi-agency public protection panels should really be something that is imminent and requires urgent action to reduce the risk. Therefore conferences need to be set up rapidly and decisions taken as quickly, and as fairly, as possible.

In her section on priorities, Stevenson (1989) refers to the sharing of confidential information as a possible barrier to effective working (p. 190). The establishment of protocols around the country appears to override any one agency concern with this matter. Thus a common policy line in this particular area might say:

> both services recognise that normal rules of confidentiality may need to be overridden in order to protect the public in respect of potentially dangerous offenders. However, any information exchanged will be subject to strict control and remain confidential between the two services unless agreed otherwise (non-metropolitan county).

Within such agreements, the aims of joint working are made explicit for both organisations, there is no room for debate. For example:

> The xxxx Probation Service and xxxx Constabulary recognise the need to identify potentially dangerous offenders who come within their remit. Moreover, both services recognise the need for effective multi-agency working, involving themselves and others, in managing the risk posed by potentially dangerous offenders.

Or:

To allow the agencies to share information about high risk offenders and devise strategies for reducing or managing the risk which each offender poses. The overriding aim is the protection of the public (large metropolitan county).

Information-sharing

The overall objective is to protect the public and the means of working towards this is to share information with other agencies and co-work on agreed plans. By definition, a failure to communicate is not an effective way to work and will not protect the public. The creation of protocols governing the sharing of information is therefore essential, especially among professionals who may not have always seen themselves as natural allies in the fight against crime. In many respects the protocols can be viewed as contracts between the agencies which spell out the expectations of each other in the knowledge that a 'breach' could lead to a serious incident. Fukyama (1995) has written of trust in another context, but one which, in many ways, could be used to describe the relationship between police and probation officers. Although talking about a decline of trust within communities, or a decline of community, he says, 'Contracts allow strangers with no basis for trust to work with one another, but the process works far more efficiently when the trust exists' (p. 150). It may sound an exaggeration to say that there is no trust between the police and probation services. However, it is fair to say that a great deal of trust has not always existed between all ranks of both services. The development of protocols, as a managerial tool, allow joint working to become institutionalised, a requirement of the job and a criteria by which to be assessed. Full and open trust may not always exist, but the management agreement does exist and cannot be ignored. The development of the shared and agreed agenda is therefore very important and further embeds joint working practice into that of each agency. To quote Fukyama again, 'As a general rule, trust arises when a community shares a set of moral values ...' (p. 153). Although, again, this quotation refers to a different context, it perfectly describes the developing shared language of police and probation officers, a language which reflects, to a certain extent, a shared set of moral values, at least around the subject of public protection. The political and practice agenda has created a shared language between police and probation officers and, perhaps to the outsider, it is the language of the probation service which has changed the more significantly. The language of public protection has many common themes which most frequently include: risk management, protection overriding rights to confidentiality, surveillance, monitoring, assessment, disclosure of information, tracking and a sense of 'managing the problem'. The establishment of protocols is then the way in which agencies, coming from different perspectives on the problem, are enabled to work together and more importantly to take down the traditional professional barriers between themselves. The protocols allow and require people to do what they might not have wanted to, or believed they could, do in the past. In Fukyama's terms, they allow trust to develop by way of formal agreements — protocols are therefore extremely important.

For example, an illustration of the type of shared agreement over possible courses of action can be seen in this extract from a press release issued by a large metropolitan area:

> Agencies attending the meeting share information which they hold and an assessment is made as to the risk which each offender represents. A course of action is then agreed, which might include a number of measures to safeguard the public. Issues to be agreed include accommodation, levels of supervision or surveillance, medical treatment (if appropriate), specialist work (for example, tackling the person's offending behaviour, with a view to preventing further crimes) and longer-term plans for rehabilitation. Additional measures may be considered, such as electronic monitoring, where further safeguards are thought to be necessary.

In this extract it is possible to see a seamless merger between police, probation and, possibly, health objectives. Even prison staff may be present to ensure continuity of the work they have begun — indeed the government would positively welcome this development. Supervision and surveillance can become interchangeable and issues such as accommodation, a traditional social work focus, are recast as protection issues, which of course they are in certain cases. The joint nature of the project is emphasised throughout the sort of documentation which now covers the country in the form of agreements and protocols. The protocol just cited makes clear that it has successfully operated working to the following aims:

- sharing information at critical stages of an agency's contact with the offender, e.g., prior to a person's release from custody;
- assessing the level of risk to individuals or the community;
- devising strategic plans to minimise risk;
- monitoring and reviewing progress and outcomes.

In this particular area, the police service, as well as other agencies, signs up to a joint agreement, affirming its commitment to public protection. Members of the police service, for example, describe their position as follows; '(we) are committed to work with the probation service to identify those dangerous and high risk offenders which come within their remit and take appropriate joint action to protect the public from harm and to attempt to prevent the commission of further offences from those offenders'. This statement is interesting in one sense, that is the emphasis on offenders coming within the remit of the probation service, rather than the other way around. This reflects a point made elsewhere in this book that it may be the police who stand to gain the greatest amount of information from the PDO process. It is they who are tapping into additional information networks more fully than the probation service, although this is not to imply that the police service is holding back. It may be that the police service is perhaps somewhat belatedly learning that the probation service holds a considerable amount of information on known offenders. It is a feature of many of the protocols that the police position statement often refers to the identification and tracking of known dangerous offenders about whom it would help them to know more. It is clear that information and intelligence remains a great priority for that organisation. One feature of the conferences is that the police service can obtain information of which it was not previously aware, although this is also the case for probation staff. Another 'benefit' of joint working may be a much greater police understanding of the range of serious and dangerous offenders that are under the supervision of the probation service at any one time, perhaps helping to dispel further some of the myths which are believed in respect of that organisation.

All protocols stress that the need for public protection outweighs any single agency's concerns over confidentiality. It is the conference that holds the information and therefore it is important that awareness of the provisions of the Data Protection Act 1998 (which, when fully implemented, will replace the Data Protection Act 1984 in its entirety), whereby subjects of information can gain access to computerised records, is constantly kept in mind. Information in this area of work can be highly sensitive and potential informants, in the widest sense of the word, could be at risk. Many conferences therefore restrict membership to those agencies who can actively contribute to a discussion on public risk and the management of dangerous behaviour in the community. This might, for example, call into question the attendance of organisations such as Victim Support who may well believe that there is a role for them at these meetings, and indeed do attend many conferences.

INTER-AGENCY PROTOCOLS

As protocols have developed around the country certain models have come to dominate and a developing national model is beginning to emerge, supported by work in ACPO and ACOP. Models such as this contain the factors already identified in this chapter, although individual areas may still operate slightly different protocols to reflect their local situation. It is clear that the requirements placed on the police service by the Sex Offenders Act 1997 have acted as a great stimulus to joint working with other agencies, but especially the probation service. One metropolitan area thus describes a protocol between police, probation, local authorities and health authorities whilst most, at least in the title, feature only the first two. For the police service the 'management of risk' in such a public way can be seen as a new departure from previous practice. The service's historical emphasis on reaction, rather than being proactive, is well documented. Therefore, to find an Act of Parliament which stresses so publicly the service's preventative role with such a potentially dangerous group of offenders, must have triggered police managers into seeking collaboration with partner agencies. Information is seen as the key, with one protocol stressing, 'The management of risk will be based on the exchange of information and the pooling of resources between the police, the probation service and other appropriate agencies'. The process of risk management, now developing as a key feature of protocol agreements, can be described as follows.

Initial Agreement

The first stage in the protection process is usually a jointly issued memorandum of agreement or protocol, released by the police and probation services and occasionally signed by other interested agencies. This agreement spells out in unambiguous terms the reason for the agreement and the rationale for collaboration. This rationale is explicit in stating that public protection is an agreed objective for all signatory agencies. An example of a broad statement of aims which aptly sums up the reason for protocols is the following from a mixed urban and rural area:

> It is acknowledged that there are a small number of people who present a significant risk of harm to themselves or others, as a result of mental disorder or deviant behaviour. Whilst all signatory agencies have a general rule of confidentiality all acknowledge that this is not absolute. The common overriding factor for sharing information is that of public protection, i.e., where there is an assessed high risk of harm to the individual or to other people.

Subjects to Include

Most protocols include the same type of offence-based list described in the next chapter, with the inclusion of catch-all phrases such as, 'those cases provoking serious professional concern'. Other protocols 'simply' refer to people who exhibit the propensity to cause serious physical injury or psychological harm to other persons and/or themselves, a group which has the potential to be very large! Clearly most of the lead work in this area has come from the probation service which, for some years now, has operated a system of registering high risk offenders and which, in most places, has established a system of regular review of supervision and other developments in these cases, often with the involvement of other agencies including the police service. Most of those included under the newly agreed arrangements are therefore likely to originate from the probation service, although there will undoubtedly be other referring agencies. Offenders referred to public protection panels are thus already likely to have been subject to risk assessment procedures by at least one agency. They may well have several factors causing concern, ranging from the baseline of their previous convictions, to threats which have been made in prison, or present behaviour which gives cause for alarm. Consequently, the meetings may not be concerned so much with a reassessment of risk factors as an evaluation of the degree and imminence of the potential risk of harm arising from those factors already identified. This is where the availability of good quality, detailed information from a range of criminal justice professionals will be indispensable.

Working Together?

As stated above, a key aim of protocols is to embed joint working into the practice of each agency. These agreements can include a requirement for the probation service to maintain an information flow to police intelligence bureaus on the arrival in the area, or changes in status, of known or registered potentially dangerous offenders. In some areas this contact may include a requirement for field probation officers to consult police intelligence or crime managers prior to the release of a prisoner, either on temporary licence or full licence. The aim of this contact would be to seek the views of the police service on any conditions it saw as appropriate for inclusion in the prisoner's licence. These licences will increasingly be used as another means of building in risk reducing measures into prisoners' post-release requirements.

Most agreements or protocols stipulate the rank of officers responsible for overseeing the joint working arrangements. For the police service this is usually a Detective Superintendent and for the probation service an Assistant Chief Officer, with heavy involvement from Detective Inspector and Senior Probation Officer ranks. Formal meetings may be planned on a regular basis, perhaps four or six times a year. These meetings are frequently known as public protection panel meetings, or something similar. In other areas there is a split arrangement between regular meetings concerning those cases registered by the probation service as being 'high risk' and those who are viewed as 'potentially dangerous'. Although this may appear to be replication it is not necessarily so. Those areas with separate systems appear to be making the point that there are many offenders who, by their previous convictions, fall within a high risk category and perhaps therefore warrant a more thorough and regular review, perhaps involving other agencies. But not all of these offenders may be demonstrating signs of the clear and vivid danger which, for many experts, is the trigger for tipping the case over the line into the area of potential dangerousness. It would appear that all areas should have a system which enables agencies to come together at short notice to consider the creation and implementation of a risk reduction plan.

Danger, by definition, is usually acute and therefore urgent action may be required. The notion of risk management, and therefore reduction, is of course a very sound one which is undoubtedly facilitated by good multi-agency planning. Regular planned reviews of a case are also essential, both to monitor the plan and potential danger and also to consider the possible deregistration of the offender if appropriate.

Including and Advising the Offender

Most protocols acknowledge that the offender has to be told of his or her registration if this is the result, or even if discussion has taken place in a multi-agency forum. Indeed some probation officers have said that this process of informing the offender has, in itself, been effective in adding to the strength of their supervisory ability. The idea that other agencies may be watching the offender may be a useful notion to plant. The probation service policy on offenders accessing information held on them could of course pose difficulties. In such a sensitive area of information disclosure as potentially dangerous offenders, any information revealed about informants, in the broadest sense of the term, could put them at risk from the offender. In such cases most protocols contain a provision not to tell the offender of the registration decision if it is felt that such notification would put someone at risk of harm. Another very important aspect of the panel process is the actual attendance of the offender for all or part of the conference (along the lines of child protection conferences). Most protocols do not allow for offender attendance but a few do, with the obvious exception that if attendance compromised public safety or the safety of an information source, it would not be allowed. Indeed it is difficult to think of many cases where, if potential danger is the subject of the discussion, this would not be the case.

The issue of offender attendance is an interesting one and replicates the discussions had over the attendance of alleged abusers at child protection meetings. The police service in particular often found this idea difficult to work with, believing that it would hinder the free flow of important information. This notion is undoubtedly present in public protection panel meetings, as well as the risk of harm from the offender to those who disclose certain information. The exclusionary model is one where decisions are taken about the offender in his or her absence and these decisions can of course include discussions concerning exclusion from certain geographical areas as a condition in a sex offender order. The aim generally here is to manage the risk and, if possible, devise strategies which might reduce the risk of serious harm befalling members of the public. The offender here is the recipient of the decision, rather than being a part of it. Words such as 'conditions' and 'requirements' are more common than 'agreements'. The community is rarely involved in the decision-making process and therefore the exclusionary focus of decisions and action is reinforced. An alternative model might be that put forward by republican criminologists Braithwaite and Daly (1994) for example, as described below.

AN ALTERNATIVE MODEL

Students of criminology will be familiar with the ideas of Braithwaite and his colleagues (Braithwaite, 1989, Braithwaite and Petit, 1990 and Braithwaite and Mugford, 1993). The general idea is one of a community conference which is based on the notion of shaming the offender by 'communities of concern'. The idea is that these communities should be empowered by the criminal justice process, not disempowered. The attendance of both victim and supporters and offender and supporters is said to be conducive to reintegrative shaming — although it does not necessarily guarantee it. In this country efforts are already being made to integrate the shaming concept into our criminal justice process, although at the present time it has not extended into very serious offences. Yet Braithwaite and Daly (1994) describe how it has been used in cases of child sexual abuse and sexual violence towards women, the type of cases perhaps most frequently referred to the newly formed public protection panels.

The authors regard violence as gendered and a consequence of masculinity (p. 189) and the response of the state is described in similar terms. They believe that the criminal process fails women and children for three major reasons (p. 191):

(1)   Most men are not made accountable for acts of rape or violence against intimates (low reporting levels, police indifference, evidential difficulties).

(2)   The men who are arrested and prosecuted for violence against women have possibly got away with it before and may have entrenched

patterns of raping and assaulting women (already hardened offenders as a result of point 1, prison becomes inevitable and rehabilitation programmes fail as a result of entrenched attitudes which have not been challenged).

(3) Women victimised by men's violence are revictimised by engaging the criminal process (complaints of intimate assault not taken seriously by police or courts, the shame of rape survivors, the way in which trials are conducted where the victim becomes the person on trial).

Exclusion or Inclusion?

The authors argue that, for example with the cases of men who assault intimates (including high levels of rape, often missed by 'public' protection panels), the community conferencing process offers better prospects for long term attitudinal change. They see a 'regulatory pyramid' (p. 197) with imprisonment at the top and therefore the final resort. Most intervention should occur at the bottom, with family and community involvement. If this does not work, the involvement of the state escalates but would also act as a means of offering safety to the victim in the form of shelters and other similar environments if the conference is not running too successfully. Braithwaite and Daly believe that the three problems identified above with the criminal process are at least partially addressed by a conferencing system, as follows.

Problem 1. Women who are victims of rape *may* be more inclined to engage in a conference process than a trial as it is private, quicker and less traumatic. The rapist can be pressured by the police to engage with the process on the basis that he may do better and get the case handled more quickly than by going to court. The victim receives much greater support from friends and family than would be possible in a court setting and she is able to confront the offender with her feelings and the consequences of his actions. The offender has the right to stop proceedings and go to court. Sanctions can be imposed by the conference which may be lighter than those imposed by the court but greater than if the matter was dismissed by the court. Empirical evidence from New Zealand and Australia suggests that many defendants admit their guilt to the conference.

Problem 2.   Here the problem is addressed through earlier intervention in the offender's life, before attitudes become fixed as a result of a lack of challenge. Picking up on the idea that adult sex offenders frequently showed very negative attitudes to women as teenagers, the idea is to use the family and community to challenge these views at an early stage and break 'patterns of exploitation and degradation of women' (p. 203).

Problem 3.   The authors believe that rape trials are about stigma and that the alleged offender is given a highly trained practitioner whose task is to deny responsibility, injury and the victim. The trial process 'institutionalises incentives for a defendant to reinforce his denials' (p. 204) and his attitudes are further entrenched by the process which calls for one side to be seen as worse than the other. Conferences, by contrast, are described as victim-centred, with participants selected on the basis of their support for 'their side' rather than capacity to exert damage.

Braithwaite and Daly do not argue that everything in the conference garden is rosy and do note some of the problems with the process in both Australia and New Zealand. However, they do believe that the conference is a process which does more to challenge current practices which leave 'patriarchal masculinities untouched and victims more degraded and defeated' (p. 210).

The purpose of community conferences therefore differs sharply from public protection panels. A public protection panel is very much a meeting of professionals who have been mandated to reduce the risk of serious harm to the public. They are there to devise and implement a plan which manages the risk, or in Floud's terminology (1981), redistributes it. There is not such a concern with long-term attitude change, which in itself may well lower the risk, but more a wish to reduce the risk in the short-term, to offer a plan which at least suggests that safety may be improved. The development of serious and dangerous offender legislation around the world would suggest that there is little opportunity for any alternative to punitive, controlling measures. Yet the gathering of multi-agency panels does surely open the door to alternatives and it is for those agencies involved to suggest it, rather than keep running with the protection baton.

WIDER DISCLOSURE

Public protection panels are required not only to set up potential
protection plans but also to decide upon who should be informed of
what. The republican model would not have such a problem with this
as the whole point would be to marshal the resources of the community
to reintegrate the offender, rather than exclude him. It is clear, however,
that Home Office guidelines have said that wider public disclosure
should be very much the exception and even limited disclosure to those
at risk or those involved with those at risk should be a rare event. In
these cases it is likely that the police service will be the final arbiters on
the decision although it is one which will be taken in discussion with
other agencies (for a fuller discussion on community notification, see
chapter 9).

There is also an issue on the amount of information which may be
disclosed to the legal representative of an offender who may be facing
another court appearance. In cases where, for example, a panel has been
activated at the pre-sentence report phase, there is great scope for the
probation service to obtain information on the defendant which could
have a potentially negative impact in the court report. Although this
information may be used in a public protection capacity there is an issue
of the defendant challenging the basis on which it was obtained. By not
appearing at the conference the defendant's legal representative may
feel justified in asking for conference notes if the result of the panel
discussion was what was viewed as harmful to the defendant's interest.
This underlines the importance of ensuring that sources of information
are anonymised in conference notes, e.g. 'the probation service' rather
than a named officer, and may also lead to police and probation services
seeking public interest immunity from the Crown Prosecution Service.
If this is not agreed by the CPS then a decision may be taken not to
proceed with the case, which was what happened in similar circumstances in many previous cases involving police informants. It could
perhaps be argued that there is a need to keep the extent of police and
probation collaboration a secret from the public, indeed some of the
protocols refer to this. However, there has been such a fanfare of
publicity in this area, with a range of media releases, that all the public
can be unaware of is some of the fine detail involved in the agreements.
The need for discretion and secrecy must be balanced by rigour and
openness in the assessment process and an ethical consideration in

discussions which may impact on the liberty and civil rights of, as yet, unconvicted defendants.

SUMMARY

Multi-agency protocols have spread very rapidly around the country. They have primarily involved the police and probation services but all include other relevant agencies. Undoubtedly, the way in which partnership features so prominently in the Crime and Disorder Act 1998 suggests that this style of working has a long future ahead of it. The way in which police and probation officers have come together and the nature of the protocols which underpin their agreements is an amazing example of culture shift on the part of both organisations. The strength of the public protection agenda, and perhaps the cost of failure, is so great as to ensure collaboration. Yet the history of multi-agency child protection conferences suggests that there is considerable scope for failure although, as yet, public protection panels do not appear to have experienced the problems of those earlier days. For some time now the probation service has been moving towards a broker or facilitator role in respect of criminal justice aims and resources. Public protection panels afford an opportunity to extend that role with a key partner in a crucial area of practice. Provided its own expertise is not diluted, this provides the probation service with a great opportunity to build its profile and credibility whilst maintaining its professional base. For the police service there is opportunity to share the load and also learn more of the offenders about whom it has most concern. Both agencies can take the opportunity to work towards the reduction of risk but both share the obligation to balance the powers involved with a sense of justice and regard to rights.

Part 2
Protection in Action

Chapter 7
Protecting the Public

The process and agreements governing joint working between police and probation services were described in the previous chapter. Of themselves, these agreements can be viewed as indicators of success. They have moved multi-agency working forward and made public protection a key priority for a variety of agencies. They have institutionalised multi-agency risk assessment and information sharing as a key element in managerial and practice agendas. However, it is important to move beyond the process and consider the outcomes. This leads to the fundamental question, 'does it work?' Chapter 1 detailed the difficulties concerning the assessment and prediction of future dangerous behaviour. This means that, in terms of effectiveness, potentially dangerous offender conferences and public protection panels are working in the area of the unknown. That is, they can claim success if the predicted dangerous behaviour does not happen, but no one can be sure if it would have happened. Possibility and probability are a long way apart, yet are often conflated in the world of dangerousness.

Yet, in terms of public reassurance, the idea that something very unpleasant might have been prevented by agreed action plans is undoubtedly comforting. An impression can be given by the agencies and, it could be argued, by the government, that something is being done about a situation where people often feel helpless and vulnerable. Any concern over whether or not something might have actually happened, is easily subsumed by the relief at avoiding the potential horrors had it happened. Police and probation services are therefore having to operate in the context of a public expectation that increased levels of safety and protection will be generated by their joint working. Despite their efforts to play down these expectations, both agencies know that they will be judged not on their successes, but on their failures. The Association of Chief Officers of Probation (ACOP) for example, in its guidance document, spoke of the need to avoid creating unrealistic expectations and that services, in their work with others, were realistic about their limited ability to protect the public. However, working within this sense of expectation lies the risk to the success of these multi-agency groups. They could well become over-cautious, wanting to include everyone that just might pose a risk. Any widening of the net in this sense would be bound to reduce the chances of effective working, if only because agency resources will not cope with massive numbers. The subjects chosen for conferencing, the way in which risk is assessed and the plans set in train to manage and reduce that risk therefore become absolutely crucial. This chapter will explore who is the type of person subject to multi-agency concern and how the process of assessment and risk management is undertaken. Some of the cases mentioned are real and have been taken from press releases issued by statutory agencies, accordingly they are in the public domain. Others are constructed from lifelike events and situations, but are not true cases, they are merely used to illustrate how the process works.

CONFERENCES IN ACTION

The large metropolitan county referred to in chapter 6 issued a major press release two years after piloting multi-agency risk assessment panels. In so doing, the county described three cases which in themselves highlight the potential for over-inclusion or net widening, but also illustrate what can be claimed as a successful intervention in what might have become a very dangerous situation. Two of these cases will be described in full from the press release and discussion will follow.

Case 1 (the Pilot Case)

Sean was due to be released from prison after an eight year sentence. His offence was the abduction and rape of a 12-year-old girl, five days after release from a previous prison sentence for burglary. He claimed not to recall the offence, despite evidence that he had planned it and refused to take part in the prison sex offender programme. He was due for release with no statutory supervision by the probation service. However, he was felt to be a risk and the panel met to decide the best way of protecting the public.

A multi-agency risk management plan was drawn up which included consideration of information and allocation of the following agency tasks:

(1) *Housing.*   An offer of accommodation on an estate with children was withdrawn. A hostel place was offered with a later planned move to a National Association for the Care and Resettlement of Offenders (NACRO) hostel.

(2) *Prison.*   The Principal Officer attended the panel and gave information, for example any links with other known sex offenders whilst in custody.

(3) *Police.*   Agreed to issue information to officers in the area and to arrange surveillance following release.

(4) *Hostel.*   Information was shared and liaison with the police agreed.

(5) *Probation Officer.*   Assumed a co-ordinating role in arranging liaison between agencies. Set up an appointment with a psychiatrist and gave practical advice.

Review

The risk management plan enabled agencies to move Sean to the NACRO hostel successfully. However, his behaviour began to deteriorate. A missed appointment and concern that he might have been driving a stolen car led the panel to review the plan. As a result of this meeting, action was taken which enabled police to link Sean to a burglary and an approach to a woman in an isolated farmhouse. He was sent to prison for these offences. It is believed that Sean was in the process of planning a far more serious offence and that the panel's action successfully prevented this.

On the face of it, this case looks to be a classic example of good preventive action. The case had several hallmarks of dangerousness, notably the denial of the offence and opportunity to address offending behaviour in prison and the very worrying combination of sexual and non-sexual offences (see the profiles listed in chapter 8). The judgment of success in this case was the removal of the offender from the community, on a burglary charge, but with the belief that he was in the process of planning a far more serious crime. The combination of previous and current behaviour would add weight to this belief. This case would then appear to be relatively clear cut. The indicators shown in previous dangerous behaviour were evident, and there was good intelligence that the offender's present behaviour and manipulation of circumstances were strongly indicative of further dangerous behaviour. If we were to apply the 'clear and vivid danger' criterion of Bottoms and Brownsword (1982), this case would be approaching that threshold, although certainty is a much more difficult concept. Other cases that might be considered by panels are, however, not so clear cut. Another case from the press release will be given before two imaginary situations are offered for the reader's consideration.

Case 2

A 19-year-old was charged with indecent assault on two women (both strangers). He denied the offences and pleaded not guilty. He was later released from prison under the automatic conditional release scheme on licence to the probation service. The following are the key points in this case:

- It is vital to have as much information as possible, and key information in this case was sought from social services.
- A condition was inserted in the offender's licence requiring him to co-operate with a probation officer and work on his sexual offending behaviour. (*This work looks at the background to his crimes and his motivation for committing them. Work of this kind can help an offender control his behaviour and reduce the likelihood of further offences.*)
- Joint work would be undertaken with a specialist probation officer dealing with sexual abuse cases.
- Information from the police regarding details of his offences would be invaluable and enable the probation service to work on his offending.

- A decision was taken not to place this offender on the 'high risk' register at this stage, but for his case to be reviewed by a senior probation officer every 12 weeks.

This case illustrates the degree to which the practice of managing dangerousness can be widened. There is little in the obvious details provided on this case to suggest that dangerous behaviour was present, that is behaviour significantly worse than that shown by a range of other sex offenders. This is undoubtedly the type of case which would have been managed by the probation service largely on its own in past years. That is not to say that this is the best or most effective way to work but, in using expensive multi-agency resources, there must be thresholds of dangerousness. It would appear that, from an initial review of the way in which agencies are working in this area, almost any sexual offence will trigger dangerousness consideration practices. In this particular case the decision was taken not to register this person as a high risk offender, but, as a result of the discussions, the probation service undoubtedly gained access to information which it probably would not have had outside of the conference. The conference therefore serves the purpose of providing the lead agency with what might be termed better tools to complete its task, even though the task of public protection in this case remained primarily with the probation service.

THE PROCESS OF ASSESSING RISK

Multi-agency conferences are concerned therefore with judgments and perceptions of danger and risk. They take a view, based on the sharing of information, as to whether or not an offender is likely to pose a fairly imminent threat of serious harm. The panels have to adopt the same caution exercised by sentencers in this area of work. In other words they have to avoid confusing frequency and severity of reoffending, and this judgment also has to be informed by the view that, with sexual offending in particular, any reoffending may be unacceptable (Grubin and Wingate, 1996). If the threat is real but distant, it is likely that preventative measures will be delayed. If the threat is imminent but not serious, it is likely to result in a decision not to progress the matter further but perhaps keep a watching brief. These decisions are very fine judgments indeed and, if we accept the received wisdom concerning prediction, are about as likely to be right as they are wrong. When the decision is one which balances the rights of individuals and the community, it is one which includes enormous pressure with a natural leaning towards caution and safety. The following list is a summary of reasons, from actual PDO conference meetings, which resulted in a decision not to progress the case any further at that stage:

- the case was not a present threat to the public;
- no immediate danger to the public;
- no immediate public safety issues;
- no immediate risk to the public;
- time since last offence and police indicate no current problems;
- risk not sufficiently serious enough.

It is clear from these few comments that immediacy of risk is the crucial issue for practitioners in their decision-making process. This is to be commended as it is important not to institute a risk management plan which has little or no immediate use. It is also extremely relevant when considered alongside the clinical research into dangerousness which suggests that, at best, short-term predictions can be made. The conferences need to assess when the risk is likely to be most serious, plan for it and keep the case under review. The issue of timing is likely to be dictated by a variety of 'decision junctures'. These might include bail assessment, involving police, probation and CPS staff as well as the courts, pre-sentence report assessment, release from custody or hospital, or transfer in from another area. In these instances professionals need to take decisions which may affect the future liberty of the offender and potential risk to the public. Because these are formal stages in the criminal justice process, it is relatively easy to control events by placing time restraints around decisions and also possibly slowing down the speed at which events may unfold. The new sex offender orders will not conveniently sit within this framework. The process of consideration will become active as soon as police officers become aware of behaviour which is causing immediate alarm. They will then need to discuss the case with other experts very quickly. The use of public protection panels which can be constituted at speed would appear to be a sound base for this sort of decision-making.

PANELS IN ACTION

Below are three cases which have been constructed to illustrate the types of situations experienced by professionals in a multi-agency public protection setting. Readers are encouraged to consider the issues raised in the cases, assess the level of risk presented and the type of risk management plan needed to reduce or at least manage it. It is quite likely that practitioners in the field will operate with as little information as is presented in these sketches, although clearly, the more information available the better the prospect for an effective evaluation of risk.

Example 1

A 32-year-old man is due to be released from an eight year prison sentence within the next three months. The sentence was imposed in respect of the attempted rape of a woman and the abduction of another woman at knife point with intent to rape. Both of the victims were prostitutes. This man has a long history of indecent exposure offences and two previous convictions for theft. He is said to have held very negative views of women in the past but now claims to have changed his behaviour and opinions. He has, however, been reported as being aggressive to female staff in prison. He is said to suffer from premature ejaculation.

He has no connection with the area in which he is proposing to settle. He has had close contact with the prison chaplain and hopes to be involved in voluntary work upon release. He will be supervised by the probation service whose first major task is to find him suitable accommodation. He has no immediate work prospects. He is very pushy and is already very demanding of information concerning his release plans. He will be subject to the registration procedures contained in the Sex Offenders Act 1997.

Police or probation officers reading details similar to these frequently have to make quite rapid assessments of the potential risk presented by the offender. Baseline indicators such as predictive scales (see chapter 8) may be used, as may personal judgment based on experience and knowledge, as well as 'gut instinct'. On a simple level, what would this person's 'risk score' be out of 10, for example? What are the indicators of dangerousness in this case? If a list were to be drawn up of dangerousness indicators what would it include? And what would be in a list of factors which might reduce that risk? What might a public protection plan include? These are the issues that police and probation officers increasingly have to consider as a part of their public protection brief.

There are several factors of grave concern in this case. The offender has already committed a rape and attempted another. In the process he has abducted a woman and used a weapon to carry out the rape. His targeting of prostitutes should be of particular concern when taken in association with his previously expressed 'bad attitudes' and aggressive behaviour towards women. The issue of potential victims being prostitutes is, unfortunately, extremely important. There has been evidence that when victims of serious sexual crime have been prostitutes, there is less public and official concern — a slower response to act than if the victim had been a 'normal' or 'respectable' woman. This statement is extremely unpalatable but is nonetheless sustainable. The evidence from the Yorkshire Ripper cases, and a much more recent series of murders of prostitutes in Glasgow could be seen, and has been seen by some people, as reflecting a less urgent sense of concern with a group not seen as deserving as much attention as others. Indeed, to counter such allegations, the Glasgow police offered to issue prostitutes with personal attack alarms and self-defence classes, saying that '[these] women have the unquestionable right to feel safe on the street' (*The Guardian*, 5 March 1998).

Does the victim being a prostitute affect the way in which risk is assessed? If the occupation of the victims had not been mentioned, would it have altered perceptions of seriousness and potential danger? In a world of scarce resources it is highly likely that public protection agencies have to scale or grade cases where they can intervene according to perceived risk, and that perceived risk is likely to be heavily victim-influenced: it is therefore frequently a moral judgment. Such a scale might place children over adults, women over men, 'normal' women over prostitutes and so on. Similar concern was expressed by the John Howard Society of Alberta in 1993 when discussing proposed dangerous offender legislation. It noted that the legislation would create different classes of victims as there was a presumption that serious harm would be caused to all child victims, but that the same assumption would not be made in respect of adult victims:

We believe that this designation of different classes of victims establishes a precedent that certain victims are more deserving of special status and protection or that there is more value placed on the hurt caused to them. This creates the possibility of further classification of victims and value judgments about assessing serious harm and deserving victims. The sentence originally handed down should have reflected the level of harm done; it should not be revisited at the time of release (p. 4).

This man has other important risk indicators in his history, according to the work of Prins (1989). In particular these can be seen as a long history of indecent exposure, an offence often viewed as petty but which can escalate into far more serious sexual offending. Prins describes this as follows:

Although the majority of exposers do not go on to commit serious sexual crimes (though they very frequently continue to expose themselves), it is worth observing that in a small number of cases where acts of exposure are accompanied by some form of threatening behaviour and where this is also associated with masturbation . . . then there is a strong possibility of progression to more serious offending (p. 107).

Indecent exposure is also an offence which many women regard as a traumatic event, not least because so few report it and therefore fail to deal with the effect of the behaviour upon them (Edwards, 1996, pp. 324, 325). This man also has a combination of (sexual) violent crime and property offending (regarded as a poor indicator (Scott, 1977, p. 133)), poor and negative attitudes towards women, aggression to women in authority, his own sexual dysfunction and a lack of supportive community ties. Reference to the rapist profiles listed in chapter 8 shows many indicators of dangerousness in this man's history and present behaviour.

A major concern in such a case would be the issue of accommodation and proximity to potential victims. It is of course impossible to keep this man away from women and prostitutes in particular if he chooses to seek them out. So why would he choose an area with which he has no ties? Does the area in which he intends to live have a significant prostitute population? If so, how might these women be protected? Could it be that community notification might take place, in this case with a warning, including a photograph of the offender, issued to known prostitutes?

Could the actions of the Glasgow police described above be replicated?
Does the risk warrant the public cost of such a measure? In such a case
police and probation services are presented with a serious problem. The
case contains many dangerousness indicators, not only previous
offending, but also a range of associated factors which a good awareness
of the literature in this field would confirm, itself suggesting the need
for specialist staff. Balanced against the perceived level of risk is a
declared intention on the part of the offender that he has changed and
that he has served his sentence and therefore should not receive further
punishment in the sense of restrictions on his liberty. Does a wider
consideration of risk factors alter the assessment of risk? Is the score out
of 10 likely to change in a situation where more information is made
available and there is greater time to consider the implications of it?
Certainly the evidence of chapter 1 would suggest that time and quality
information are the most useful tools in assessing dangerousness, but
they both may not always be available.

The case just described poses great problems for public protection
staff. The risk of serious harm is real and will soon be imminent. A
known target group of victims could be at risk, yet the balance to be
struck between the offender's right not to be 'punished' for what he has
not yet done and the potential victims' (not a named individual, but a
community of women) right to protection is a difficult one. Indeed
'balance' may be an inappropriate word to use here and it may be that
action leans more towards protection than rights of the individual. The
next case does not offer such a clear-cut distinction.

Example 2

A 60-year-old man, a former church volunteer, was convicted of
indecently assaulting boys and is shortly to be released from a ten month
prison sentence. He has no previous convictions of any type. The
offences occurred during a camping trip associated with his church, and
occurred following the man having had a major row with his wife. She
had said that she never wanted to see him again. Periodic minor assaults
had occurred for a period of 15 months following the first incident. None
of the assaults involved violence or strong verbal coercion and were
usually characterised by genital fondling. As a result of the conviction
the offender's marriage has ended and he is now looking for accommodation through local church groups. He has asked for voluntary contact

with the probation service. He will be required to register as a sex offender but will not be under statutory supervision.

Is this case more or less serious than that described above? Would it have a higher or lower score out 10? What are the factors which might be regarded as aggravating or mitigating the seriousness of his offending behaviour? Is there a sense of imminency of risk? Does it appear more or less imminent and vivid than the risk posed by Example 1? A closer examination of these sketchy details might offer a few clues. The offender's age of 60 years might be regarded by some as a sign that he is not really a risk. Indeed, judges have often remarked in court when sentencing an offender that the sentence is of such a length that, by the time of release, the offender will be too old to pose a risk, a statement frequently made in the case of sexual offenders. Is this true? There is certainly a typology of paedophile offender whose risk does not appear to diminish with the passage of time. For example, Prins (1986) describes the 'pre-senile or senile paedophile', an individual whose sexual predilections are not dulled by age, although their sexual ability may be. Prins argues that it is foolish to regard these people as potentially less dangerous as they grow older, indeed the opposite may be true. They may become more easily frustrated and less in command, or powerful, than they thought themselves to be previously and as a result may resort to violence including homicide (p. 174). In other words their physical ability may lag behind what their mind is telling them and the resulting frustration finds a vent in violence. What other factors might lead to increased levels of concern with this case? The offender has clearly abused a position of trust and has repeatedly offended over a long period of time. He is retaining contact with church groups and is looking for accommodation through them. Will he therefore be able to return to voluntary activity involving children? On the other hand, what are the positive factors that a dangerous offender conference might consider? His offending appears to be of a relatively minor nature and he has not shown any signs of violence or coercion. He has requested voluntary contact with the probation service and his whereabouts should be tracked by the sex offenders' register. Is this man as great a risk as the rapist above? His target group is young boys. In an age obsessed with protecting children would he be viewed as a greater risk? If so, would church organisations be informed of his previous behaviour? What would and could a panel do if a church group were aware of his behaviour but allowed him to continue his voluntary work (a not uncommon decision in a forgiving organisation)? Which, if any, of the paedophile profiles described in chapter 8 does this man fit? If he is compared with those profiles, does the estimation of his risk increase or reduce?

Example 3

A man is referred to the multi-agency public protection panel by the police service. He has been reported by the public as being seen loitering near and in children's playgrounds and speaking with children. Further police inquiries reveal that he plays a money game with the children. This involves them having a coin placed in their (usually her) clothing by the man and then rolling it up to obtain the coin, showing parts of their body as they do so. Police records reveal that this 23-year-old man has a history of similar behaviour since the age of 16 and has served two short prison sentences as well as a probation order, but none of these sentences were imposed for sexual offences. Members of the local community are aware of him and his record and he is generally tolerated by them, there is no evidence that he is likely to suffer any form of vigilante activity. He is living with his family who say that he is 'backward' and awkward, but harmless. He has never physically harmed a child and is usually regarded by children as a soft touch for money, they generally seek him out. He is to be interviewed by police officers who will have to decide upon their next course of action. His previous offences include burglary and a physical assault on an adult male.

What might be the score out of 10 for this man? In an age of paedophile panic, can a potentially dangerous offender panel afford to ignore this man's behaviour? Is he a risk to children and if so what is the basis for the evaluation? How serious is the risk and what is it a risk of? He has no record of sexual offending but he clearly does have a history of age-inappropriate behaviour with children. He has other convictions so should he be considered a greater risk for having a combination of 'ordinary' offending and unacceptable sexual behaviour? What account should be taken of the views of his family and the apparent general level of tolerance by the community and children? What should the police do with this man? This is clearly a case where as much information as possible will be of assistance to the decision-making process. Information will be the key to deciding upon a level of risk. This case is one where there is a good chance of erring on the side of caution. The facts are that this person is behaving age-inappropriately and has other previous convictions. It is likely that the potential for serious harm will outweigh the likelihood of him simply reoffending and he would be viewed by public protection staff as a serious risk — but is this a case of the public protection tail wagging the dog?

The first and third of the examples just mentioned are very loosely based on real events and have been discussed by multi-agency panels. The third case was viewed overall as presenting the strongest signs of potentially dangerous behaviour and this decision was almost totally based on the potential victims being children. The first case appears on paper to present a greater number of verifiable serious risk indicators, although the reader may not agree. It is, though, an example of how public concern and fear of certain crimes, added to a pushy, blaming political climate, might impact upon the judgment of criminal justice agencies. Dangerous behaviour can take many forms and can include a very broad spectrum of potential victims, yet there is a real 'danger' that dangerousness becomes pigeonholed around certain offenders and offences. When recidivism rates for sexual offences are added to the argument the position becomes even less clear. A fuller discussion of these difficulties, summarised by Grubin and Wingate (1996) will take place in chapter 8.

CONFERENCE ISSUES

Who is a Suitable Subject for a Dangerous Offender Conference?

The cases already mentioned in this chapter have all concerned sexual behaviour and it is clear that sexual offending, particularly against children, has driven the dangerousness agenda. Although most formal protocols suggest a list of serious offending behaviour which is all encompassing, sexual offences appear to dominate both people's thoughts and the conference process. One example of an inclusive, offence-based list will demonstrate the parameters in which criminal justice professionals are operating. This list is composed of defendants brought to court who are charged with/convicted of:

- homicide and attempted murder;
- rape;

- arson and criminal damage endangering life;
- firearms offences;
- section 18 or section 20 wounding (Offences against the Person Act 1861);
- serious offences against children including sexual offences;
- false imprisonment and kidnapping;
- robbery, assault with intent, aggravated burglary;
- serious drugs offences;
- indecent assault.

Added to this list might be those currently in prison, special hospital or serving community sentences who have committed these offences, and all those on life licences. The catch-all final group is any other person about whom there is serious professional concern. Undoubtedly all the offences included in this list could include serious and potentially dangerous behaviour, but can all these offences/offenders be screened fully, yet alone be subject to a range of community protection measures? At the other end of the spectrum, can all of them serve very long or even indeterminate sentences? The answer has to be in the negative, therefore risk assessment, which the probation service has said must take place in every case, must be targeted to those posing the type of vivid and imminent danger suggested by many writers in this field. The problem with such a wide list is that all offenders become grouped together as it is easier than assessing individual risk on the basis of the detailed evaluation suggested by Scott (1977) and Prins (1989). Public protection panels are also prone to be driven to make judgments in favour of risk in offences which concern the public at any one time, in other words perceptions of and reaction to perceived risk will vary over time and place. Undoubtedly the development of predictive devices which formulate a risk indicator score helps agencies to make difficult judgments within limited time scales, and can be used as a sign that evaluation is rational and almost scientific. These devices will be discussed in more detail in chapter 8.

During the evaluation of a pilot Potentially Dangerous Offender scheme mentioned earlier mentioned earlier in this book, several practitioners were asked who they thought might be suitable subjects for the dangerous offender conferences. Some of the replies are listed below, with the occupation of the speaker in parentheses:

'... they should be pretty exceptional I think' (probation)

'... offenders who presented a significant danger to the public because their target group, the type of people they could have offended against, was fairly wide, it wasn't necessarily within the family. It tended to show that they were targeting people outside of the family. They tend to be people who have been sentenced to quite a long period of time and who were offending against members of the public that we considered were in need of protection' (probation)

'... where it involves children who are outside that person's family' (police)

'any offender who would put the public at risk' (police)

'... people who are likely to kill, rape, abduct, cause serious harm to the public' (police)

'it's generally the child protection and public protection issues, the victims or potential victims have invariably been under the age of sixteen, the offenders have either a pattern of behaviour which implies that sexual offending has happened, will happen or the offences are actually representative of a pattern of behaviour that is of concern to the public' (probation)

These suggestions span the specific to the all-inclusive, although the focus remains upon child sex offenders. In another pilot of multi-agency working, a small rural county had 23 cases; 15 of the cases were sexual offences, 14 of which were offences against children (schedule 1 of the Children and Young Person Act 1933).

It is perhaps worthy of note that offences within the home do not appear to trigger as much concern among those practitioners working in the public protection field. This is reminiscent of the scaling of 'sympathy' mentioned above. This is not to say that agencies are not understanding of assaults on family members, or prostitutes, or indeed not condemning of it, but that when compared with other behaviour it is viewed less seriously. This is itself a dangerous idea. Experts in child protection have long argued that the greatest danger of sexual assault against children comes from within the family (Sampson, 1994). More recently, similar concern has shifted towards the offence of rape. On 17 June 1998 *The Guardian* newspaper reported that the traditional stereotype of the stranger rapist was now true in only 8% of cases. Home Office research (1998b) had shown that 50% of rapes were carried out by a close acquaintance. One of the most worrying results of this trend was a significant fall in rape conviction rates, from 25% in 1985 to 10% in 1996. The report stressed the muddied waters of consent that victims faced in court proceedings and one criminologist, Professor Sue Lees, suggested that experienced rapists were seizing upon the opportunity presented by this situation. They formed a brief acquaintance with the victim, knowing that it could considerably assist their defence if caught. The Home Office categorises rapes as stranger, acquaintance and intimate. Acquaintance can be judged on the basis of 24 hours or less. Lees therefore regards many men classified as date rapists (a term thoroughly disliked by Professor Stanko, *The Guardian* 17 June 1998) as actually being serial rapists, who know the system well enough to cover their tracks and significantly increase their prospects of escaping punishment. The figures may also include attacks on prostitutes but are as likely not to do so. What these kinds of research findings mean is that panels considering risk really do need to undertake the detailed kind of assessment indicated by Scott (1977) and must not be swayed by publicly held stereotypes which may have increasingly less relation to real risk. 'Stranger danger' may fuel the public fear of crime but it is private danger which demands greater recognition and attention from criminal justice practitioners. Another area of sexual assault which has received little attention is that of the rape of elderly women. *The Independent* newspaper (23 January 1994) carried a story by Linda Grant which explored the extent of this problem, citing several cases where the victims were aged between 68 and 100 years. A marked feature of these cases was that they were accompanied by severe violence and little public attention. In investigating the story, Grant had discovered a lack of research in the area and could find no one within the prison service sex offender programme who could comment upon it. It was argued that there was a social taboo anyway around elderly sex and the rape attacks fitted within this. Undoubtedly society would view such attacks with horror, but if it is so little discussed it is unlikely to feature highly on the list of dangerousness concerns. There may be some time before dangerousness is routinely considered within the full range of situations in which it occurs.

In terms of those cases considered by public protection meetings, it is clear that male offenders are in the majority. Risk of serious harm is associated with men and the majority of violent and violent sexual crime is undoubtedly committed by them. Crimes such as that reported in *The Guardian* on 18 July 1998 are rare. In this case a female teacher was given a two year prison sentence for having sexual intercourse with a 15-year-old boy and giving him drugs (cannabis). The judge declared that he would sentence her in the same way as if she were a man, that gender should not make any difference. Had the offender been a man and the victim a girl, it is possible that the press reporting might have been different. It will be extremely interesting to see if this woman is assessed as presenting a danger to young boys upon her release in the same way that a man might be seen as presenting a risk to young girls in the same circumstances. Unusual cases such as this are treated by the press with a good deal of fascination or even voyeurism, which very much reduces the sense of risk transmitted to the public. In other cases, though, journalists will swing to talk endlessly about the nature of evil inherent in certain women. Consistency is not a feature of the reporting of serious crime committed by women.

Men have dominated the conference process evaluations seen by the author. In one county all 23 cases were men with an age span from 20 to 73 years (average age 35). It would be interesting to compare this age profile with that of the so-called normal offender caseload of the probation service, for example. Public protection referrals will therefore be based upon an offence-based classification list with the addition of those cases causing 'serious professional concern'. Within these broad lists it would appear that both age and gender of the potential victim will carry weight as will the gender of the offender. Indeed one set of guidelines asks the question, 'Is there a risk specifically to: children, old people, black people, women, gay/lesbian?'. The only group not really covered here are heterosexual white men, perhaps because they are seen as the most likely perpetrators. As indicated in the discussion on conference procedures, there is a possibility that members of the police service will increasingly take a lead role on sex offender risk assessment due to their responsibility under the Sex Offenders Act 1997. This begs a series of questions. Do police officers view risk of offending in the same way as probation staff? Does an organisation still dominated by men, especially in the CID, take a 'gendered' view of sexual offending? Do men and women share the same professional perceptions of risk and seriousness of crime (Nash, 1995)? If the victim of violence is a man will the case be considered as serious and potentially dangerous as when the victim is a woman?

Trigger Behaviour?

In this context of 'uncertainty' it is natural for practitioners to seek an indicator of 'probability' and it is here that panels will no doubt turn to actuarial predictive tools. There is a variety of these instruments in existence and it may be that a national predictive tool will be sought to attempt a degree of consistency around the country. Certainly those agencies who are less experienced in assessment and prediction but are now charged with that task, such as the police service, are looking to make full use of these devices. Some of these will be discussed in the next chapter. Alongside these, however, must continue the detailed analysis of offending behaviour and offender history which is so necessary for an evaluation of potential dangerousness. If both police and probation officers have in mind their own set of trigger factors it may well serve as an invaluable aid to their own professional and personal antennae. Acordingly, the following aspects of behaviour might be useful in considering dangerousness.

- Are there any unusual characteristics to the behaviour? For example, is it bizarre or sadistic?
- Is the behaviour isolated, frequent, escalating?
- Is there a specific type of victim and how are they selected?
- Is there a good deal of planning in the crime or grooming of potential victims?
- Is the offender a good trickster or con artist?
- Is he or she good at finding out information?
- What are the motivations for the crime?
- Is the 'true' motive for the crime masked by a less serious one (e.g. in domestic burglary cases)?
- What is the offender's attitude to the crime and what was their behaviour like both before and after the event?
- Is there or has there been a history of mental illness?

Many other points could be added to this list but this should be sufficient to stress the need for a detailed consideration of the case. When police officers are investigating an apparently 'ordinary' offence, are there any of these features present? When probation officers are preparing an apparently 'ordinary' pre-sentence report, are there clues in what the offender says that open up the possibility of something more sinister taking place? It is important to pursue the matter and not close the mind to other possibilities. This is a skilled task which demands a knowledge of the literature, good listening skills and a preparedness to ask the unthinkable. Probation officers in particular will come across people who will demonstrate some of these 'qualities' in all aspects of their work, including in prisons, in the field and in other settings such as family court welfare. Dangerousness does not inhabit particular settings or live within certain offence categories. Probation officers are skilled in this area of work and can contribute enormously to the process of risk assessment. Of course they need to be guided by a range of criteria but should not abandon some of the relevant social work skills. It is to be hoped that the new probation officer training programme will encourage the development of a range of professional skills allied to a sound theoretical knowledge base in this important area of practice.

Conference Outcomes — Costs and Benefits

There is an accepted wisdom now that multi-agency information sharing is, by definition, a good thing. This wisdom suggests that the very process of working together should assist in the process of managing and hopefully reducing the risk of harmful behaviour. Less is made of the quality of the information and the use to which it is put, which are in themselves crucial issues. So what are the real benefits of PDO conferencing and conversely the potential costs? A review of a multi-agency conferencing pilot in one specific area (Nash, 1997), indicated the following:

Potential benefits
- a sharing of information between police and probation services far in excess of that which preceded it;
- probation officers gained access to higher ranking police officers and with it a higher quality of information, used in supervision plans, pre-sentence reports and bail information schemes;
- very limited community notification had taken place which was very well managed and raised no difficulties, other relevant agencies had been brought into the process;

- the process of conferencing was quick and simple, with a minimum of bureaucracy;
- all staff involved in the conferences found that the decisions taken were supportive and gave them additional strength for what had become a collective responsibility;
- probation staff gained considerable support from police officers in respect of staff safety measures;
- police officers predominantly and probation officers to a lesser extent, gained access to new information.

Potential costs
- the desire by police officers to use 'probation' information poses potential difficulties in terms of role clash, but this is likely to be minimised as an issue by the strength of the public protection arguments;
- the use of 'police' information by the probation service in its pre-sentence reports may cause difficulties with defendants and their legal representatives;
- the focus on child sex offenders is understandable but may cause those involved in conferences to underestimate risk in some areas and overestimate it in others;
- some police officers believed that the new, additional information gained by them from the conference process was useful but may still only lead to increased detection opportunities rather than a more proactive prevention role.

At a national conference for senior police and probation officers, held in April 1998, the author again asked a group of people, some of whom had experience of PDO conferences, and some of whom were about to embark upon the process, for their views on the potential costs and benefits of the system. The benefits results tended to cluster into three key areas of practice under the broad headings of intelligence/ information, sharing and practice. Comments made by the practitioners under these headings are summarised below to give an indication of what benefits people expect from multi-agency working.

Information and intelligence
Generally police and probation officers spoke of the ability to access more information and better quality information. Phrases such as getting

the full picture, confirming information and facts and better information were common. It was also noted that both police and probation officers saw greater opportunities to increase their knowledge and intelligence and probation officers in particular noted opportunities to increase power and access.

Sharing
Many of the comments made at the conference came within this category and centred on particular themes. One of these was shared responsibility and contained phrases such as sharing the load, equal responsibility, shared and informed decisions. Another theme was that of gaining strength through shared working and better understanding. This was shown in phrases such as mutual understanding, defensible decisions, common language and clarity of roles, credibility of the service, increased confidence in and between agencies and enhanced reputation. This last point is important. Many of the protocols established around the country emphasise the importance of agencies agreeing a media and public relations strategy to deal with problems if they arise and also to foster the image of working together towards one end — public protection. For the probation service there is likely to be benefit in associating with the police — at least in the eyes of the public if not their own clientele.

Practice
This section is perhaps more outcome oriented than the others which focused on process. Here phrases such as increased solutions, earlier intervention, coherent action and objective assessment dominated. Issues were also raised about more efficient resource allocation, easier access to multi-agency resources, and shared skills. It was suggested by one person that this method of working was 'relevant and modern'.

What was interesting in these comments was that it was not really possible to break them down by agency. That is to say that a probation officer was as likely to talk about intelligence opportunities as police officers — the only real difference perhaps being the use of the words intelligence or information. There was a strong sense of shared language and it was evident that the more these agencies worked together the more coherent their practice was to become. Perhaps the only cloud on the multi-agency horizon was that nearly all of the conference attenders were middle to senior managers. It remains to be seen how far this degree of sharing and collaboration extends down the respective organisations.

The potential costs of multi-agency working can be examined under the same three headings.

Information and intelligence

The opposite of the potential benefits would be expected here and it is fair to say that most of the reservations were expressed by police officers. Phrases such as a concern for the integrity of intelligence, a risk of inappropriate disclosure, a worry over potential leaks and overall concern with confidentiality dominated this section.

Sharing

It was in this section that issues were raised which have been covered elsewhere in this book and represent a challenge to the 'multi-agency is best' orthodoxy. Phrases such as losing separate identities and differing perspectives came to the fore (these of course should be a central rationale in favour of multi-agency working). Other words and phrases which emerged were: mistrust, separate expectations, the dominance of one agency, a clash of cultures and hidden agendas. Also raised were issues such as the challenge to established working practices with particular reference to the attendance of the offender at meetings. A lack of practitioner involvement in the process (see the dominance of management referred to earlier) and scepticism of the grass roots also featured.

Practice

Under this heading the main focus was on what could actually go wrong, so issues such as breach of agreements and breach of the legislation featured heavily. However, there was a wider concern with the downside of the whole process and in this context words such as net widening, labelling and overcaution were used. Finally in this section concern was raised about resources, not that of gaining more but of using more, especially that most precious one of time, about working in a context of heightened expectation and anxiety and finally, but of course importantly, about civil liberties.

SUMMARY

At the beginning of this chapter the question, 'does it work?' was asked of multi-agency conferencing of potentially dangerous offenders. The point was also made that knowing if something has actually been prevented from happening is very difficult to establish, if not impossible. Judging success then becomes problematic in terms of outcomes and attention may therefore shift to the process. That process, one of multi-agency working, is generally regarded as good practice and agencies involved in it are, by default, effective agencies. Is this good enough, however, when the costs involved are huge in terms of agency resources and are matched by raised public expectations? On certain indicators this new form of working is a success. It is undoubtedly the case that police and probation services are collaborating to a degree that has never been seen before. The exchange of information between them is now required by a range of protocols covering the country and failure to exchange would undoubtedly invoke management sanction. Sharing quality information and using it effectively will undoubtedly assist in the process of public protection.

The range of cases considered for inclusion into the parameters of the meetings is in most cases all-inclusive and this reflects the concern of agencies not to be seen as missing any category of serious risk. This is of course to be expected but stands the risk of overcaution and net widening, a serious threat to resources and effective practice. There is also a risk of a pigeonholed approach to dangerousness, both by offence category and staff specialism. A wider approach based on the use of quality information in the assessment process might be more helpful and particularly avoid the driving of the agenda by paedophile offenders. Finally there is a risk to agency integrity in the rush to adopt the shared language and practice of public protection. Both police and probation staff have unique skills to bring to this process and these should not be diluted in an attempt to be seen working together.

Chapter 8
Possible rather than Probable – the Lowering Threshold of Prediction

The political and penal climate in which dangerousness assessments are made will determine, to a great extent, the acceptable threshold in terms of the accuracy of the prediction. In other words, if there is not a great public fear of violent crime, if the media has not been filled with horror stories of sexual predators and if there is a feeling of safety, then the threshold may be higher. This means that the 'scientific base' of the predictive tool, its accuracy, should be at a higher level of probability than the norm of 'one in two' which has tended to dominate dangerousness prediction. The public, being less afraid, may be more concerned with rights and justice and demand more safeguards before those rights are violated. Conversely, at times of fear and panic, concern for those safeguards may diminish and the efficacy of predictive tools will not really be questioned, as communities demand that the authorities err on the side of caution and detain and incarcerate more people for longer periods. Indeed, at times such as this, a scientific attempt to predict may be overridden by a blanket wish to protect, on whatever basis. This feeling was summarised by the John Howard Society of Alberta, in their occasional paper, *Assessing Dangerousness* (1995),

What is judged to be an acceptable risk is bound to change over time. In the current political climate, it is reasonable to assume that public pressure to detain potentially dangerous individuals will result in more offenders being judged as high risks.

This comment reflects the view of judges who took part in the HMIP thematic inspection of sex offenders (Home Office, 1998a). They suggested that the threshold level of high risk of serious harm had been lowered as probation officers were concerned not to make mistakes in their reports, in effect to make sure that their backs were covered. This is inevitable in an area of practice where the stakes are so high. Everyone is judged by their failures, not by their successes. Although believing the issue to be a moral one, Floud concluded that politics play an equal, if not greater part:

> The question whether certain ills are tolerable or should prevented, even by measures which carry the risk that a legally sane person will be unnecessarily deprived of his liberty, is essentially a moral one. Though, in practice, what people actually have to put up with is decided by government and the agencies of law enforcement and is in this sense a political matter, the question is one of principle (Floud, 1982, p. 221).

A range of criminal justice practitioners is now involved in the risk assessment business and it takes place throughout the whole process. From the earliest stage, police, probation, CPS and court staff take decisions in respect of bail, a decision which requires that fine but vital balance of often unconvicted defendant and public rights. Probation officers have to assess risk in their pre-sentence reports and sentencers need to consider it in their decisions. Throughout a prisoner's sentence it is important that risk of repeated serious behaviour is assessed and wherever possible work undertaken to reduce that risk, both in custody and upon release. Release discussions relating to those prisoners who might pose a risk of further serious offending crucially require good, informed decision making, based on sound risk assessment methods. Community sentences, increasingly involving serious offenders, need to be operated with the potential risk to the public clearly in mind.

Raising the Threshold

Predictive tools such as the parole predictor (and its revised version), the sentence planning predictor and the CLASP model (see p. 167) described below, are all intended to assist in the risk assessment business and introduce greater consistency into the decision-making process. However, in most cases the value of the tool has always been stressed as being a component of the assessment process alongside the clinical or qualitative interview. New legislative requirements, such as the sex offenders register (Sex Offenders Act 1997) and the sex offender orders (Crime and Disorder Act 1998, ss. 2, 3), place onerous responsibility on the police service, in association with other experts, to assess risk. Looking for a tool that assists that process, and can therefore be used to demonstrate that assessment has taken place, is essential for those agencies in the public eye. Therefore, despite the reservations outlined in chapter 1, it is important to assess the usefulness of predictors as they will undoubtedly be used with much greater frequency in the future than they have been in the past. Good practice increasingly emphasises the use of such tools and bad practice can be characterised by their absence. A society increasingly characterised by the acceptability or otherwise of various risk situations demands evidence that all efforts to reduce perceived risks have been taken and predictive tools may offer that reassurance, even if their predictive value is somewhat limited and may run the risk of over rather than under inclusion. There is of course something of a potential downside to the use of predictive tools and that is their application in place of individual case consideration. Writing in 1975, van den Haag argued that, 'Once it is possible to predict violence better than the toss of a coin, predictive methods should be used to identify and determine the disposition of dangerous offenders'. He argued for a period of 'post-punishment confinement', whereby offenders would be detained at the end of their period of custody if their prediction stood in favour of further offending (in Conrad, 1982). It is significant that Conrad was sceptical of legal systems developing a constitutional innovation which would allow for continued detention. The seventeen years since his article was written have shown that all sorts of constitutional arrangements can be made to accommodate any form of criminal justice development, and some will be made *in spite of* such safeguards. Predictive tools can therefore be used as an aid to structured decision-making or to replace professional decision-making which is regarded as fraught with the potential not only for mistakes but also discrimination. Their use should always form a part but not the whole of good assessment methods but should equally serve to introduce multi-agency consistency into the definition of risk. This point is made by Broadhurst and Loh (1993):

> ... actuarial estimates should not be neglected in the formal assessment of the risks of reoffending or in identifying potential 'dangerousness' or 'high risk' offenders. We would argue that such base-line risk assessments constitute the starting point for the important qualitative decisions correctional agencies are frequently required to make. They also have the virtue of making the criteria for decision making explicit and thus go some way towards addressing concerns about fairness and consistency in the management and identification of high-risk offenders (in Pratt, 1997, p. 175).

PREDICTIVE TOOLS — A SAMPLE REVIEWED

One of the criticisms of actuarial methods in predicting dangerousness, identified in chapter 1, is that they have greater application to so-called normal offender populations operating within a band of more predictable behaviour. It is agreed that dangerous behaviour generally occurs at the extreme and therefore becomes much more difficult to predict because the indicative factors themselves are less quantifiable and regular. The result of this general reaction against a more actuarial approach in the past has been a preference for the clinical interview, although Scott (1977) did say that a detailed casework approach undertaken by non-clinicians could yield equally positive and effective results. Naturally this has meant that much of dangerousness assessment and prediction methodology to date has been in the hands of mental health practitioners, but that is a changing situation. Those practitioners now involved in the new world of risk assessment are not health experts and will not have the clinician's knowledge or often the caseworker's time to evaluate the information in front of them. A reliable method of utilising that information is therefore required and one which avoids the subjectivity which has been said to dominate psychiatric assessment at times (Quinsey and Mireille, 1986). It has to be a method which is relevant to all agencies and applicable by those not fully trained in psychiarty, psychology or even social work. That said, major decisions involving the liberty of individuals should always be based upon a consideration of all the evidence available and subject to detailed multi-disciplinary scrutiny. Decisions concerning the loss of liberty have to be defensible and based on strong evidence. The tools that are used by police and probation officers should then perhaps not be seen as ends in themselves, but rather as devices to focus thoughts and ensure that each agency at least starts the process from a common base-line.

Assessment and prediction methods are clearly a developing area of expertise, not least due to the need to find methods which can easily be accessed by non-clinicians and applied in relatively short time spans. Cohen (1997) describes three generations of prediction thinking. The first generation was characterised by what Cohen called natural history experiments, in which the recidivism of individuals who had been released against expert advice was assessed. The second generation combined actuarial tables and clinical material, or those tables which included static variables such as type of crime, age and sex of victim, age at onset of criminal behaviour and so on. The third generation described by Cohen is an attempt to produce a standard for the clinical prediction of dangerousness, based on a standardised conditional model, which is geared to the relative probability of future violence in given situations.

Cohen developed a theoretical model of dangerousness assessment which is based on the following components. One of his first points was to express his difficulty with the term 'prediction' itself and a preference for 'assessment'. That assessment should also be one which is based on multi-variables such as personality and situational factors, making use of the disciplines of biology, psychology and sociology. Cohen also supports the view that assessment of dangerousness cannot take place in the absence of a pattern of violence, pattern in this case meaning at least two previous similar behaviours to the one being assessed. A crucial element in this analysis of previous behaviour should be an attempt to answer not only the question, 'why was something done?', but also the questions, 'why then?', 'why to that particular victim?', 'why that behaviour and not some other?'. Finally he makes a clear point about the situational aspects of assessment, in other words that assessment requests are usually situation specific. Thus a 'safe' assessment for a short period of home leave may not be the same as one for a longer period of parole. Police and probation staff considering the risk presented by offenders in the community should accordingly allow for the situation specific assessments that may form a part of their information portfolio (as well as, of course, the situational specific context of the original offending behaviour itself). Institutional reports have in the past been notoriously situational and were of limited use to an assessment of risk in the community. In other words, safe institutional behaviour is quite different from safe community behaviour. It is fair to say that now, institutional and community assessments represent much more of a continuum.

Having taken all these factors into consideration, Cohen proposed a formula which he believes is useful for a thorough assessment of future dangerousness, represented as follows:

$$P(D2) = [(B2P2E2) - (B1P1E1)]$$

$P(D2)$ is the probability of future dangerous behaviour and B2, P2 and E2 are biological, psychological and environmental factors valid at the time of the assessment, whereas B1, P1 and E1 are those same factors at times in the past when dangerous behaviour was observed. The greater the similarity between the past and the present, that is, the closer $P(D2)$ is to zero, the greater the probability that dangerous behaviour will repeat itself. Cohen believes that much of the information required to make this type of assessment is available to practitioners in the form of records held by various agencies and by way of detailed interview. It should also be noted that, as in offence assessment for the court, many of these factors may be viewed negatively or positively, or as aggravating or mitigating the situation.

The first sight of such a mathematical looking model may be rather daunting to the criminal justice practitioner, although it is one way of making sense of a variety of information sources. A less formulaic method of assessing risk was issued by the Royal College of Psychiatrists in 1996, which, although referring to a standard psychiatric assessment, is a useful tool for criminal justice practitioners and may more realistically reflect the reality of their working situation. The suggested areas of enquiry and nature of the questions to be raised when taking a case history, should include investigation of:

- previous violence and/or suicidal behaviour;
- evidence of rootlessness or social restlessness, for example few relationships, frequent changes of address or employment;

166 Possible rather than Probable – the Lowering Threshold of Prediction

- evidence of poor compliance with treatment or disengagement from psychiatric aftercare;
- presence of substance misuse or other potential disinhibiting factors, for example a social background promoting violence;
- identification of any precipitants and any changes in mental state or behaviour that have occurred prior to violence and/or relapse;
- evidence of recent severe stress, particularly of loss events or the threat of loss;
- evidence of recent discontinuation of medication.

Further questions need to be asked concerning the accessibility of potential victims and notice taken of any threats, especially thoughts of persecution or of being controlled by external forces. Is the person showing emotions related to violence, such as irritability, anger or hostility? In assessing this information, it should be used by the practitioner to attempt to answer the following questions:

- how serious is the risk?
- Is the risk specific or general?
- How immediate is the risk?
- How volatile is the risk?
- What specific treatment, and which management plan, can best reduce the risk?

Both the accessing of this information and the evaluation of it should be made easier by an open relationship between offender and practitioner and one which is based on knowledge built up over time. This model very much reflects a quality approach, and is precisely what probation staff can and should bring to multi-agency dangerous offender assessment. It is a means of interrogating information and looking for clues — this should also be familiar practice for police officers.

Risk assessment can be viewed as the probability of a specified behaviour occurring and a consideration of the consequences of such occurrences (Towl and Crighton, 1996). For police and probation staff operating under conditions of great public pressure, it is essential to be clear about the criteria of 'specified behaviour'. It must not be a general risk of reoffending but of specific and serious offending behaviour, that which has a serious impact upon the potential victims's physical or emotional wellbeing. Consideration of the consequences of that behaviour is, of course, crucial but practitioners need to remember that it could be dominated by concern with certain types of behaviour, such as harm to children. It is quite possible that risk indicator scores could be skewed in this particular direction. Naturally these offences will provoke the greatest concern but could also generate overcaution on the part of those undertaking the assessment.

Needs and Towl (1997) suggest that there is a risk in over reliance upon information gained solely from the offender alone as there is a possibility of deception and also selective bias in recall and interpretation by offender and worker (p. 14). They suggest that a degree of subjectivity must remain as part of the process of assessment. They believe that the subjectivity of the individual being assessed may yield crucial information concerning the crime which a more rational, statistical approach would not allow for. They recommend what is known as the CLASP model, which was developed to aid in the assessment of life sentence prisoners. The acronym stands for context, life history, agenda, sequence and personal meanings. A brief explanation is offered as follows:

Context   This is essentially an examination of the offender's behaviour and lifestyle in the months leading up to the offence, focusing on relationships, employment and health. On the basis that many serious offences follow an accumulation of negative events, it is important to note how the offender contributed to these events or may react in similar situations on the future.

Life history   This is the background of the offender and includes the key influences on their development. Relevant factors here would include upbringing, approaches to problems, peer influences and psychological trauma.

Agenda   This includes the individual's reasons for being in the situation where the offence occurred, intentions, expectations, planning, preoccupations and any fantasies, issues for resolution, or emotional priming.

Sequence   Sequence is the narrative of the offending episode, extending to subsequent actions, with the focus on the sequence of actions. Escalating factors can include physical characteristics of the situation and the behaviour of the victim.

Personal meanings   Needs and Towl see this as running through all of the other factors and it embodies the way in which the individual makes sense of other people, self, situations and life in general.

Once again, what runs through these factors is the need for quality information and a detailed examination of it. Clearly that information is likely to be more complete when it comes from a variety of agencies, therefore this has to be the basis of multi-agency working. Sharing and pooling information should be focused upon the quality of that information and the uses to which it will be put. Needs and Towl (1997) make a telling summation of the need for quality and indeed, a degree of subjectivity:

> Risk assessment is complicated by the issue of human subjectivity, the tendency of people to be guided by what makes sense to them. In sum, offences arise out of one frame of reference and are made sense of in another. Subjectivity is not the enemy of good practice. The real problem is oversimplification — assumptions, bias and lack of clear focus. Any 'objective' approach which ignores the subjectivity of the individual being assessed is at best incomplete, while the potential limitations imposed by the frame of reference of the assessor can be reduced by knowledge, critical awareness and a concern with evidence (p. 17).

Decisions regarding future risk are taken in a variety of situations and at various rates of speed. Much of what has been discussed already in this chapter requires a reasonable amount of time. Case records need to be fully studied. Staff who know the offender in other situations need to be consulted. A detailed analysis of available information has to take place in an attempt to locate the risk in place and time. The offender needs to be interviewed fully and a constant watch kept for the type of risk trigger factors identified by the foregoing process. The opportunity for such detailed investigative work may not, however, always be available. Police officers with a responsibility to protect the public under the provisions contained in the new sex offender orders may wish to move fairly quickly to minimise the risk presented from sex offenders. In these cases, one of the clear triggers will be that the offender has a previous record of qualifying sexual offences (as determined by the Sex Offenders Act 1997). From this point it will be that the offender has demonstrated behaviour which causes concern and that members of the community will be at risk of harm from him. Although being seen loitering in a particular area may trigger the concern, it is to be hoped that in the light of the potential penalty for breach, there will be a more substantive, evidence-based assessment. The police service will consult with other experts and it may be that some of those people will have access to the kind of detailed information described above, although this will not always be so. In forming a base-line judgment police officers may well resort to the use of risk predictor tools to test whether they should proceed further with the matter, or as a basis for discussion with other professionals.

SPEED IS OF THE ESSENCE — SHORT CUTS TO ASSESSMENT

In a sense there is a need for a streamlined test for dangerousness which fulfils the need to protect the public whilst maintaining the rights of the offender. Is this possible? This question was posed by the Parliamentary Office of Science and Technology (POST, 1996) over the issue of gun control laws. Assessing the way in which firearms certificates had been issued until that point, it was responding to a call for a more 'scientific' evaluation than had been in place until that time. It was the tragic events of the Dunblane killings which had provoked the review and a desire to try to identify more readily the sort of person seen as a psychopathic loner. In line with much of the information above, POST concluded that dangerousness was best assessed when based on an overview of all available knowledge gleaned from other agencies as well as several in-depth interviews with the offender. Even then, POST believed that assessment required the full co-operation of the subject and that time was needed to obtain this. In the gun control context, POST concluded that cost, insufficient resources, a lack of collateral information (confidential medical records for example) and the fact that applicants, once they were aware of the process, could be 'briefed', all made the clinical approach to assessing dangerousness a non-starter in the community context. The POST paper then went on to examine the possibility of a more streamlined test offering the opportunity for a reasonably accurate prediction. They examined the issue of 'profile' characteristics, that is the types of factors frequently found in certain types of offenders. The paper cited the results of an American study of psychiatric patients which revealed the following characteristics:

- drug and alcohol abuse combined with a mental disorder (increased the risk of violence three- to fourfold);
- poor anger control and impulsivity;
- being unable to function independently in daily life;
- having violent fantasies and pervasive delusions;
- having frequent changes of residence.

POST believed that in principle much of this information could be obtained through self-report questionnaires but doubted the effectiveness of this measure. However, this paper does hint at the adoption of profile type information which might be useful to those attempting to identify future dangerousness. Police officers are increasingly familiar with the idea of offender profiling (Ormerod, 1996, Cantner, 1994), especially in the process of detection. Profiling has been described as, 'information gathered at a crime scene, including reports of an offender's behaviour, used both to infer motivation for an offence and to produce a description of the type of person likely to be responsible' (Ormerod, 1996, p. 865). In assessing dangerous offenders in the community, the identity of the person is known and what is at issue is the likelihood of their reoffending. Some of the information used from profile techniques may assist in the prediction of risk and a few examples may illustrate the point. The more familiar staff are with data or information sets, the more confortable they may feel in examining that material in a new way and for a different purpose — both police and probation officers work in this context.

Profiling Danger

In a recent paper Turvey (1997), reviewed some of the predictive factors associated with recidivism in violent sex offenders. He dealt with rape in particular and noted a shifting pattern in rape victims in the USA. This change was related to the age profile of the victim, with the number of victims in the 12–19 age band increasing from 35% of the total to 50%. He also noted that 16% of all rape victims were under the age of 12 years. Turvey goes on to cite the work of Doctor Vernon Quinsey from Canada, which Turvey believes demonstrates a clear correlation between inappropriate age selection (of victim) and future recidivism, had concluded that 'sex with children was the most highly related to victim damage ... compared with others, subjects who had injured their victims engaged in violence or sadism during the rape, showed little sexual interest in adults and a lot of interest in coercive sex with children'. In a 1991 follow-up study Quinsey had found that out of 136 released extra-familial child abusers, 43% had committed another violent or sexual offence. Professional concern with child sex offenders may therefore be quite appropriate, not just on the grounds that it is such a morally heinous crime, but because of the high probability of recidivism. Turvey therefore summarised Quinsey's work as indicative of the following factors for prediction:

- psychopathy is positively correlated to recidivism;
- violence/sadism are positively related to recidivism;
- inappropriate age choice of victim is a consistent predictor of recidivism;
- patient self-reports of sexual preferences have no bearing on recidivism;
- psychiatrists tend not to be very objective about dangerousness assessment.

This last point related to a comment made by Quinsey in 1986, 'Perceptions of treatability, however, may be more like moral judgments or judgments of likeability than they appear to be. If perceptions of treatability are moral judgments, then the negative correlation of dangerousness and treatability makes sense'. The involvement of the views, feelings and attitudes of the worker have already been mentioned in the work of Needs and Towl (1997), above. It was also a key point made by Prins (1988) when he discussed the concept of 'ambivalent investment'. This is where the recognition of your own feelings concerning the crime and the offender, a sense of responsibility to the community and a desire to see something positive, may well lead to the missing of signals that the situation is actually going wrong.

Holmes and Holmes (1996) offer a detailed guide to serious offender typology in the context of it being an investigative tool, but its use for assessing risk is evident. In looking at paedophile offenders they begin with a definition taken from the *Diagnostic and Statistic Manual of Mental Disorders*, produced by the American Psychiatric Association in 1994. A definition of paedophilia is useful in the context of its widespread use and the widespread condemnation of a range of offenders tagged with this label:

> The acts or fantasy of engaging in sexual activity with prepubertal children as a repeatedly preferred or exclusive method of achieving sexual excitement (Holmes and Holmes, 1996, p. 135).

The authors proceed to describe different types of child molesters thereby offering clues for practitioners engaged in risk assessment, as it is clear that even within the category of child abuse, there will be degrees of risk which demand different levels of protection plans. Two types of child molesters are discussed: situational and preferential. The first is a person described as not having a true interest in children but who experiments and could well abuse any vulnerable person. Within this category are four sub-types described by Holmes and Holmes which are worth repeating here:

- *The repressed paedophile*: children are used as a temporary measure, usually as a result of changes in self-image. This person has normal adult relationships and the child (victim) may be experienced as a pseudo-adult. Girls are the most likely victims and the offender usually has a stable, employed, and married background but suffers from low self-esteem. This person may offer a reasonable prospect of rehabilitation.
- *The morally indiscriminate paedophile*: this person is described as an abuser of all available persons.
- *The sexually indiscriminate paedophile*: a sexual experimenter, a 'trysexual' with a wide variety of victims.
- *The naive and inadequate paedophile*: a person probably suffering from a mental disorder who is unable to determine right from wrong concerning sex with children. This person is probably a loner, is not usually violent and does not feel threatened (but for a contrasting view see Prins, 1986, p. 175).

The second type of child molester discussed was the preferential child molester, identified by Holmes and Holmes as the more likely to be very dangerous. In these cases children are preferred for pleasure, and two sub-types are noted:

- The sadistic molester who associates sexual gratification with fatal violence. Features of their offending behaviour may include abduction with force, pain and death. This person has no 'love' for children.
- The second sub-type is the seductive molester who courts or lures children with gifts and affection. These offenders are fixated at an earlier age and stage of emotional development. They have a persistent and compulsive interest and generally prefer male victims. They are likely to be single and immature (Holmes and Holmes, 1996, pp. 135–140).

Readers may question the value of applying such characteristics to the real offenders that they face in their daily working lives. Yet, much of this information is known. The police service, working with others in the multi-agency forum, should know in detail the characteristics of the offence and the offender because these people have already been caught and punished. Probation, prison and possibly health staff can add flesh to the bones in terms of their interviews with the offender over a period of time. By assembling a profile of how and possibly why an offender did what he did, the assessment of future risk might be slightly more accurate. This may not necessarily indicate the likelihood or probability of harm, but could assist with the nature of that harm, which should be an essential component of the assessment process. It may suggest that differentiation is needed between categories of offenders rather than a blanket assumption of high risk for all.

Holmes and Holmes (1996) also offer typologies of rapists which again might be useful in assessing the magnitude of risk offered by individual offenders. However, these should be observed in the context of most violent sexual assault occurring within personal relationships as discussed in chapter 7. Holmes and Holmes describe the stranger rapist as a predominantly young male with 80% under the age of 30 and 75% under 25. They note four categories of rapists which offer clues as to their offending style: the power assurance rapist, the anger retaliation rapist, the power assertive rapist and the sadistic rapist. These profiles are offered below not for detection purposes, but as clues to the potential harm such offenders might present if they offend again.

- The power assurance rapist is described as the least violent and aggressive. Characteristics include a background of single

174 Possible rather than Probable – the Lowering Threshold of Prediction

parents, and being non-athletic and passive. Their aim in rape is to elevate their own status. They are described as having some concern for the victim (although this characteristic may be hard to believe). They are frequently local, on foot and operate at night. They tend to believe that the victim enjoys the act and may well return. According to the authors these rapists have a 7 to 15 day cycle of attack which, if anywhere near accurate, should be an alarming figure for those assessing dangerousness and imminence of risk. In such cases a profile of this type of rapist could be extremely useful.

- The anger retaliation rapist is characterised by a desire to hurt women physically and to get back at what they view as injustice by women. The background of these offenders is said to be characterised by the following: divorced homes (80%), physically abused as a child (56%), raised by single women (80%) and adopted (20%). These offenders hold negative and hostile feelings towards women and see themselves as masculine and athletic. Their intention is to harm, and their behaviour ranges from verbal and physical assault to murder. They enjoy sexual degradation of the victim and may ejaculate in the face. They frequently use a car and operate close to home and tend to engage in blitz attacks with little planning. They have a six to twelve month offending cycle.

- The power assertive rapist is characterised by a belief in male superiority and his entitlement to rape (see a discussion by Los (1990) on the 'right' to rape in Canada). This rapist's behaviour is characterised by aggression which is used to secure compliance, the victim must do as she is told. The background history of these offenders is characterised by single parent homes (70%), foster care (33%) domestic problems and unhappy marriages. They tend to be loud and boisterous individuals who drive fast and flash motor cars. They occasionally carry out multiple assaults on the same victim and may suffer from retarded ejaculation. They often have a steady partner. Their aggression escalates as they carry on offending and they may resort to the use of a weapon. They offend on a 20–25 day cycle (readers may wish to consider the case in chapter 7 in the light of this profile).

- Finally Holmes and Holmes describe the characteristics of the sadistic rapist. They regard this person as the most dangerous of all and expressive of sexually aggressive feelings. They have an anti-social personality and are normally aggressive. They are typically married and regarded as a good family man. Many of these rapists have a compulsive personality and make intricate plans for their attack. They demonstrate a knowledge of police work and procedures. They take care in victim selection and use a range of paraphernalia to terrorise their victims, maybe using excessive profanity and degradation. They may well call the victim by another name, which might belong to their wife or mother. Their behaviour is characterised by ritual and they may need certain things said to them to bring on arousal.

Is information such as this of any use to police and probation officers involved in assessing risk? It could be argued that the background of most offenders or characteristics of their behaviour can be fitted into one or several of these models, so classifying a rapist as one type or another may induce over- or underestimation of risk. This may be the case, but a base-line of behavioural characteristics, associated with different types of offending behaviour, may be useful. It could be said of course that all rapists released in the community pose a serious risk of further offending and if so, the risk of harm is extremely serious. If so, can public protection plans, which require surveillance and prevention plans, be set up for all of them? The realistic answer has to be no, so the issue of imminence becomes crucial and it is possible that some of this profile information may be useful in assessing that particular issue.

A model which has become popular around the country is a combination of actuarial methods enhanced by clinical and/or casework evaluation. In *Structured Anchored Clinical Judgement* (Thornton, 1997), actuarial classification acts as the basis for prediction and utilises three risk levels, as does the American system related to community notification schemes. A point is scored for each of the following: the index offence having a sexual element, previous convictions including a sexual element, the index offence including a non-sexual assault, previous convictions including a non-sexual assault, and conviction on more than three occasions prior to the index offence. Scoring one point puts the offender at level 1 (lower risk), scoring two or three points places the offender at level 2 (medium risk) and four or more points at a higher risk. A list of possible aggravating factors adds further information and if two of these are present the offender should be raised one risk category. This list includes: contact sex offences with a male victim, non-contact sex offences, sex offence with a stranger victim, never having been married nor having lived with a lover for two years, having been taken into local authority residential care, substance abuse problems and deviant arousal scores. Added to this may be more qualitative judgments such as likelihood of repetition, consequences of repetition and the pattern of events threatening harm. The final stage in the assessment would include an assessment of positive or negative factors. These might include failing to comply with treatment or group programmes as a sign of added risk, or completion of treatment and improvement within programmes as a sign of risk reduction.

Utilising a model such as this may well overcome some of the difficulties inherent in various agencies attempting to agree a common definition of risk. Without such agreement, the prospects for implementing effective strategies to reduce and manage risk would be lowered. Catherine Staite made several telling points in her contribution to a national conference devoted to the issue of sharing information to manage risk, which offer excellent guidance for people working in a multi-agency forum. She identified differing agency approaches to the assessment of risk and differing individual perceptions of risk as barriers to effective communication. She noted that all were subject to bias based on personal experience but tended to see this as a consequence of rule of thumb assessments rather than objective (mathematical) assessments of risk. There were difficulties over what constituted likely or probable, and there was a good deal of either talking down or talking up the degree of risk depending upon group constitution and dynamics. Her view was that professionals needed the complete picture of what led up to violence in the past, rather than relying on the fact that violence had simply happened in the past. There were three points relating to information which Staite regarded as essential: it should be timely, accurate and relevant. For her there were four lessons to be learned from previous mistakes in risk assessment:

- be aware of the limitations of risk assessment and of the biases which existed in the judgments of everyone;
- make information sharing and effective communication a key part of the strategic planning process of organisations, not an afterthought;
- identify ways such as e-mail or encryption to overcome the technical problems of sharing information quickly and confidentially;

- when, in spite of all efforts, things did go wrong, it was usually a mistake to look for someone to blame. Most failures were the result of a lack of resources, systematic or organisational inadequacies rather than individual fault.

(Home Office, 1997, pp. 19–20.)

USE OF PREVIOUS CONVICTIONS

Throughout this book two points have constantly been made concerning the prediction of future dangerousness. These are that previous behaviour has already occurred and that this behaviour has been from a specific list of such behaviour; in other words, previous convictions assume great importance. But is this out of proportion to their value? Doubts have already been cast upon an over-reliance on the offence-based criteria. Scott (1977) for example, argued that:

> It is axiomatic that all behaviour can be reached by different paths, each of which has different implications for the future. To put it another way, offence entities all tend to comprise a majority of benign cases which have made a single and temporary crossing of the threshold, and a malignant minority which are firmly entrenched across that threshold. Just as some of the major offences do not qualify for dangerousness, some of the lesser offences (drunkenness, theft) may (p. 130).

Further doubts have to be expressed about the use of previous convictions. For example, in chapter 1, Gunn's (1996) negative view concerning the retrospective application of data to individual cases, usually based on conviction-type, was noted. Two issues arise when previous convictions are used as a means of prediction. One is the likelihood of a further similar offence taking place (not just any offence) and the other is, how long is the period of risk — does time diminish the risk of reoffending? For prison, probation and police officers assessing the risk of prisoners about to be released in the community the further question arises of the account to be taken of time spent in prison. In other words, does the ticking of the clock start with the onset of the sentence or at the point of release?

Grubin and Wingate (1996) argue that public concern about the recidivism of sex offenders is in contrast to their low levels of sexual reoffending. They review a range of sex offender recidivism studies which suggest sexual reoffending rates of between 10% and 19% over a period of five years. When considering more serious sexual offenders (those serving prison sentences of four years and over), the rates were a little higher. For example, 15% of rapists and about 35% of child molesters were reconvicted for a sex offence, but this time the follow-up period was 10 years (Thornton and Travers, 1991). Previous convictions will therefore offer another base-line for assessment but can by no means be regarded as the definitive predictor that many people make them out to be — at least not without a full consideration of all the associated variables.

SUMMARY

Predicting future dangerousness in an individual is a very difficult task — any reading of the literature confirms this. Yet the agencies charged with public protection are expected to do this on a daily basis and in a variety of settings. In the present climate there does not appear to be too much concern expressed if they get it wrong in the sense of 'over-predicting'. However, in the opposite case they know that the media and politicians are waiting to pounce if they underestimate the risk. There is consequently a degree of safety in utilising predictive tools. They prove that a method which approaches the scientific has been used and, if mistakes are made, it could be argued that the predictive tool is wrong, rather than the person using it. Blame can therefore be diverted. There is a growing sense of confidence in the ability of predictive tools to forecast future offending but there remains a large amount of scepticism considering their usefulness with danger-ous behaviour, in itself so unpredictable.

Good quality information clearly lies at the heart of effective risk assessment and it is here that the multi-agency approach is invaluable. The exchange of information and its assessment by a group of professionals each coming from a different perspective offers the best way forward. Those individual agencies should strive to retain their own perspective, even if they move towards more generally agreed defini-tions of risk and danger. The pressure is on criminal justice practitioners to assess risk quickly and it is natural to look for ways to short-cut the process. The evidence suggests that there is not a short cut. The stakes are too high, on both sides of the equation, for mistakes to be made due to pressure of time. Over- or under-caution could have significant effects on people's lives. Professional judgment and experience, gut feeling, detailed interviews and predictive tools all have their place. Particular agencies or even practitioners will be better at one or more of these than others. All should contribute fully to the process. The threshold for a safe and just assessment and prediction of risk should not be lowered.

Chapter 9
Rights and Wrongs — Balancing Possibility with Probability

Any considered reading of what has become known as the 'Dangerousness Debate' of the late 1970s and early 1980s will reveal a major preoccupation with the issue of rights (Floud and Young, 1981, Walker, 1980, Bottoms and Brownsword, 1982). An essential point in that debate was a consideration for the rights of offenders who might be punished, or receive additional punishment, for something that they had yet to do, and based upon what they had done in the past. This consideration was set against the rights of those who might be victimised by their actions. In the late 1990s that concern with the rights of the offender appears to be singularly absent from the debate on dangerousness which had gained ground throughout the Conservative government's last term in office and gathered even greater pace in the early stages of the New Labour government. This chapter will explore that decline in a libertarian conscience and a concern with rights and justice. The development of community notification laws in the USA and the discussions on rights provoked there, will be used as a case example to consider the issues that might arise in this country.

RIGHTS FOR ALL?

In asking whether Britain needs a Bill of Rights, Dworkin (1996) eloquently spelt out the tradition of freedom which he saw as having been eroded in recent years:

> Great Britain was once a fortress for freedom. It claimed the great philosophers of liberty — Milton and Locke and Paine and Mill. Its legal tradition is irradiated with liberal ideas: that people accused of crime are presumed to be innocent, that no one owns another's conscience, that a man's home is his castle, that speech is the first liberty because it is central to all the rest (p. 59).

Although Dworkin goes on to argue that Britain now offers less legal protection to central freedoms than its neighbours in Europe, he does not see it becoming a police state. Yet he argues that freedoms are under threat from what he terms, 'a decline in the culture of liberty'. In a culture of liberty, freedoms would only be abridged in order to prevent a 'clear and serious danger — a calamity — and even then only so far as is absolutely necessary to prevent it' (p. 60). This point was picked up by the Lord Chancellor in a speech in the US Supreme Court on 11 May 1998. In talking about the introduction of a Human Rights Bill into parliament by the Labour government he was publicly acknowledging Dworkin's concerns. He said:

> UK law is undoubtedly deficient ... (it) possesses no statute which sets out citizens' rights ... (and) there is no obligation on governmental and other public authorities to respect substantive human rights ... more generally, the UK lacks a legal culture of rights: for instance, no institutional procedure exists which seeks to ensure that new legislation conforms to human rights norms.

It is interesting to ponder how recently introduced dangerous offender legislation would have fared in the face of such scrutiny. It may be that the 'competing rights' argument would have been found in favour of the majority, but at the very least, the debate would have been held. In summarising his argument, Lord Irvine said, 'British citizens will, at long last, be empowered to vindicate their fundamental rights before British courts'. These rights are those enshrined in the European

Convention on Human Rights and include: the right to liberty and the security of the person (which can be seen as a clear competing right in the dangerousness context); freedom from inhuman or degrading treatment and right to a fair hearing (but in most public protection panels the offender is not represented or present). As in America, where many offenders have sought the court's decision on 'cruel and unjust punishment' claims, it would appear that a Bill of Rights in the UK could open the door to a great deal more litigation from offenders whose rights and freedoms have been impaired by decisions taken within public protection panels or potentially dangerous offender conferences. Undoubtedly the issue of rights does appear at these conferences but, as described elsewhere in this book, they can quickly be subjugated by the overriding aim of protecting the public. Police and probation staff need to retain as much of their professional judgment as they can in the face of changing state definitions of risk.

LOSING RIGHTS

Dworkin's description cited above perfectly fits the debate over the rights, or lack of rights, to be had by offenders who have, by their past behaviour, shown themselves to have posed a risk of serious harm to the public. The key issues here are the extent of the potential danger; by using the term 'calamity' Dworkin suggests great seriousness and of course this must be accompanied by a very strong indication of certainty. As seen in chapter 7, one or both of these elements may be missing in the profile of people subject to discussions in public protection meetings.

    Dangerous offenders, according to protagonists of preventive deten-tion, have forfeited the right to enjoy the same freedom and liberties afforded to the non-dangerous population. This forfeiture is different even from that experienced by so-called 'normal' offenders and can therefore excuse action which may not be normally acceptable in a democratic society. Morris (1994) for example discussed the dangerous offender in the terms of modern warfare, 'In the criminal law, if not in international relations, the pre-emptive strike has great attraction; to capture the criminal before the crime is surely an alluring idea' (p. 241). However, it could be argued that the pre-emptive strike is not really playing according to the rules, it is not how civilised communities operate (but does of course considerably improve the prospect of victory). In an incisive analysis, Pratt (1997) sees dangerousness as a creation of modernity and the development of the risk society as affording neo-liberal governments an opportunity to retain a major stake in social control, even when they are exhorting the public to become involved in 'care of the self' (p. 139). The ongoing commitment to protect the public is reflected in the right of the public to be given public protection, and this will be written into the laws of the country as numerous laws around the world, especially in the early 1990s, demonstrate. Pratt argues that the climate of fear escalates to demand ever greater protection, whereby this right defeats all other competing rights in terms of the individual offender's rights as a citizen of the country:

> Indeed, it is as if the increasing crime fears and insecurities generated by their neo-liberal programme of government are turned back on the state itself, as the right to protection from ungovernable risks, such as those posed by the dangerous offenders of this period, is claimed as one of those inalienable rights of modern society, and is likely to find forceful expression in the campaigns of social movements representing victims' and women's rights (p. 158).

Pratt goes on to argue that the issue of rights is a politicised one which feeds off the general perception of a punitive-minded public:

> By enacting new laws against the dangerous, politicians can thus be seen as responding to citizens rights and expectations while at the same time enhancing their own popularity with the public by appearing to guarantee these rights and expectations (p. 159).

The assumption by politicians is that the public are prepared to accept a wider attack on rights — which can of course indirectly affect their own rights — if the target of state intervention is a specific named offender or type of offender. The rationale behind this is that the risk to innocent members of society outweighs the rights of those who would cause serious harm. This is what Floud and Young (1981) termed the just distribution of risks, in that protective sentencing could be morally justified because dangerous offenders, by their previous behaviour, had forfeited the right to be presumed harmless and the state was therefore justified in removing their rights. The debate engendered by the Floud report was heavily focused on the rights issue and it is an indicator of the changing penal climate that this debate has been almost entirely absent during the 1990s when, it could be argued, a much greater erosion of rights has been proposed and has already taken place.

Rights and Freedom

Laws concerning dangerous offenders infringe upon the liberty and freedom of the individual. These laws give rise to policies which can take the form of 'longer than desert' sentencing, detention at the end of the original sentence, extended supervision in the community, intrusive supervision, electronic tagging, measures to prevent the offender frequenting certain public places as well as measures to establish surveillance of their movements. The power taken by the state and its agents over the individual is enormous, yet, in the 1990s especially, this has provoked scarcely a dissenting voice. History may tell us that late twentieth century society saw this erosion of rights as morally justified and defensible, it was after all a worldwide movement. The philosophical debate has never been so clear cut as this apparent public consensus might indicate. Henman (1997) reviews the ethical and rights issues in relation to sentencing policy. He identifies four main positions running throughout the argument. The first approach, which encompasses the second approach, is that additional punishment is warranted for those offenders who seem likely to commit harmful offences in the future, even if this punishment outweighs desert considerations. He describes this as both a reductivist approach and a utilitarian approach, in that the perceived social utility of the measures outweighs the cost to the few dangerous people and their families (there remain problems with sorts of harm and likelihood of them occurring). Having described these two positions, Henman argues that the third position finds the previous two unacceptable because probability of future harm is insufficient to trigger the measures, the criterion should be one of certainty. The fourth position that he cites is that of the retributionist who always regards precautionary sentences as unjustifiable, since they consist of punishment for crimes not yet committed (Henman, 1997, p. 46). He summarises the position as follows:

These views, therefore, represent ethical assumptions which form the moral basis for justifying the ascription or derogation of individual offender's rights in a situation where they are adjudged dangerous (p. 47).

What we then see is a debate around the nature of competing rights, a notion which had been developed by Bottoms and Brownsword (1982):

> However, the right can ... be set directly against the competing rights of potential victims not to be assaulted, for those citizens are entitled to insist upon their right to go about their business without attack ...

This had built upon the work carried out by the Floud committee (Floud 1982), who regarded the issue of competing claims as a moral choice that society has to make:

> We have to make a moral choice between competing claims: the claim of a known individual offender, not to be unnecessarily deprived of his liberty; and the claim of an innocent (unconvicted), unknown person (or persons), not to be deprived of the right to go about their business without risk of grave harm at the hands of an aggressor (p. 219).

Floud saw that providing the risk is real and the anticipated harm is grave, the notion of diffused risk (unknown victim therefore a communal or collective claim to protection) is acceptable in permitting protective sentencing. The growth of fixed, mandatory life (or long) sentences for certain classes of offenders to a certain extent overcomes the problems, both moral and real, of predicting future dangerousness. By focusing on certain crimes, such as serious violence or sexual offences, which have been repeated at least once, the law says that the offender has given up the opportunity to be given the full citizenship rights which might (and should) be accorded to the so-called normal offender who reoffends. By choosing the first course of action — the serious crime — and then choosing to repeat something similar, the offender has, by default, chosen to give up some of the rights normally associated with citizenship.

The last two decades have seen this issue of competing rights brought into sharp focus by suggesting that it is the rights of those most vulnerable in society that are at risk, people perhaps not even able to defend their rights. The most frequently cited potential victims are children, and the most likely offence is one of serious sexual assault. By framing the debate concerning rights within this context, those supporting the abrogation of rights can completely nullify any discussion. A case reported in *The Guardian* (25 August 1996) illustrates the issue. A man was released into a New Jersey community having served 16 years of a total 53 year sentence for murder and sodomy. He had been a model prisoner and pronounced 'cured' by counsellors in prison. The community was aware of his offences due to the community notification laws in existence. The man challenged the community notification (and the threatened vigilante activity which accompanied it) saying that he had already been punished. The parents of children living in the same street had this to say at the time, 'Doesn't our daughter's right to exist in safety take precedence over this sex offender's right to a secret past?'. When framed in this way the question becomes quite easy to answer and it has become an example of how the issue has been presented around the world. Yet no threats had been issued by this man and there had not been any official or public concern with his behaviour. People who have committed heinous crimes in the past lose their rights in the present and as a result, innocent victims should find their position strengthened by the implementation of preventative and protective measures. By demonising the offender the concern for their rights sharply diminishes. Thus, when the chemical castration law was debated in California, the Women's Coalition who had proposed the measure said, 'If this doesn't pass, we'll bring it back again and again and again. We're not talking about cutting off their testicles. Maybe someday, but not now'. The American Civil Liberties Union promised a legal challenge saying; 'This bill poses serious, unresolved legal problems regarding some very fundamental constitutional rights, including the right to privacy, the right to procreate, and the right to exercise control over one's body' (ACLU news release, 3 September 1996).

Tough measures, whether in the form of harsher sentencing or community notification laws (explored in greater detail further on), appear to be quite acceptable to a public in fear of predatory violent and sexual offenders. Yet little is said of the way in which these measures might develop and expand. The demonisation of sex offenders in particular has been extremely effective and countered any suggestion that their rights have been compromised. As reported in *The Guardian* (23 June 1996), American politicians were unwilling to speak out against tougher measures whereas civil liberties groups did at least express concern:

> The American Civil Liberties Union has warned of dangerous precedents — today paedophiles, tomorrow armed robbers? But faced with a conflict between the rights of a known abuser and those of a child, the public has no such problems.

More recently, the issue of rights has spread out into the area of housing provision, an indicator that public protection is becoming an all-including agenda for the public sector. A case was reported in which Hounslow council in West London won the right to make a convicted paedophile homeless. The High Court ruled that the circumstances of the 65-year-old offender's past history were ample justification for the council to refuse to house him (*The Guardian*, 20 February 1997).

The issue of community notification of the whereabouts and offending history of known sex offenders in particular raises very serious personal liberty concerns which will now be discussed. It is interesting to note that concern with violent offenders, or rapists of adults has not manifested itself to a similar degree, although there is evidence, especially from the USA, that all sex offenders are lumped together. Community notification clearly raises the primacy of community rights over those of the individual. It also raises protectionism over rehabilitation. It does not easily allow the repair of a broken social contract.

COMMUNITY NOTIFICATION

Community notification laws have attracted widespread public and political support which has eased their subsequent implementation. Notification essentially begins with a requirement for certain types of offenders (most commonly sex offenders) to register their current whereabouts with the police service in the area in which they live. That in itself should be enough and be the end of the process, but a more likely development, at least from the American experience, is a degree of notification of that information to people outside the police service and other law enforcing agencies. There are three common levels of notification: (1) broad community notification; (2) notification to organisations and individuals at risk; and (3) access to registration information. In describing these models, the John Howard Society of Alberta says that, 'In making a decision about notification, justice agencies must try to achieve a balance between the public's safety and right to know and the offender's right to privacy' (1997 p. 1). In practice it is not so much a balancing of rights as a decision as to whose rights are the more important, on the basis that they compete with each other.

TELLING WHOM? LESSONS FROM NORTH AMERICA

There are various examples of the levels of notification required by certain states in America and Canada which will be discussed below. Laws recently introduced into the UK have not gone as far as many of these although the opportunity is there, if the agencies involved in public protection, particularly the police service, deem it to be necessary. Public access to sex offender registration information is a contentious issue. The registers themselves frequently fail to distinguish between types of sexual offences and offence severity, or fail to take account of the time that has elapsed since an offence was last committed. The public can therefore, in some cases, access information which may be dated and concern a relatively minor offence, yet the named individual instantly stands to become one of the demonised group of predatory sex offenders. In California, for example, a member of the public can telephone their law enforcement office to find out whether someone they know is a registered sex offender. Other information may not necessarily be given, yet the naming itself and confirmation of sex offender status, may be enough to provoke a possible violent community reaction. An example of limited notification occurs where certain vulnerable members of the community only are notified of a prisoner's impending release. The notification is carried out by the chief of police or state trooper.

A more extreme example of broad community notification is found in Louisiana. Here the State Board of Parole requires a sex offender to notify the public by mail of his name, address and the offence for which he was convicted. The requirements are very specific, so that people must be notified who live within one square mile in rural areas, or three square blocks in urban areas, of the proposed release address. Offenders may also be required to conduct any other form of notification deemed necessary by the board, for example bumper stickers, signs or handbills (John Howard Society of Alberta, 1997, pp. 3, 4). Such measures may appear to be excessive and perhaps unlikely to take place within these shores, yet the rapid importation of registration schemes, in the face of limited opposition, certainly opens the door to wider notification procedures. It is likely that once a serious offence is committed by someone who is already on the register, the clamour for wider community notification will considerably increase. The registration process will have been deemed to have failed and the public and press will clamour for much greater access to registration information.

In Alberta, Canada, the law relating to community notification is found in the Freedom of Information and Protection of Privacy Act (an interesting home for legislation which again is likely to decide that one person or group's rights are more important than another). The legislation stipulates that notification can only be carried out by the police department. A protocol governs the decision to notify, a decision which would be told to the offender. The protocol calls for disclosure if it is in the public's best interest and must serve the task of enhancing public protection (John Howard Society of Alberta, 1997). One interesting development in Manitoba is the establishment of a community notification advisory committee, whose task is to balance the public's right to information with the offender's right to privacy, described by the committee as: 'an important and delicate task, requiring the expertise of individuals from a wide range of disciplines' (John Howard Society of Alberta, 1997, p. 6). The decision to notify, be it in limited fashion or more broadly, invariably resides with the police service, although it may well take advice from other criminal justice professionals. The potential is, however, present for quite subjective decisions to be made. Considering the potentially negative effects of notification to the community — for example vigilantism — it is a decision which needs to be taken with great care.

However, it is the criteria for registration which are arguably the most important. The mass registration of all sexual offenders, no matter what the degree of risk to the public, accompanied by a fairly liberal policy on notification, can put large numbers of people at risk of severe community reactions. In some American states, for example Minnesota, it is enough to be charged with a sexual offence to trigger the registration process (Hebenton and Thomas, 1996).

Finding Out Information

The levels and means by which sex offender information is communicated in the USA are now quite sophisticated. The Internet is a

major provider of information on this subject and many law enforcement agencies and commercial organisations provide information in
response to individual requests — Texas, for example, offers a
web-based sex offender search for a credit card payment of 25 dollars.
Registration schemes have to run a parallel community notification
scheme which is required by statute. The Jacob Wetterling Crimes
Against Children and Sexually Violent Offender Registration Act, a
national law, more commonly known as 'Megan's Law', links federal
anti-crime funding with the sexual offender warning system. When
President Clinton signed the law in May 1997, states were given until
September of that year to comply or lose federal money. Information is
conveyed based on a three tier level of risk, namely low (1), medium
(2) and high (3), with wider notification taking place the greater the
perceived level of risk. One example, posted on the Internet by
Pembroke (USA) police department will illustrate the system. The web
page announces the number of offenders under each risk level registered
in the area and states the purpose of the scheme, which is to 'provide
Pembroke residents with the means to obtain information concerning
registered sex offenders who reside or work in the Town of Pembroke'.
The guidelines for obtaining information are clear, restricted to people
over 18 years of age, who must appear in person at a police station and
provide proper identification (including a photograph). The requesting
person must state that he or she requests sex offender registration
information (SORI) for his or her protection or for the protection of a
child under 18 for whom they have responsibility, care or custody. The
request may concern a specific person, or an offender who lives within
a one mile radius of a specified address or whether any sex offenders
live or work on a specific street within the town. For level 1 offenders,
the following information is disclosed to the requesting person:

- the name of the offender;
- the home address of the offender if the address falls within a one
  mile radius or if the offender lives on a specific street identified
  by the requesting person;
- the work address of the offender (conditions as above);
- the offence for which the offender was convicted or adjudicated
  and the relevant dates;
- the offender's age, race, height, weight, eye and hair colour;
- a photograph, if available, at a cost of $1.50.

For level 2 offenders the amount of community notification increases, requiring the police, within two days of receipt of the information, to notify the following:

- all schools, public and private, known to the police department, sent for the attention of the principal;
- All licensed day care facilities, sent for the attention of the person in charge;
- all the organisations eligible to receive such notification and who have provided a mailing address and a point of contact;
- individual requests as described in level 1.

For level 3 offenders the notification moves beyond named individuals to the whole community:

- The *Pembroke Mariner* and *Pembroke Reporter* newspapers and local cable television;
- all people and organisations as for levels 1 and 2;
- public notices posted at Pembroke Town Hall, Pembroke Library, Pembroke Police department, private establishments with their permission and the Pembroke Police Department Web site.

In discussing the extent to which the community would inquire after sex offender registration information, much was made of the low take-up in the USA. Those supporters of wider notification argue that it is the requirement to visit a police station in person and have the reasons for the information request recorded that have kept the numbers low. As a result, people have taken the matter into their own hands and posted full details on the Internet. One site, www.sex-offenders. net, has put details on-line for anyone to access with the introductory message: 'The information here gives you another tool to help protect your children and your loved ones from harm. Over 63,000 child molesters and adult rapists live in California. Many will now obey the law; thousands will strike again. Studies show that half will be re-arrested, 40% of them for another sex crime'. The terminology of this message is exactly that which enables the further spread of community notification with all the possible negative effects it might have, although all police web sites seen carried a legal warning concerning vigilante or similar activities. In reviewing the development of registration schemes in the USA,

Hebenton and Thomas (1997) noted that harassment of the offender had been recorded in 10% of cases. The same report also noted that there was little research so far into the deterrence or displacement effect of registers, although they mentioned that one study had shown that offenders subject to registration were no less likely to offend than non-registered groups. However, a quicker arrest time for a new offence was noted (25 months as against 60 months), a result, it was felt, of increased surveillance. This last point reflects the observations made by some of the police officers spoken to during the course of researching this book, namely that the measure would increase detection but not do as much for proactive work.

Notification in the UK

The debate over registration in the UK was not noted for a major discussion on the issue of rights — it was as if it was taken as read that the rights of the community to be protected outweighed any rights that might be claimed by sex offenders. The sub-text of the registration debate, that of community notification did, however, provoke a little more discussion. That discussion was one joined by civil liberties groups, although it was not on the same plane as the American debate. Here the issue was not one of rights to privacy, but more one of protecting the offender from community vengeance and the main player in the discussion was the police service. The Sex Offenders Act 1997 made the registration of sex offender information with the police service a requirement in law (the detailed requirements of the Act were discussed in chapter 4). There had been little real debate over the proposed legislation in parliament, it was another of those issues which had become politically neutralised, as one party sought to outmanoeuvre the other. The initial proposals came from the Conservative government, with Michael Howard saying, 'This Bill will provide the police with the information they need to apprehend sex offenders and help them to protect the public from those who would seek to do harm to children' (*The Guardian*, 19 December 1996). This statement shows the politics of the Bill, however, the suggestion being that it was paedophile offenders who were to be registered, whereas it was to be a much more extensive list of sex offenders. Indeed, John Wadham, director of the civil rights organisation, Liberty, was moved to say that the register would include thousands of people who had never been a danger to children. The whole issue was therefore conflated so as to neutralise the opposition and indeed effectively challenge anyone to counter the proposals to protect the most vulnerable. But, as we have seen already in the chapter on the politics of protection, reasoned opposition to any of the government's measures was sadly lacking. Instead the Labour Party in opposition had attempted to raise the stakes considerably. By February of 1997 it was tabling amendments to the Bill suggesting notification to schools and in some cases members of the public (*The Independent*, 19 February 1997). The same report quoted a survey of the 43 police forces in England and Wales which showed the police as opposing the idea of greater disclosure, fearing an increase in vigilante activity and the risk of driving paedophiles underground. The Labour Party had proposed what it termed a 'sophisticated version of Megan's Law, where there are circumstances in which members of the public are told . . . they should be made aware of the risk due to people coming into their neighbourhood' (*The Times*, 2 February 1997). The same report asked the spokesman, Alun Michael, if he was concerned about the civil rights issues. His reply aptly reflects the mood and political context of the time, 'I can't accept it, because the protection of the child is very important'.

'Outing' by Newspapers

It could be argued that the Labour Party was responding to the popular mood and was attempting to outflank the government on its own ground. During the Bill's passage through parliament, several newspapers took the matter into their own hands and indeed pushed the debate much further than the government probably intended. These newspapers pursued a policy of what became known as 'outing'. In practice, this was the naming and occasionally provision of photographs of convicted paedophiles in mostly local newspapers. One of the leading newspapers in this field was the *Bournemouth Evening Echo*, which ran a 'Protect our Children' campaign. The newspaper compiled a register of those convicted of child sex offences over the previous six years and promised to make it available to organisations and groups working with children. Naturally the opportunity for this information to become available outside these groups is considerable, a concern noted by Liberty:

We are very worried. Newspaper registers are bound to contain mistakes and will not be comprehensive. We are not against a properly held and regulated register. But it is for the police to know who and where paedophiles are — and for them to decide who has a right to know (*The Guardian*, 21 July 1996).

The spread of the practice of outing led to an increase in the number of vigilante attacks around the country. Some of the more respectable newspaper coverage of these events took the line that the prospects for protecting the public were being hampered by the naming of offenders, as those involved fled the area and the police and probation officers lost contact with them. Generally speaking the police were fairly united in their opposition to notification and outing. Tony Butler, the Chief Constable of Gloucester and the ACPO speaker on this issue repeatedly called for the matter to be left to the police, 'There are real dangers of public over-reaction and violence. Such action could drive offenders underground' (*The Independent*, 24 February 1997). Examples such as the beating of a 67-year-old man in Manchester, mistaken for an abuser whose photograph had been published in the *Manchester Evening News*, were relatively common for a period of time. The response of the newspaper to the incident again shows a lack of concern with justice, even when mistakes were made. The editor accepted no responsibility, saying that the newspaper was reflecting public concern, a stance which was supported by 92% of those who took part in a telephone poll conducted by the newspaper. Other police chiefs referred to a concern over lynch mob justice by people usually acting on false rumours. However, some senior officers did not take this line. For example, a detective chief inspector in Liverpool called for a new law allowing community notification in the case of 'an incredibly dangerous man' (*The Independent*, 10 June 1997). However, in an article in the *Police Review*, Potter (1997) reported a detective inspector in Manchester as saying:

> (we would not want to have to tell the public) on the same statutory basis as Megan's Law. We would not want the same sort of situation as in Washington in the US, where it is a criminal offence not to inform the public about a convicted paedophile, and an officer who fails to do so can face a jail sentence (p. 19).

Concern with paedophiles was of course closely associated with the difficulties of providing suitable accommodation for them. On 9 January 1997 *The Independent* reported a case of a council housing official in

Birmingham facing disciplinary action for allegedly alerting mothers that a paedophile was moving into the area. Residents from the council estate concerned sent a 1,000 name petition to the housing department in support of the official. The concern of residents is understandable yet almost certainly inflated beyond what is a reasonable estimation of risk. The determination to protect a small part of the world overcomes any idea that, in the bigger picture, child sex offenders, if in the community, need to be supervised so that warning signs can be observed and acted upon if at all possible. This work can only take place in the context of professional relationships, not with people being driven from pillar to post.

Even within the limited amount of notification that has taken place in the UK, there has been legal challenge to the decision. In one case a couple were asked to leave a caravan site as a result of the owners being informed by the North Wales Police of their previous convictions. The judgment is worth noting in some detail as it covers many of the issues raised by the notification debate. The actions of the police were held not to be unlawful as the principles were in accordance with section 28(10) of the Data Protection Act 1984 and with the policy recognised by the court in *R v Brown (Gregory)* [1994] QB 547 and *Hellewell v Chief Constable of Derbyshire* [1995] 1 WLR 804. Those principles included: a general principle that information should not be disclosed; a strong public interest in ensuring that police were able to disclose information about offenders where necessary for the prevention or detection of crime or the protection of young people; and each case must be considered carefully on its particular facts. The final words of the law report raise many of the issues which were apparently so easily overlooked in the discussions which took place before and after the 1997 general election:

It was not acceptable that those who had undergone the lawful punishment imposed by the courts should be the subject of intimidation and private vengeance, harried from parish to parish like paupers under the old Poor Law. It was not only in their interest but in the interest of society as a whole that they should be enabled to live normal lives. While the risk of repeat offending might in some circumstances justify a very limited measure of official disclosure, a general policy of disclosure could never be justified, and the media should be slow to obstruct the rehabilitation of ex-offenders who had not offended again and were seriously bent on reform. (*R v Chief*

Constable of North Wales Police, ex parte AB; Queen's Bench Divisional Court (Lord Bingham, Lord Chief Justice and Mr Justice Buxton) at p. 813.)

Yet again the voice of reason emanated from the court and of course it should be noted that this judgment was delivered under a Labour government — the official opposition continued to remain the senior judiciary no matter who was in power. These comments aptly reflect those cited earlier by the Lord Chief Justice and suggest that the courts continue to have a role in curbing the excesses of parliament. However, the evidence to date is that the wider public interest has been given precedence over the rights of the individual.

As indicated above, the raising of the rights issues in the new dangerousness debate has not come from politicians but from a few academics, senior judges and occasionally the serious newspapers. For example, *The Guardian* newspaper ran an editorial under the title, 'Paedophiles have rights as well' relating to the issue of police disclosure of information. *The Guardian*'s view was that, 'The current law is far too vague. It should not be the police who establish the principles of disclosure, but Parliament. The civil rights issues are far too important to be left to the police'. They concluded that, 'Paedophiles should expect closer supervision, more systematic risk analysis and more challenging prison treatment programmes, but they do have the right to be free from lynch law when deemed ready for release'. Those subject to registers, formal or informal, stand a good chance of finding themselves the subject of information-sharing, either between agencies, or more widely if judged appropriate. In *R v Norfolk County Council, ex parte M* [1989] 2 All ER 359, Waite J recognised the potential of any system of registration to protect the vulnerable (in this case children) but, 'A child abuse register nevertheless remains (at all events as regards the abusers named on it) in essence a blacklist, and as such it also has the dangerous potential as an instrument of injustice and oppression' (Russell, 1998). Russell argues that although there is a clear recognition of the rights of sex offenders and the potential risk to those rights inherent in registration, their rights will nevertheless take second place to those of children (p. 96). The public furore surrounding the release of convicted paedophile killers Cooke and Oliver shows how easy it is for information to slip out and make the lives of those trying to protect the public very difficult.

SUMMARY

The issue of rights has featured very little in what might be termed the second dangerousness era. This is because the right of the public to be protected, a right demanded of the government, outweighs individual offender's rights to be treated the same as other citizens. It has essentially been a non-debate. As Britain increasingly adopts the litigation culture so prevalent in the USA, the issue of rights will undoubtedly assume greater importance. For a long while, the legality of dangerousness assessments has been challenged in the American courts and as a result clinical judgment has very much been called into question. The most recent raft of legislation gives much greater powers of assessment and subsequent labelling to non-clinicians and must lead to legal challenge. As more information gained from public protection panels feeds into the criminal justice decision-making process, so the potential for legal challenge will increase. The sharing of information means that it will be used in a wider range of criminal justice junctures, from bail assessment right through to prison release and indeed after prison release. At the present time there is little if any offender or legal representative presence at the panels — how much longer can that be sustained? So far, the need to protect the public, which has meant that, by default, the offender must not be aware of measures put in place to offer that protection, has countered any argument about attendance. If the public mood calms a little and if the professionals involved reassert a degree of independence from the government, this matter may be one which demands much greater attention than it has so far merited.

The concern must be that the lack of consideration for rights is missing the main issue — that is that the rights of more people than paedophiles are at risk of being compromised. The fact is that the state, ostensibly for political reasons, and not for any reason based on sound evidence, has defined dangerousness in such a way as to make the rights issue a nonstarter. If the state can do this for one group of people it can do it for others. Those involved in the process need to be aware of the way in which the process they are engaged in can be used, and they must make certain that their professionalism ensures the *just* redistribution of risk.

Chapter 10
Conclusion

This book has argued that the activities of a small number of dangerous and potentially dangerous offenders have driven the wider criminal justice agenda in recent years. These activities have led to the development of a very specific form of public protection agenda which, it has been argued, has had significant impact upon both legislation and the practice of criminal justice agencies. Despite no hard evidence that societies in Britain and elsewhere were increasingly at risk from these people, governments appeared content to allow the issue to be inflated by the popular press. As a result they were able to present themselves as responding to the 'new' dangerousness issue and thereby offer public reassurance and protection (Pratt, 1997). In Britain, the reported release from prison of a hundred or so dangerous paedophiles in the next few years was seen as sufficient reason to justify significant legislative development (chapter 4), much of which has considerable 'rights' issues within it, despite an absence of political debate on this matter. It is very difficult to know if there are more 'dangerous' offenders in the community or about to be released into it. What is clear, however, is that more information is known about them and, as a result, governments have felt it necessary to be seen to be offering the degree of protection the public is said to have demanded. Undoubtedly the activities of this small group of offenders can cause public alarm and there is an obvious need for legislative and policy development to curb the potential harm that they may cause. Yet, in mid-1990s Britain, little was said by the government to reassure the public that these offenders represented a *very small* part of the offender population. Public fear and concern was allowed to rise and, to a great extent, was exaggerated by the knee-jerk response of politicians. This book has argued that this particular public protection agenda served a clear political purpose, in Britain and other countries. That purpose was to attempt to differentiate between government and opposition political parties. This differentiation appears not to have occurred anywhere. The issue became politically neutral and as result escalated in 'toughness' in its attempt to produce that difference. Clearly, there was a need to respond to public concern, but there was also arguably a moral duty to deflate the situation, something which politicians of all parties were either unwilling or unable, given the political context, to do.

The absence of dissent, political or practitioner, from the public protection agenda, is unsurprising. It was framed largely in the context of protecting children and, as such, opposition was likely to amount to political or professional suicide. Reasoned debate therefore gave way to a form of bidding process in which proposed criminal justice legislation and agency practice was to be affected in major ways. The police and probation services in particular have had to examine the way in which they have traditionally worked and have come together in significant areas of daily working practice. Although the government, especially the probation inspectorate, has encouraged this, it also appears as if both agencies felt the need to 'share the load' and seek allies within the criminal justice sector. Undoubtedly the probation service has been vulnerable for some time and has transformed itself to ensure survival under successive Conservative administrations. Yet in the climate promoted by Home Secretary Michael Howard during the last Conservative government, that survival looked increasingly less likely. An association with the police service may well have been beneficial to the organisation, although it is difficult to pinpoint distinctive time periods when this shift occurred, and even more difficult to find too many public pronouncements on it. For the police service, despite continuing to enjoy high levels of public support, its political support was beginning to wane. For it too, the idea of someone else with whom to share the load (and blame?) was increasingly an organisational necessity.

Police and probation staff working together means a joining of cultures which have not always easily sat alongside each other. The rapid development of the public protection agenda gave common purpose to these two organisations and facilitated the creation of protocols which built shared working into daily practice. Public protection had long been a mandate for the police service and was widely accepted as part of its brief in the mind of the public. For the probation service, however, this task was much less in the public's mind, its image being one associated with caring for the offender more than the victim. Although it is argued in this book that this public conception was ill-informed, it nonetheless retained currency, making the probation service vulnerable in harsher penal climates. The task for probation service managers and practitioners, therefore, is to take on the service's enhanced role whilst utilising its practice with serious and dangerous offenders which has worked remarkably well for many years. Members of the probation service should not feel the need to become police officers by another name. Its expertise is well recognised by those who know but is much less well known on a wider front. In its formal meetings with police officers, the probation service should be demonstrating its skill and expertise as part of a multi-agency response to dangerousness, not as aids to the police service. For its part, the police service has already become much more of an organisation prepared to work with others but in so doing has frequently remained the lead agency which dominates the agenda. It too should work with others and not see others as a means of simply fulfilling its own agency goals. Successful public protection will depend upon free and full information flow, based upon trust and shared aims. Respect must be given to the work of the other without having to compromise traditional working practice and expertise. In researching this book the author did not detect that the probation service had shifted its value or professional base a long way from its routes but a shift was definitely occurring. This may represent a reality shift by probation officers as they find themselves increasingly subject to public scrutiny. However this shift should not have to involve adopting the language and values of the police service whose role remains quite different. It could be argued that within the field of public protection the aims of each are much closer, yet the impact is likely to be felt on practice outside this narrow but nonetheless important brief. In researching this book that trend was definitely apparent.

It has proved very difficult to pin down the origins of public protection, as described in this book. What came first? Was it a real public concern over the activities of certain offenders, inflated by the popular press? Was it a populist Home Secretary who saw his chance of political glory by unleashing a tide of penal populism not warranted or justified by any hard evidence? It is also worth considering why agencies signed up to this new agenda so readily, although the answer seems relatively clear — organisational survival was the priority. In the changed political circumstances of a new government, will the public protection agenda continue as before or will greater realism enter at the expense of rhetoric? Whatever the political situation it is clear that the agency agenda has turned for good. It is difficult to see any slowing down of the development of inter-agency working and many would argue that this is essential in any case, if the criminal justice process is to be effective, although previous good practice should not be forgotten. It is to be hoped that, even if the political situation does once again demand a call for more punitive measures, the professionals working within the field will be confident and competent enough to argue their own particular corner. The comments in the postscript may offer some hope for the future.

Postscript

A New Message

At the time this book was completed it appeared as if, for the time being at least, media and public hysteria with dangerous offenders had died down. Since the media circus had followed released paedophile killer Sydney Cooke in April 1998, there had been relatively little in the way of press reporting. This had not, however, stopped the process of public protection as agencies continued to develop their partnerships in response to constant pressure from the government to increase the amount of multi-agency working. It is clear that the Crime and Disorder Act 1998, will cement a range of partnership agreements into the daily working practices of a variety of public agencies. The Act will be a cornerstone of the Labour government's criminal justice strategy[1] and will focus on a range of measures aimed at increasing public safety, as expressed by the Home Secretary in a speech on 25 June 1998, 'building safer communities, through new local partnerships and by giving better protection against anti-social behaviour, sex offenders and drug misusing offenders' (Straw, 1998).

---

[1] So important is the Act to the Labour government that it was announced that the Home Secretary was to drop one of its key measures (the lowering of the age of consent to homosexual activity to 16 years from 18), in the face of opposition to this clause in the House of Lords and obvious threat to the implementation of the Act.

The use of the term 'partnership' is central to the message of the Act and so crucial is it that it will be put on a statutory footing. In working together to devise strategies to build safer communities these partnerships are expected to consult with the local community in order to set targets to reduce crime and disorder. It will be interesting to see if this public consultation process, which is clearly ongoing, will be extended to the work of public protection panels. We have already seen that, in its early days, this process has not included a great deal of public consultation, although the best of the schemes perhaps make their intentions clear. In so doing they hope to give out a strong message that they work together in order to protect the public, a message they hope will be heard by potential offenders. However, the sensitivity of the intelligence used and the need to protect operational policing practice has certainly narrowed the field of involvement. As yet, there is no real sign of the type of community conferences envisaged by Braithwaite and Daly (1994) (see Chapter 6 of ths text) operating in this area of practice. Yet it appears to be quite clear that the Home Secretary is envisaging the fullest of community involvement in crime reduction strategies; the issue therefore is to what extent this will apply to all forms of crime, including the most serious. The Home Office has already issued draft guidance on statutory crime and disorder partnerships and in his foreword the Home Secretary said that prescription from the government will be avoided as, 'The people who live and work in an area are best placed to identify the problems facing them and the options available for tackling those problems' and goes on to say, 'It is self evident that we cannot make communities safer if we do not find out the extent to which local people currently perceive them as unsafe; and it is clearly right that these people should be invited to participate actively in the process of tackling local problems, not just passively consulted about them'.

Yet again, however, the question must be raised about the type of behaviour to which this will relate. For example, the housing of a released paedophile offender is most clearly a local problem. Home Office guidance has already said emphatically that community notification about these offenders should be very limited. Police officers have already said that community notification risks driving offenders underground, thereby increasing the risk to the public. The kind of consultation envisaged and proposed by Straw is one of community empowerment but, in some areas, such as sex offenders, can communities be trusted to be empowered by the agencies of public protection?

Much of the strategy proposed by the Labour government is about long-term solutions, crime prevention in the full 'social' as well as the situational meaning of the term. In the case of the paedophile offender, the empowered community would therefore know the whereabouts of the offender but be working with public protection agencies to manage the level of risk — not to keep their area safe and pass on the risk to someone else. Empowerment must mean an acceptance that there will always be levels of risk, but that good quality, shared information, not only shared between agencies but also (selectively perhaps) with the public, may reduce those levels of risk to manageable proportions.

July 1998 also saw a quite astounding turn around in penal rhetoric. This book has already argued that the Labour administration appeared to wear the clothes of the previous Conservative government very easily in its law and order policies. The process begun with such gusto by Michael Howard made an almost seamless transition into the new government's thinking. Many of the measures discussed in this book, whilst perhaps commendable in many respects, have also responded to the populist streak unleashed in the media. Scant attention was given to the reasoned arguments put by the judiciary in particular and a small group of academics. Equally scant regard was had to the emerging research findings from the USA, namely that many of the measures proposed were unlikely to increase public protection significantly, but ran the very real risk of inflating the prison population with the 'wrong' people. From Tony Blair's famous soundbite, 'tough on crime, tough on the causes of crime', only the former appeared to have found favour with the government. Then, on 22 July 1998, the Home Secretary announced what amounts to a significant reversal of the punitive ethos of recent years and a major shift towards social crime prevention. Coinciding with details of the government's comprehensive spending review and what was described as 'seminal' research by the Home Office, several of the recent dogmas were debunked, including one very highly regarded by Jack Straw, that of zero tolerance policing. Police effectiveness was back on the agenda as the Home Secretary announced that it would no longer be immune from the efficiency reforms faced by the rest of the public sector.

Some Things Work!

The new message was that funding would follow 'evidence based' work which could demonstrate effectiveness. Thus the probation service, anticipating a cut in its 1998–9 funding of £6 million, found that cut reversed and replaced by a proposed £18 million increase — provided that the money found its way into programmes that work. Those that cannot demonstrate effectiveness risk losing their funding. Added to this amount was a £250 million social crime prevention fund, aimed at long-term investment in children, families and schools. The police service is encouraged to focus and target its activities more than it does now, to consider adopting more problem oriented or intelligence led policing activity. This would include targeting repeat offenders, directed patrols in crime hot spot areas and targeting repeat victims. For the probation service, the endorsement of the 'what works' research of recent years suggests that, yet again, it will have a future and that community penalties can be a major focus of the criminal justice system. Yet there must be a few words of caution here. The linking of funding to what the government sees as effective work resurrects the view of previous Conservative governments and ensures a considerable degree of central direction of practice. Sex offender programmes were identified as one area of good practice, but in terms of the wider community goals of empowerment and integration, Worrall's comments (1997) in chapter 3 of this text should be noted. In terms of public protection the creation of clear systems will be helpful but so will the intuition of individual police and probation officers. The skills needed to spot what might be going wrong are based on a variety of life and professional experiences and the Home Office must be careful not to encourage an overreliance on one method of working which runs the risk of squeezing out this notion of individuality. The use of such words as 'unfocused' can be used to denigrate practice which does not fit the new mould, but the best systems and group programmes can still miss the obvious. 'Unfocused' personal relationships have much to offer — of course alongside clear and effective joint working systems.

The announcement by the Home Secretary fully endorsed Home Office research published on 21 July 1998, Goldblatt and Lewis (1998). Included in the research was a call for closer collaboration between the prison and probation services, so as to facilitate the continuation of offence-focused work in prison being continued in the community. No doubt the prisons/probation review, established by the Labour government, will ensure that this closer collaboration will happen. In its newsletter, the National Association of Probation Officers (*NAPO News*, July/August, 1998) suggested that the number of probation areas would reduce from 54 to 43 within the next 18 months or so and that, in the longer term, it might be reduced to nine, jointly with the prison service under the auspices of a new national agency. This would be used to deliver more integrated working between the two agencies. In an interview in the same edition of *NAPO News*, Joyce Quinn, Minister responsible for prisons and probation (itself a significant innovation), said that:

> The enthusiastic working (of the probation service) in local partner-ship already, the openness in exchanging information and ideas; probation, prison and police co-operation in terms of risk assessment of dangerous offenders, for example, mean that we are working with the grain of changes that are already taking place in the probation service.

In his meeting with NAPO, the Home Secretary had also said that, although he saw a clear role for the probation service in terms of community punishment, he did see it as necessary for it to improve effectiveness and raise public confidence. NAPO's response was that ministerial statements affected public confidence and these of course have not always been very complimentary in recent years. So what does the future hold for the agencies of criminal justice in the next few years?

One press report of the Home Secretary's speech and the Home Office research was, 'prison doesn't work: official' (*The Guardian*, 22 July 1998). It is highly unlikely that such a headline would have been predicted in the first few weeks of the Labour government's term of office and it of course remains to be seen if the policy will be adhered to in the light of the inevitable press reports of serious violent, sexual offending or large scale public disorder. It is to be hoped that this new policy does at the least represent a return to reason in the making of criminal justice policy and a listening to research findings. Yet in no sense can this substantial shift in policy be seen as a return to some kind of golden age. The intention of the government to take control of probation and prisons practice, as well as that of the police service, is quite clear. The prisons/probation review has clearly laid out the ground for more formal links between these two organisations and will undoubtedly leave open the door to some form of eventual merger. Yet this book has focused on collaboration between the probation service and the police service, which has developed to a considerable degree and without the formal process of review attached to prison and probation work.

The July/August 1998 *NAPO News* also led with a significant headline, and this was the speculation over the new name for the probation service. There has already been discussion over whether or not probation officers should be corrections officers (apparently favoured by Jack Straw) or community justice workers (favoured by ACOP). The headline suggested another title for the new national agency which itself would oversee the work of the probation service. The one apparently favoured in the Home Office is the National Public Protection Service. Whether or not probation officers would change their title along the lines suggested above, or whether the probation service itself would have to change its title under the ambit of the new agency is not yet clear. What is clear from the various leaks and guesses, is that the focus of the probation service is changing at a rapid rate. It has, to a certain extent, already anticipated many of the developments and responded in various ways. Jack Straw's wish for greater public confidence is met in part by the closer collaboration with the police service. Working jointly with the police under the public protection mandate undoubtedly increases both public profile and public awareness of role. The police still enjoy popular support and the probation service will undoubtedly benefit from the type of association outlined in this book. Profile is important and, in an advertisement for the new Chief Probation Officer for Merseyside (*The Observer*, 26 July 1998) this was recognised as a key achievement of the retiring chief. Undoubtedly there has been a strong leaning towards the literature on 'what works' and many probation service groups tackle a range of offending behaviour under this particular banner. This has also enabled the probation service more easily to demonstrate that it is doing something and is doing it well.

One Step Forward, Two Steps Back

Yet any progress in terms of taking the heat out of the criminal justice agenda could be quickly reversed. This chapter began by saying that the media concern over paedophile offenders had died down during the months from April until July 1998. Indeed, it could be questioned whether the Home Secretary would have so enthusiastically endorsed the Home Office research if the media climate and public mood had been in July 1998 what it had been but a few months earlier. But this mood is never far below the surface. Only on 19 July 1998 *The Mail on Sunday* carried front page headlines over the suspension of probation workers 'after a convicted pervert attacks boy of five'. The main newspaper headline was 'How did they let a child suffer?'. The substance of the allegation was that a man who was previously convicted of gross indecency with a young child (and sentenced to imprisonment), was subsequently reconvicted of criminal deception and ordered to serve a community service order. Upon release from his earlier prison sentence he had been categorised as a high risk offender and 'green flagged', with a warning that he should not be allowed to work near minors. For whatever reason this warning appears to have been missed or disregarded (he was working with a group of other offenders), and he allegedly indecently assaulted the five-year-old son of a single mother whose home was being decorated under the community service scheme. In response to the allegation Joyce Quinn said, 'This is an horrific case. Urgent steps are being taken to improve communications between the probation service, prisons and police generally'. Yet this book has charted how that communication has already reached unparalleled levels and received widespread support and acclamation from Her Majesty's Inspectorate of Probation. This was not, however, the message that was put out for public consumption, although the comments by Surrey's chief probation officer, that this was the first such incident in 23 years of community service schemes in that county, was reported, albeit somewhat down the article and off the front page. The more kneejerk response was that consideration should be given to preventing the making of any community service orders on convicted child sex offenders because of the risk of contact with children. This statement of course flies in the face of successful orders served by this group of offenders for years. Yet this very message had been given out in the HMIP report (1998a) on sex offenders where it said that chief probation officers should, 'issue guidance to staff that it is inappropriate to propose community service in a pre-sentence report on a sex offender unless they are assessed as presenting minimal risk and the proposal is approved by an SPO' (p. 17). It could be argued that this message should have been heard by the Surrey staff but yet again the implication is one of searching for perfect safety in the face of evidence that most of the time a problem is not encountered. The blame culture is still alive and the quest for perfect safety remains high on the public and media agenda. Herein lies the real threat to what must be regarded as a sincere attempt by the government to take forward criminal justice policy.

Further indications that the public safety agenda was still riding high appears in a further announcement arising from the comprehensive spending review, this time from the health service budget. The government announced that £1 billion would be allocated to a major overhaul of care in the community. Many critics have argued that this system has failed the mentally ill and the wider community. However, the review announced by the government was framed in the context of public safety, the need to protect the public from the type of high profile murder such as that committed by Christopher Clunis. These though remain very rare and, as *The Guardian* report indicated (25 July 1998), mentally ill patients have a much higher rate of self harm than random killings, with at least 20 committing suicide each week. A letter in the same newspaper on 17 July 1998 had suggested that, of the 50 'psychotic' murders recorded each year, 46 of these involved family tragedies, with only 4 of strangers, a rate that the author, Dr Birley, claimed had been steady since 1978. The association of dangerous behaviour with mental illness, often made in the public mind, is perhaps an erroneous association. This book has not really dealt with the mental health issue. One reason for this is that other texts would do this much better. Another is that this text concentrates more on those offenders who frequently do not come to attention wearing the mental illness label. If they do, it is likely that psychiatric opinion will be available and generally police and probation officers will defer to their expertise. This is of course a generalisation but is likely to be true. The decisions concerning offenders at public protection panels are more likely to be located in the grey area of dangerousness, arguably a much more difficult area in which to work.

So what does the future hold for the police and probation services in this delicate area of practice? There is, as yet, no hint of a departure from the kind of results culture so beloved of successive Conservative administrations. This means that public accountability and mana-gerially dominated practice agendas are set to continue. The evidence to date is that the more acute the political situation, the more heated the criminal justice agenda, so the more managers have influenced practice. The determination to be seen to be doing what has been set as the task, has overridden professional scruples and doubt. Public protection has assumed a dominant role in practice and yet the risk presented to most people going about their everyday lives is minimal. Public protection has managed to shift the cultures of both police and probation services and created a full and frank exchange of information between them. Yet there must be questions about the extent to which this cultural shift can take place without totally compromising the values of these organisations and particularly that of the probation service. Undoubtedly a new set of values had to be found for the probation service of the 1990s, but this should not involve throwing out 90 years of values and experience. For its part the police service has been moving towards more partnership for some years but it has managed this without such a change in its daily practice. The overall aims of the public protection agenda clearly involve less change for police than they do for probation officers, although recognising the changes which have already occurred within the probation service requires a considerable mind shift from police officers.

Undoubtedly the whole issue of public protection arose out of an acute political context and not out of evidence which suggested that society was suddenly becoming considerably less safe. The speed of legislative development and its knock-on effect on practice was quite spectacular and has now established a range of measures which attempt to provide public protection from every conceivable angle. It is difficult to think of any loopholes being left. (That said, on 24 January 1999 *The Observer* reported that the government were to make available a 'previously secret' register of known paedophiles to employers and voluntary groups dealing with under-18-year-olds.) The ready absorption of public protection ideology by police and probation officers says more of the fear of the blame culture than it does of an acceptance of a well thought out practice agenda. If that blame culture can be given a back seat, and if professionals are allowed to develop their expertise whilst retaining a sense of their own agency values, we may yet see public protection set within a context which values rights and justice for all.

References

ACOP (1993) *Guidance on Management of Risk and Public Protection*, Wakefield: ACOP.

ACPO Quality of Service Committee, *Getting Things Right*, London: New Scotland Yard.

Ashworth, A. (1989) 'Criminal Justice and Deserved Sentences', *Criminal Law Review*, 340–355.

Ashworth, A. (1993) 'Victim Impact Statements and Sentencing', *Criminal Law Review*, 498.

Audit Commission (1993) *Helping with Enquiries: Tackling Crime Effectively*, London: HMSO.

Barker, M. (1995) 'What works with sex offenders?' in G. McIvor (ed) *Working with Offenders*, Research Highlights in Social Work 26, London: Jessica Kingsley.

Beck, U. (1992) *Risk Society*, London: Sage.

Bingham, Lord (1997) 'The Sentence of the Court', *Police Foundation Lecture*, 10 July 1997, Lord Chancellor's Press Office.

Blagg, H. and Stubbs, P. (1988) 'A Child-Centred Practice?', *Practice*, II, 1, 12–19.

Bottoms, A. E. (1977) 'Reflections on the Renaissance of Dangerousness', *Howard Journal of Criminal Justice*, 16: 70–96.

Bottoms, A. E. and Brownsword, R. (1982) 'The Dangerousness Debate After the Floud Report', *British Journal of Criminology*, Vol. 22 (3), 229–254.

Bottoms, A. E. and McWilliams, W. (1979) 'A Non-treatment Paradigm for Probation Practice', *British Journal of Social Work*, 9, 159–202.

Bottoms, A. E. and Preston, R. H. (1980), The Coming Penal Crisis: A Criminological and Theological Explanation, Edinburgh: Scottish Academic Press.

Bowden, P. (1996) 'Graham Young; the St Albans poisoner: his life and times', *Criminal Behaviour and Mental Health,* 17–24.

Braithwaite, J. (1989) *Crime, Shame and Reintegration*, Sydney: Cambridge University Press.

Braithwaite, J. and Daly, K. (1994) 'Masculinities, violence and communitarian control' in T. Newburn and E. A. Stanko, (eds) *Just Boys Doing Business*, London: Routledge.

Braithwaite, J. and Mugford, S. (1993) 'Conditions of successful reintegration ceremonies: dealing with juvenile offenders', *British Journal of Criminology*, 34, 139–171.

Braithwaite, J. and Petit, P. (1990) *Not Just Deserts: A Republican Theory of Criminal Justice*, Oxford: Oxford University Press.

Brake, M. and Hale, C. (1992) *Public Order and Private Lives. The Politics of Law and Order*. London: Routledge.

Broadhurst, R. and Loh, N. (1993) 'Sex and Violent Offenders: Probabilities of Reimprisonment', paper presented to the Australian Institute of Criminology, in J. Pratt (1997) *Governing the Dangerous*, Sydney: The Federation Press.

Brody, S. R. (1976) *The Effectiveness of Sentencing*, Home Office Research Study No. 64, London: HMSO.

Brody, S. R. and Tarling, R. (1980) *Taking Offenders Out of Circulation*. Home Office Research Study No. 64, London: HMSO.

Brooks, A.D. (1984) 'Defining the Dangerousness of the Mentally Ill: Involuntary Civil Commitment' in Craft, M. and Craft, A. (eds) *Mentally Abnormal Offenders*, London: Baillière, Tindall.

Brownlee, I. (1998) *Community punishment: A critical introduction*, Harlow: Longman.

Bryant, M. (1989) *The contribution of ACOP and probation services to crime prevention*, Wakefield: Association of Chief Officers of Probation.

Butler, A. J. P. (1996) 'Managing the future: a chief constable's view' in F. Leishman, B. Loveday and S. P. Savage, *Core Issues in Policing*, London: Longman.

Butler Committee (1975) *Report of the Committee on Mentally Abnormal Offenders*, Cmnd. 6244.

Cantner, D. (1994) *Criminal Shadows: Inside the Mind of the Serial Killer*, London: Harper Collins.

Cavadino, M. and Dignan, J. (1997) (2nd ed.) *The Penal System: An Introduction*, London: Sage.

Cleveland (1988), Report of the inquiry into child abuse in Cleveland 1987, Cm 412, London: HMSO.

Cohen, D. A. (1997) 'Notes on the Clinical Assessment of Dangerousness in Offender Populations', *Psychiatry On-Line* (http://www.priory.com/psych/assessin.html).

Coker, J. B. and Martin, J. P. (1985) *Licensed to Live*, Oxford: Blackwell.

Conrad, J. P. (1982) 'The Quandary of Dangerousness. Towards the Resolution of a Persisting Dilemma', *British Journal of Criminology*, 22(3) 255–267.

Cornick, B. (1988) 'Proceeding Together', *Community Care*, 17 March, 25–7.

Dale, P., Davies, M., Morrison, T. and Wayers, J. (1986) *Dangerous Families: Assessment and the Treatment of Child Abuse*, London: Tavistock.

Dingwall, G. (1998) 'Selective Incapacitation After the Criminal Justice Act 1991: A Proportional Response to Protecting the Public?' *The Howard Journal*, Vol. 37 (2), 177–187.

Ditchfield, J. (1997) 'Actuarial Prediction and Risk Assessment', *Prison Service Journal*, 113, 8–13.

Douglas, M. (1986) *Risk Acceptability According to the Social Sciences*, London: Routledge and Kegan Paul.

Downes, D. and Morgan, R. (1997) 'Dumping the "Hostages to Fortune"? The Politics of Law and Order in Post-War Britain' in Maguire, M., Morgan, R. and Reiner, R., *The Oxford Handbook of Criminology*, Oxford: Clarendon Press.

Dunbar, I. and Langdon, A. (1998) *Tough Justice: Sentencing and Penal Policies in the 1980s*, London: Blackstone Press Limited.

Dworkin, R. (1977) *Taking Rights Seriously*, London: Duckworth.

Dworkin, R. (1996) 'Does Britain Need a Bill of Rights?' in Gordon, R. and Wilmot-Smith, R., *Human Rights in the United Kingdom*, Oxford: Clarendon Press.

Edwards, S. (1996) *Sex and Gender in the Legal Process*, London: Blackstone Press Ltd.

Ericson, R. (1994) 'The division of expert knowledge in policing and security', *British Journal of Sociology*, Vol. 45 (2), 149–75.

Family Research Council (1997) *Policing Sex Offenders: An Update,* (http//www/nationalreview.com/frc/insight/is97g3cr.html).

Field, S. (1990) *Trends in Crime and Their Interpretation: A Study of Recorded Crime in Post War England and Wales,* Home Office Research Study No. 119, London: HMSO.

Fielding, N. F. and Conroy, S. (1994) 'Against the Grain: Co-operation in Child Sexual Abuse Investigations' in Stephens, S. and Becker, S. (eds) *Police Force, Police Service,* Basingstoke: Macmillan Press Ltd.

Floud, J. (1978) 'Dangerousness: is it a Valid and Necessary Concept?' (abstract), in *Proceedings of the Annual Conference of the British Psychological Society 1978,* Leicester: British Psychological Society.

Floud, J. (1982) 'Dangerousness and Criminal Justice', *The British Journal of Criminology,* Vol. 22 (3), 213–228.

Floud, J. and Young, W. (1981) *Dangerousness and Criminal Justice,* London: Heinemann.

Fukyama, F. (1995) *Trust: The Social Virtues and the Creation of Prosperity,* London: Hamish Hamilton Ltd.

Geis, G. (1996) 'A Base on Balls for White-Collar Criminals' in D. Shichor and D. K. Sechrest, *Three Strikes and You're Out; Vengeance as Public Policy,* California: Sage.

Gendreau, P. (1995) *What works in community corrections. Promising approaches in reducing criminal behaviour,* IARCA Journal 6.

Gendreau, P. and Ross, R. (1987) 'Revivification of Rehabilitation: Evidence from the 1980s', *Justice Quarterly,* 349–407.

Gillespie, A. A. (1998) 'Paedophiles and the Crime and Disorder Bill', *Journal of Current Legal Issues,* Issue No. 1, Web Journal in association with Blackstone Press Ltd (http:webjcli.ncl.ac.uk/1998/issue1/gillespie1.html).

Gilling, D. (1997) *Crime Prevention: Theory, policy and politics,* London: UCL Press.

Goldblatt, P. and Lewis, C. (eds) 'Reducing Offending: An Assessment of Research Evidence on Ways of Dealing with Offending Behaviour', *Home Office Research Study No. 181,* London: Home Office.

Greenwood, P., Rydell, C., Abrahamse, A., Caulkins, J., Chiesa, J., Model, K. and Klein, S. (1996) 'Estimated Benefits and Costs of California's New Mandatory-Sentencing Law', in D. Shichor and D. Sechrest (op. cit).

Grubin, D. and Wingate, S. (1996) 'Sexual offence recidivism: prediction versus understanding', *Criminal Behaviour and Mental Health*, 6, 349–359.

Gunn, J. (1996) Supplement 'Let's Get Serious About Dangerousness', *Criminal Behaviour and Mental Health*, 51–64.

Harris, R. (1992) *Crime, Criminal Justice and the Probation Service*, London: Routledge.

Hawkins, K. (1983) 'Assessing Evil', *British Journal of Criminology*, 23, 101–127.

Hebenton, B. and Thomas, T. (1996) 'Tracking Sex Offenders', *The Howard Journal*, Vol. 35 (2), 97–112.

Hebenton, B. and Thomas, T. (1997) 'Keeping Track? Observation on Sex Offender Registers in the U.S.', *Police Research Group Crime Detection and Prevention Paper 83*.

Henman, R. (1997) 'Protective Sentences: Ethics, Rights and Sentencing Policy', *International Journal of the Sociology of Law*, 25, 45-63.

Hills, S. (ed) (1987) *Corporate Violence: Injury and Death for Profit*, Totowa, NJ: Rowman and Littlefield.

Holden, A. (1974) *The St Albans Poisoner, The Life and Times of Graham Young*, London: Hodder and Stoughton.

Hollway, W. and Jefferson, T. (1997) 'The risk society in an age of anxiety: situating fear of crime', *British Journal of Sociology*, Vol. 48 (2), 255–266.

Holmes, R. M. and Holmes, S. T. (1996) *Profiling Violent Crimes: An Investigative Tool*, (2nd ed) California: Sage.

Home Office (1984) *Tougher Regimes in Detention Centres*: Report of an Evaluation by the Young Offender Psychology Unit, London: HMSO.

Home Office (1988) *Punishment, Custody and the Community*, Cm 424, London: HMSO.

Home Office (1990) *Crime, Justice and Protecting the Public. The Government's Proposals for Legislation*, Cm 965, London: HMSO.

Home Office (1990b) *Supervision and Punishment in the Community: A Framework for Action*, CM 966, London: HMSO.

Home Office (1993) Monitoring the Criminal Justice Act 1997: Data from a special data collection exercise, Home Office Statistical Bulletin 18/92, London: Home Office.

Home Office (1995) *Dealing with Dangerous People: The Probation Service and Public Protection*, Report of a Thematic Inspection (HMIP), London: HMSO.

Home Office (1996) *Protecting the Public*, Cm 3190, London: HMSO.

Home Office (1997a) *Inter-Agency Work with Dangerous Offenders: Sharing Information to Manage Risk*, Liverpool: Home Office Special Conferences Unit.

Home Office (1997b) *The prevalence of convictions for sexual offending in England and Wales*, Home Office Research and Statistics Report No. 55.

Home Office (1998a) *Exercising Constant Vigilance: The Role Of the Probation Service in Protecting the Public from Sex Offenders*, Report of a Thematic Inspection (HMIP), London: Home Office.

Home Office (1998b) *The Processing of Rape Cases by the Criminal Justice System*, London: HMSO.

Hood, R. and Shute, S. (1996) 'Protecting the Public: Automatic Life Sentences, Parole and High Risk Offenders', *Criminal Law Review*, 788–800.

James, A. and Raine, J. (1998) *The New Politics of Criminal Justice*, London: Longman.

John Howard Society of Alberta (1995) *Assessing Dangerousness* (http://www.acjnet.org/docs/assesjhs.html).

John Howard Society of Alberta (1993), Briefing Paper on Dangerous Offender Draft Legislation (http:/www.acjnet.org/docs/draftjhs.html).

John Howard Society of Alberta (1997a), *Community Notification*, ACJNet Publications (http:/www.acjnet.org/docs/commojhs.html).

Johnston, L. (1997) 'Policing Communities of Risk', in Francis, P., Davies, P. and Jupp, V. (eds) *Policing Futures; The Police, Law Enforcement and the Twenty-First Century*, Basingstoke: Macmillan Press Ltd.

Kozol, H. L., Boucher, R. J. and Garofalo, R. F. (1972) 'The Diagnosis and Treatment of Dangerousness', *Crime and Delinquency*, 18, 371–392.

Kvaraceus, W. C. (1966) *Anxious Youth*, Ohio: Columbus.

Laycock, G. and Pease, K. (1985) 'Crime prevention within the probation service', *Probation Journal* 32, 43–7.

Leishman, F., Loveday, B. and Savage, S.P. (eds) (1996) *Core Issues in Policing*, London: Longman.

Los, M. (1990) 'Feminism and rape law reform' in Gelsthorpe, L. and Morris, A. (eds) *Feminist Perspectives in Criminology*, Buckingham: Open University Press.

Martinson, R. (1974) 'What Works? — Questions and Answers about Prison Reform', *The Public Interest*, 35, 22–54.

May, T. (1991) *Probation: Politics, Policy and Practice*, Buckingham: Open University Press.

McWilliams, W. (1985) 'The mission transformed: professionalisation of probation between the wars', *Howard Journal of Criminal Justice* 24 (4), 257–74.

McWilliams, W. (1986) 'The English probation system and the diagnostic ideal', *Howard Journal of Criminal Justice* 25 (4), 241–60.

McWilliams, W. (1992) 'The rise and development of management thought in the English probation system' in Statham, R. and Whitehead, P. (eds) *Managing the Probation Service, Issues for the 1990s*, Harlow: Longman.

Morris, N. (1994) '"Dangerousness" and Incapacitation' in Duff, A. and Garland, D (eds) *A Reader on Punishment*, Oxford: Oxford University Press.

Nash, M. (1995) 'Aggravation, Mitigation and the Gender of Probation Officers', *The Howard Journal of Criminal Justice*, Vol. 34, No. 3 (August), 250–258.

Nash, M. (1997) *Multi-Agency Conferencing Of Potentially Dangerous Offenders in Hampshire*, University of Portsmouth: Probation Evaluation and Research Unit.

Nash, M. and Savage, S.P. (1994) 'A Criminal Record? Law, Order and Conservative Policy' in Savage, S. P., Atkinson, R. and Robins, L. (eds) *Public Policy in Britain*, Basingstoke: Macmillan.

National Association of Probation Officers (1984) *Draft policy statement; crime prevention and reduction strategies.*

Needs, A. and Towl, G. (1997) 'Reflections on Clinical Risk Assessments with Lifers', *Prison Service Journal*, 113, 14–17.

Newburn, T. (1995) *Crime and Criminal Justice Policy*. London: Longman.

Ormerod, D.C. (1996) 'The Evidential Implications of Psychological Profiling', *Criminal Law Review*, 863–877.

POST (1996) Technical Report No. 87: *Psychological Evaluation and Gun Control*, Parliamentary Office of Science and Technology.

Potter, K. (1997) 'The right to know', *Police Review*, 21 February 1997.

Pratt, J. (1997) *Governing the Dangerous*, Sydney: Federation Press.

Prins, H. (1986) *Dangerous Behaviour, The Law, and Mental Disorder*, London: Tavistock Publications.

Prins, H. (1988) 'Dangerous Clients: Further Observations on the Limitation of Mayhem', *British Journal of Social Work*, 18, 593–609.

Prins, H. (1989) The Importance of Previous Convictions in Assessing Criminal Motivation — the Need for Detail, *Medical Science and Law,* Vol. 29 (2), 107, 108.

Prison Reform Trust (1997) *The Effect of American Sentencing Policy Changes on the Courts, Prisons and Crime*, London: PRT.

Quinsey, V. and Chaplin, T. (1988) 'Penile Responses of Child Molesters and Normals to Descriptions of Encounters with Children Involving Sex and Violence', *Journal of Interpersonal Violence*, Vol. 13 (3), 259–274.

Quinsey, V. and Mireille, C. (1986) 'Perceived Dangerousness and Treatability of Offenders: The Effects of Internal Versus External Attributions of Crime Causality', *Journal of Interpersonal Violence*, Vol. 1 (4), 458–471.

Radzinowicz, L. and Hood, R. (1978) 'A Dangerous Direction for Sentencing Reform', *Criminal Law Review*, 713–724.

Reiner, R. (1992) (2nd ed.) *The Politics of the Police*, London: Harvester Wheatsheaf.

Rice, M. E. (1997) 'Violent Offender Research and Implications for the Criminal Justice System', *American Psychologist*, 414–423.

Russell, F. (1998) 'Getting the balance right', *New Law Journal,* 23 January 1998.

Sampson, A. (1994) *Acts of Abuse*, London: Routledge.

Sampson, A. and Smith, D. (1992) Probation and community crime prevention', *Howard Journal*, 31, 105–19.

Savage, S. P. (1990) 'A War on Crime? Law and Order Policies in the 1980s' in Savage, S. P. and Robins, L., *Public Policy under Thatcher*, Basingstoke: Macmillan.

Savage, S. P. and Nash, M. (1994) 'Yet Another Agenda for Law and Order: British Criminal Justice Policy and the Conservatives', *International Criminal Justice Review*, Vol. 4.

Shichor, D. and Sechrest, D. K. (1996) 'Three Strikes as Public Policy' in Sichor, D. and Sechrest, D. K. (eds) *Three Strikes and You're Out; Vengeance as Public Policy*, California: Sage.

Scott, P. (1977) 'Assessing Dangerousness in Criminals', *British Journal of Psychiatry*, 131, 127–42.

Scottish Council on Crime (1975) *Crime and the Prevention of Crime*, Edinburgh: HMSO.

Shaw, R. (1996) 'Supervising the Dangerous in the Community' in·
Walker, N. (ed) *Dangerous People*, London: Blackstone Press Ltd.

Skolnick, J. (1995) 'What Not to Do About Crime', *Criminology*, 33, 1–14.

Soothill, K. and Francis, B. (1997) 'Sexual reconvictions and the Sex
Offenders Act 1997', *New Law Journal*, September 5 and 12, 1285–6
and 1324–1325.

Stephens, M. and Becker, S. (1994) *Police Force, Police Service. Care
and Control in Britain*, Basingstoke: Macmillan.

Stevenson, O. (1989) 'Multi-Disciplinary Work in Child Protection'
Stevenson, O. (ed) *Child Abuse: Public Policy and Professional
Practice*, Hemel Hempstead: Harvester Wheatsheaf.

Straw, J. (1998) Speech to Magistrates' Association, Blackburn, 25 June
1998, (http://www.homeoffice.gov.uk/cdact/magsp. htm).

Thomas, D. A. (1998) 'The Crime (Sentences) Act 1997', *Criminal Law
Review*, 83–92.

Thomas, T. (1988) 'Working with the Police', *Social Work Today*, 20,
19–20.

Thompson, K. (1998) *Moral Panics,* London: Routledge.

Thornton, D. (1997) *Risk Assessment: Structured Anchored Clinical
Judgement*, (personal communication).

Thornton, D. and Travers, R. (1991) *A Longitudinal Study of the
Criminal Behaviour of Convicted Sexual Offenders*, Proceedings of a
Prison Psychologists' Conference, HM Prison Service.

Towl, G. J. and Crighton, D. A. (1996) *The Handbook of Psychology for
Forensic Practitioners*, London: Routledge.

Turvey, B. E. (1997) *Dangerousness: Predicting Recidivism in Violent
Sex Offenders*, Knowledge Solutions LLC (http://www.corpus-delic-
tii.com/danger.html).

Van Den Haag, E. (1975) *Punishing Criminals: Concerning a Very Old
and Painful Question*, New York: Basic Books.

Von Hirsch, A. and Ashworth, A. (1996) 'Protective Sentencing Under
Section 2 (2) (b): The Criteria for Dangerousness', *Criminal Law
Review*, 175–183.

Walker, N. (1980) *Punishment, Danger and Stigma: The Morality of
Criminal Justice*, Oxford: Basil Blackwell.

Walker, N. (1996) 'Ethical and Other Problems' in Walker, N. (ed)
Dangerous People, London: Blackstone Press Ltd.

Wasik, M. and Taylor, R. D. (1994) (2nd ed.) *Blackstone's Guide to the
Criminal Justice Act 1991*, London: Blackstone Press Ltd.

Weatheritt, M. (1986) *Innovations in Policing*, London: Croom Helm (Police Foundation).

Worrall, A. (1997) *Punishment in the Community: The Future of Criminal Justice*, London: Longman.

Young, A. (1996) *Imagining Crime*, London: Sage.

Zedner, L. (1997) 'Victims' in Maguire, M., Morgan, R. and Reiner, R. *The Oxford Handbook of Criminology* (2nd ed), Oxford: Clarendon Press.

Zeigler, F. A. and Del Carmen, R. (1996) 'Constitutional Issues Arising from "Three Strikes and You're Out" Legislation' in Shichor, D. and Sechrest, D. K. (eds) *Three Strikes and You're Out; Vengeance as Public Policy*, California: Sage.

Index